Russia's Communists at the Crossroads

Russia's Communists at the Crossroads

Joan Barth Urban and Valerii D. Solovei

 WestviewPress
A Division of HarperCollinsPublishers

Copyright © 1997 by Westview Press, A Division of HarperCollins Publishers, Inc.

Published in 1997 in the United States of America by Westview Press, 5500 Central Avenue, Boulder, Colorado 80301-2877, and in the United Kingdom by Westview Press, 12 Hid's Copse Road, Cumnor Hill, Oxford OX2 9JJ

Library of Congress Cataloging-in-Publication Data
Urban, Joan Barth, 1934–
Russia's communists at the crossroads / Joan Barth Urban and
  Valerii D. Solovei.
    p. cm.
  Includes bibliographical references (p.   ) and index.
  ISBN 0-8133-2930-2.—ISBN 0-8133-2931-0 (pbk.)
    1. Kommunisticheskaîa partiîa Rossiĭskoĭ Federatŝii.
2. Communism—Russia (Federation) 3. Russia (Federation)—Politics
and government—1991– I. Soloveĭ, V. D. II. Title.
JN6699.A8K638 1997
324.247'075—dc21
                                                                        96-53174
                                                                            CIP

Typeset by Letra Libre

10   9   8   7   6   5   4   3   2   1

To our Russian and American families

Contents

Preface

In May 1993, I spent three weeks in Moscow searching for a local scholar with whom I might collaborate on a study of the communist movement in post-Soviet Russia. This was no simple task; the Russians, I was told, had turned their backs on communism. In due course, however, I met Valerii D. Solovei, a young researcher at the Gorbachev Foundation who shared my hunch that communism in Russia had not yet run its political course.

Over the next three years Valera and I worked together collecting documents, conducting interviews, scanning the communist press, and pondering the fortunes of a power elite which had so recently controlled the Soviet empire and its East European neighbors. For a time many of our acquaintances, in both Moscow and Washington, thought us a bit wacky. But during the Russian election season of 1995–1996, it became apparent to all that communism in Russia was not a spent political force.

Many colleagues and institutions have helped us to bring this project to fruition. The United States Institute of Peace awarded me a research grant, from March 1994 through August 1995, which provided funds for (among other things) my frequent travel to Moscow and Valera's collection of the necessary documentation in between my trips. We are both very grateful for this support. Thanks are due as well to the Catholic University of America for two faculty research grants which enabled me to observe firsthand the Russian parliamentary elections of December 1995 and the presidential race in 1996.

I would also like to express my gratitude to the Institute of Scientific Information on the Social Sciences of the Russian Academy of Sciences (INION RAN), to its director, Academician Vladimir A. Vinogradov, and to all my friends on its research staff for hosting me during the many field trips required for the completion of this book. A special word of thanks goes to Valerii P. Liubin for his facilitation of my institutional invitations and to Vadim V. Ishutin, the editor of INION's weekly press review, *Raznogolositsa*, which is an indispensable research tool for all observers of contemporary Russian political parties and movements.

The idea for this book originated with Jane Leftwich Curry. At the 1992 convention of the American Association for the Advancement of Slavic Studies, Janey expounded with her customary brilliance upon the need to investi-

gate and compare the successor communist parties of the former Soviet
Bloc. If Janey gave me the idea, it was my husband, Laszlo, who inspired in
me the confidence to undertake this project. With my background in Soviet
studies and my work on the non-ruling communist parties of Western Europe, he argued, why should I not examine the development of the non-
ruling communist parties in post-Soviet Russia?

For research assistance and logistical help of many different kinds, Valera
and I are indebted to the following individuals: Michael D. Braun, Andrei P.
Filippov, Sergei V. Gretsky, Nikolai V. Ivanitsky, James M. Quirk, Andrei V.
Riabov, Rebecca G. Urban (my daughter, who by the time she was nineteen
had traveled four times to Russia), Maia A. Vinogradova, Audrey A.
Whitaker, and Tamara G. Zagladina. We also warmly acknowledge our frequent interlocutors on contemporary Russian politics as well as readers of
various draft chapters of this book: Robert Otto, Peter Reddaway, Heinz
Timmermann, and Marc Zlotnik. The many key personalities in the post-
Soviet Russian communist movement who shared with us their insiders'
knowledge of our subject are cited in endnotes throughout the text.

Professor Robert Vincent Daniels played a unique role in the writing of
this book. His seminal work, *The Conscience of the Revolution*, enormously
influenced my own intellectual development as a graduate student many
years ago. Our personal paths finally crossed during our parallel odysseys
into the world of Italian communism during the Brezhnev era. Valera and I
are grateful beyond measure that he agreed to serve as a reader of the manuscript for Westview Press. This volume owes much to his prompt and pene-
trating critiques of each chapter.

We have dedicated this book to our Russian and American families. I have
already mentioned my American family. Valera's Russian family and my
"adoptive" one in Moscow have yet to be given their due. To each of them
go our love and gratitude for their unstinting attentiveness to our well-being
during the course of this project.

Joan Barth Urban
Chevy Chase, Maryland

Abbreviations

ACPB	All-Union Communist Party of Bolsheviks
BP	Bolshevik Platform in the CPSU
CC	Central Committee
CEC	Central Executive Committee
CIM	Communist Initiative Movement
CPRF	Communist Party of the Russian Federation
CPSU	Communist Party of the Soviet Union
DP	Democratic Platform in the CPSU
DPCR	Democratic Party of Communists of Russia
LDPR	Liberal Democratic Party of Russia
MP	Marxist Platform in the CPSU
NSF	National Salvation Front
PPUR	People's-Patriotic Union of Russia
PPFR	People's Party Free Russia
RCP	Russian Communist Party
RCWP	Russian Communist Workers' Party
RPC	Russian Party of Communists
RPRF	Republican Party of the Russian Federation
R.S.F.S.R.	Russian Soviet Federated Socialist Republic
RUSO	Russian Scholars of Socialist Orientation
SLP	Socialist Labor Party
UC	Union of Communists
UCP-CPSU	Union of Communist Parties–Communist Party of Soviet Union
UFL	United Front of Labor
U.S.S.R.	Union of Soviet Socialist Republics

Russia's Communists at the Crossroads

1

Introduction

This book is about the evolution of the communist movement in the Russian Federation from the last years of the U.S.S.R.'s existence through Russia's presidential elections of June–July 1996, when the chief contenders were the incumbent president, Boris N. Yeltsin, and his communist challenger, Gennadii A. Ziuganov. Our main protagonist is the Communist Party of the Russian Federation, or CPRF as it is commonly called. But the CPRF was a latecomer to the post-Soviet communist playing field. Its formal establishment came only in February 1993, well after the formation of a number of more doctrinaire communist parties which initially competed with the CPRF and influenced its political profile and conduct in numerous, if not always readily apparent, ways. All of these new Russian CPs emerged from the rubble of what had been the mighty and supposedly monolithic Communist Party of the Soviet Union (CPSU). On the Marxist-Leninist political spectrum, however, the range of the official positions espoused by these post-Soviet neocommunist groups was more comparable to that of the international communist movement as a whole in the post-Stalin era than to the CPSU under Nikita S. Khrushchev and Leonid I. Brezhnev.

The post-Soviet Russian CPs began to take embryonic shape during the last year or so of Mikhail S. Gorbachev's tenure in power (1985–1991). With the reforms "from above" beginning in 1987–1988, the freedom from fear to publish what one wished (*glasnost*), and the promise of pluralist politics to come, multiple grassroots pressures developed for yet more far-reaching democratic changes in Russia and some of the other Soviet republics. Similar pressures "from below" developed within the CPSU. But these intra-party tendencies, somewhat muted at first because of the long-standing Leninist ban against any manifestation of factionalism, embraced both conservative anti-reformers and reform-minded groups. Moreover, the diverse political-ideological factions that openly surfaced among CPSU activists in the U.S.S.R.'s twilight years were grounded in long-standing differences of opinion which had been concealed from public view by the Soviet party-state's enforced code of unanimity. For reasons that have yet to be sat-

1

isfactorily explained, before Gorbachev's *perestroika* most Western Sovietologists dismissed the relevance, indeed often even the existence, of these genuine ideological and policy cleavages within the CPSU elite.

The Soviet elite, for the purpose of our analysis, included the senior CPSU functionaries in the full-time party bureaucracy, or *apparat*, as well as the far more numerous holders of upper-level positions in the multiple, all-embracing state bureaucracies, those whose job appointments required party certification of their political reliability. As a group they constituted the so-called *nomenklatura*. The Soviet-era elite may also be said to have included the many establishment intellectuals who populated the academic institutes and party-sponsored think tanks and whose prestige and perquisites set them apart from the rest of the population. From the collapse of the Soviet Union in late 1991 if not earlier, numerous members of these groups rushed to bare to the world the political differences that had in fact divided their ranks for decades.

Many of these individuals in the Russian Soviet Federated Socialist Republic (R.S.F.S.R.), as Russia was then known, supported Gorbachev's policy initiatives and later backed the market reforms of President Yeltsin. A large number were also able to execute successfully a personal transition from Soviet bureaucrat to manager, businessman, or government official in the new post-Soviet order. Here, however, we wish to make one point clear: our purpose in undertaking this book was not to examine the career patterns of these figures from the former CPSU elite, nor was it to evaluate the policies and conduct of President Yeltsin and his administration.

Our concern was with those lower or middle level Soviet-era bureaucrats, researchers, and ordinary employees who were not so easily able to navigate the shoals of system change, let alone repudiate their political convictions. They, too, soon began to expatiate upon the behind-the-scenes character of the former CPSU party-state. However, they stressed the chasm that had always existed within the U.S.S.R.'s ruling party between those who joined it for reasons of personal career advancement and those who did so because of genuine ideological commitment. All too quickly, moreover, the distinction they drew between careerist motives and Marxist-Leninist conviction was transformed into a dichotomy between traitors and patriots. One cannot emphasize too strongly the pervasiveness of this way of looking at things among the neocommunist activists in the post-Soviet Russian Federation. Regardless of specific group affiliation, they were all but unanimous in denouncing Gorbachev, Yeltsin, and their respective inner circles as self-serving opportunists who were, to boot, guilty of high treason.

For students of the international communist movement in the Soviet era, the notion of a cleavage between careerism and conviction among communist party members was taken for granted. A fundamental difference between ruling and non-ruling CPs involved precisely this type of differentiation. The presence or absence of authentic ideological belief contributed to a crucial psychological gap between members of non-ruling CPs and members of ruling communist parties, between individuals devoted to the cause of somehow, someday bettering their societies and those already in power who were concerned primarily with maintaining their status and privileges. Nevertheless, the rapid emergence of semi-clandestine Marxist-Leninist groups in Russia in late 1991, in the wake of the ban on the Soviet and Russian communist parties after the hardline coup attempt that August, furnished telling evidence that in the CPSU too, even in the "era of stagnation," there had been pockets of true believers in the official ideology. Elaboration of this point is one of the basic themes of this book.

There is one characteristic common to all of the post-Soviet Russian CPs: their shared view that the results of the Yeltsin government's economic "shock therapy" and pro-Western orientation vindicated once and for all the writings of Marx and Lenin. On the one hand, economic conditions in the Russian Federation bore witness to Marx's views regarding mass impoverization, social polarization, and the degradation of the human spirit under capitalism. On the other hand, the influx of consumer goods and food products from Europe and the newly developed periphery of East Asia, along with the export of Russian raw materials to the West, corroborated much that Lenin had to say about imperialism. Russia, they insisted, was being transformed into a colonial outpost of Western powers, led by the U.S.A.

Another idea held by all Russian neocommunists is that the dissolution of the U.S.S.R. was an act of treason on the part of both Gorbachev and Yeltsin. Never mind that Gorbachev had struggled to the last to preserve the Soviet Union on the basis of a new and equitable federation treaty. Never mind, too, that Yeltsin had acted in concert with the chiefs of state of Ukraine and Belarus in signing the early December 1991 Belovezhskie agreements dissolving the Soviet Union, or that most of the leaders of the Central Asian and Caucasian republics of the former U.S.S.R. later appended their signatures to this act. For the post-Soviet Russian communist parties the lowering of the Soviet flag over the Kremlin on December 25, 1991, was a symbol of high treason rather than national liberation. It was a move undertaken, so they argued, at the behest of Yeltsin's Western "bosses" as well as his spurious democratic cronies in Russia.

It is important to keep in mind these shared perceptions within the post-1991 Russian communist movement for two reasons. First of all, this book focuses largely on the *differences* among the many neocommunist formations in post-Soviet Russia. Under these circumstances, it is easy to lose sight of the broad areas of agreement which explain the emergence and strength of the Russian communist movement in the mid-1990s. Secondly, all too often the beliefs of the "born again" Russian Marxist-Leninists were disregarded by Western observers of contemporary Russian developments. If it was commonly thought before *perestroika* that the Soviet order could never really change, it was just as frequently assumed after 1991 that communism in Russia was somehow dead and gone forever.

At the same time, a countervailing conclusion which emerges from our study is that the development of the post-Soviet Russian communist movement was just one facet of the explosive, if fitful and incomplete, growth of a democratic political culture in the Russian Federation. We ask the many persistent skeptics in this regard to reflect for a moment upon the political profile of Soviet Russia in 1985–1986 compared with that of 1995–1996. During the former time frame, as Gorbachev began his tenure as the last CPSU General Secretary, Andrei Sakharov was still under house arrest in a city that was still called Gorky (now Nizhnii Novogorod) for daring to endorse democratic civil liberties and condemn the Soviet invasion of Afghanistan. Ten years later, under a constitution approved by popular referendum (however flawed), competitive and relatively fair elections were held for the new State Duma (the lower house of parliament) as well as for the presidency of the Russian Federation. Russia was plainly a tortoise rather than a hare in the modern industrial world's march to create democratic institutions. But the Russian people, once released from the grip of communist dictatorship, have shown themselves to be quick and determined learners. One of the purposes of the present volume is also to shed light upon this phenomenon.

The book as a whole has two major focal points. One pertains to the political profiles of the multiple, diverse components of the post-Soviet Russian communist movement as well as the infighting among them. To this end we analyze, on the one hand, the ultra-leftist Marxist-Leninist groups which emerged in 1991–1992 and, on the other hand, the mainstream Communist Party of the Russian Federation formed in early 1993. Chapters 2 through 4 as well as the last section of Chapter 5 deal with these topics, including the question of where the individual CPs fit on a broadly conceived Marxist-Leninist ideological spectrum.

The other major focus involves the CPRF's organizational and programmatic development as well as its political conduct in general, especially during the election campaigns of 1995 and 1996. In Chapter 3 and again in Chapters 5 through 7 we examine in particular the theoretical positions and political strategy of the CPRF chairman, Gennadii Ziuganov, whose writings have led some in the West to view him as a potential "national Bolshevik," or fascist. We also, however, explore two other major tendencies within the CPRF, which we label "Marxist reformers" and "Marxist-Leninist modernizers." At times their influence has been as great, if not greater, than that of Ziuganov and his nationalist associates.

Throughout our discussion of the multi-faceted communist movement's evolution, we also touch on various aspects of overall developments in post-Soviet Russia. Highlights include the events leading to President Yeltsin's

September 21, 1993, dissolution of the Soviet-era legislature, the Russian Supreme Soviet and the Congress of People's Deputies. That step sparked, in turn, the immediate takeover of the parliament building by opposition deputies and their supporters and the eventual outbreak of armed conflict in the center of Moscow on October 3–4, 1993. It is obviously of critical importance to examine the role of the different communist groups in that bloody conflagration, in which over 150 civilians perished.

The new constitution framed by the Yeltsin administration and approved by popular referendum on December 12, 1993, along with the electoral system implemented during the parliamentary contests of 1993 and 1995, were also important benchmarks in Russia's post-1991 evolution. These institutional developments provide the background and political context for our examination of the CPRF's organizational growth and political conduct. As the only communist party to run in the 1993 elections and to be represented in the State Duma, the Ziuganov party enjoyed significant access to offices, funds, and communication links which were unavailable to the extra-parliamentary CPs.

A brief overview of the chapters that follow may be useful to the reader. Chapter 2, "From the Debris of the CPSU: The Rebirth of the Communist Movement," deals with the creation in late 1991, early 1992 of a half dozen or so small Marxist-Leninist parties, tracing their origins back to anti-reform factions which emerged within the CPSU during 1990–1991. That, of course, was the period when the Soviet political system as a whole as well as the CPSU party bureaucracy, or *apparat*, were fragmenting under the dual impact of Gorbachev's halting steps toward democratization and the rush by the Soviet republics to assert their sovereignty vis-à-vis the Kremlin's central authority.

Chapter 3, "Unity in Diversity: The Founding of the Communist Party of the Russian Federation," focuses on the party that would soon become the most important communist organization in post-Soviet Russia. The proceedings of the CPRF's February 1993 congress suggested the presence of three more or less discrete political-ideological tendencies among the party's activists. The most prominent one at that time was represented by Marxist reformers, individuals who had supported many of Gorbachev's changes but had balked at their ultimate denouement: the disintegration of the CPSU and the dissolution of the Soviet Union. A second tendency, the one led by the party's newly elected chairman, Ziuganov, was characterized by unvarnished ethno-centric Great Russian nationalism. The third and weakest current was more orthodox Marxist-Leninist in outlook. Although not nearly as doctrinaire as some of the neocommunist groups described in Chapter 2, it sought to update traditional Soviet ideological precepts to fit the modern world. We thus call its proponents Marxist-Leninist modernizers.

Chapter 4, "The CPRF, the Radical CPs, and the Constitutional Crisis of 1993," addresses the escalating tensions between the executive and legislative branches of government during 1992 and the first half of 1993, which culminated in Yeltsin's dissolution of the Russian Congress of People's Deputies and the bloody clash that followed. During the months leading up to the ultimate confrontation, Ziuganov opted for caution, calling for the creation of a broad national front coalition to oppose the Yeltsin government by peaceful, non-violent means. Most of the more radical neocommunist parties, in contrast, were prepared for a violent showdown with the regime. As we shall see, however, when push did come to shove between the president and the defenders of the Russian parliament (the so-called White House), all of the communist groups including the CPRF were to some extent implicated in the events culminating in the outbreak of mob violence on October 3. That explosion, which included the armed storming of the Moscow mayor's offices next to the White House and an abortive assault on the state-run Ostankino TV station several miles away, prompted the president's decision to order the military bombardment of the White House at dawn the next day. The honeymoon of Russian democracy was over, and Yeltsin's standing in the eyes of many of his fellow citizens would never be the same again.

Chapter 5, "Ziuganovism in Theory and Practice," examines some of Ziuganov's political writings during 1993 and 1994. In these works the CPRF chairman revised many of the basic tenets of Marxism-Leninism, expounded upon his thinking regarding the special character of Russia through the ages, and set forth his views on Russia's relations with the rest of the world. While Ziuganov's theoretical ruminations embraced extreme Russian nationalism, his prescriptions for practical political action were rather moderate. Thus, as already mentioned, the CPRF alone among the post-Soviet communist groups took part in the December 1993 elections for the State Duma, winning over twelve percent of the popular vote and ten percent of the parliamentary seats. At the same time, the very fact of its participation in the elections aroused the fury of the extra-parliamentary CPs and provoked them into a polemical and organizational campaign against the CPRF. This radical neocommunist challenge made the CPRF more vulnerable than it might otherwise have been to pressures from its more orthodox members at all levels of the party structure.

Chapter 6, "The Political Evolution of the CPRF, 1994–1995," analyzes the interplay among the party's three main tendencies as successive drafts of a formal party program were discussed at all levels of the party's organizational structure. For reasons having to do in part with the strengthening of its regional network and the input of its rank-and-file membership, the end result was the approval at the CPRF's January 1995 congress of a program document in which Ziuganov's nationalist views were watered down and the Marxist-Leninist modernizers gained the upper hand over the Marxist reformers.

The crux of Chapter 7, "On the Campaign Trail: The CPRF's Electoral Strategy," has to do with the impact of the foregoing developments upon the CPRF's electoral fortunes. After analyzing the political profile of the top party leadership following its January 1995 congress, we turn to an examination of the 1995 parliamentary elections. As we shall discuss in some detail, the CPRF's striking gains on that occasion were not to be translated into victory in the two-round presidential race of June–July 1996. During the course of the latter contest, it would become all too clear that the CPRF's multiple personality was its Achilles' heel.

In Chapter 8, "Whither Communism in Post-Soviet Russia?," we take a look at some of the sources of the CPRF's electoral support during the 1995–1996 campaign season as well as the alternative strategic choices the party faced if it was ever to become a partner in a democratic government rather than simply a vehicle of social protest.

By way of conclusion, a few words are in order regarding the sources we used in writing this book. Most important were the various communist opposition newspapers which we collected on a regular basis as well as the extensive primary documentation which we received from the CPRF's Duma offices. We also conducted numerous interviews with leading figures in many of the communist parties, including above all the CPRF. Our analysis of the overall Russian context in which the various communist groups operated was, however, based primarily on secondary sources, in both Russian and English.

2

From the Debris of the CPSU: The Rebirth of the Communist Movement

The failure of the August 1991 hardline coup attempt against the Gorbachev regime gave Russian President Boris N. Yeltsin the opportunity to strike what seemed at the time a fatal blow against his erstwhile comrades and now chief political opponents, the Soviet and Russian communists. On August 22, 1991, he imposed a temporary ban on the publication of communist newspapers. The next day he decreed a suspension in the activity of the Russian Communist Party (formally entitled the Communist Party of the R.S.F.S.R.), and two days later the nationalization of all party property on the territory of the Russian Republic. Yeltsin's measures were reinforced when, on August 29, the Supreme Soviet of the U.S.S.R., then in the last days of its existence, suspended the activity of the CPSU throughout the territory of the Soviet Union.

The wording of Yeltsin's August 23 decree against the Russian Communist Party (RCP) had a temporizing character, however. For it spoke of the "suspension" of the RCP's activity until a final resolution of this question in court and thus gave some ground for hope to the communists and their supporters. Therefore, in order to "bury" communism in Russia once and for all, the president would later issue a decree *banning* the communist party on the territory of the Russian republic. Symbolically, it was announced on November 6, the eve of the Soviet Union's most hallowed day of celebration, the anniversary of the Great October Socialist Revolution.

In the course of several days, if not hours, one of the twentieth century's most powerful organizations, which had for more than seventy years almost completely controlled the Soviet state and society, ceased to exist. The country and the world observed in amazement bordering on disbelief the inglorious wreck of the colossus whose might, though undermined during the years of *perestroika*, still seemed enormous. Particularly startling were the

speed and manner in which the multi-million member communist party dis-
appeared without any resistance or protest. The overwhelming majority of
rank-and-file members said farewell to the CPSU—some with feelings of regret, others indifferently, but in general peacefully and without thought of
further participation in politics. The top party leaders turned out to be especially paralyzed.[1] The virtual absence of overt resistance suggested that communism, deprived of any kind of mass support and so quickly defeated in the
country that had been its chief stronghold, had indeed exhausted its vitality.

This assessment, while entirely comprehensible, turned out to be hasty
and mistaken. Already on November 7, 1991, the first anniversary of the
Great October Revolution to be celebrated in post-communist Russia, tens
of thousands of people came out into the streets for demonstrations in
Moscow and other cities in Russia. In contrast to previous years, they were
not required to do this, thus indicating that the communist idea had not
lost its attractiveness for a certain number of Russians. They voluntarily
marched under the red banner, some carrying hand-made posters recalling
that Hitler's first act after coming to power in 1933 had been to ban the
Communist Party of Germany. And by the end of 1991 there had emerged
in Russia five not inconsequential parties claiming communist legitimacy to
one or another degree, not to mention a multitude of smaller leftist groups
and organizations.

The Banning of the Communists
as a Spur to Struggle

The formal legality of Yeltsin's decrees looked extremely doubtful. The constitutional powers of the president as they had evolved under Mikhail S.
Gorbachev did not give him the right to ban political parties or to national-
ize their property. The suspension of public associations was possible only
under conditions of martial law, which had not been declared on August 23.
In reply to these arguments, the president's advisers took the position that
after October 1917 the CPSU had become a "state-political organization of
a criminal type" and not a political party.[2] For Russia it was all too customary
for politicians, especially those in power, to conduct themselves according to
the principle of "revolutionary expediency." In this sense the democratically
elected president was no exception. By outlawing the organizational structures of the communist party and depriving it of its material and financial
basis, Yeltsin had not simply made a political point but he had also gotten rid
of a powerful rival.

But just how did the ban of the communist party itself affect the prospects
of the diverse neocommunist movements in Russia? As mentioned above,
the impact of the government's decrees turned out to be ambiguous. On the
one hand, they put a decisive end to the all-embracing crisis that had struck

the CPSU during the years of *perestroika*.[3] Had it not been for the August events, it would most likely have disintegrated into a series of movements and parties competing with one another for a monopoly on ideological "purity" and for the right of succession to their historical progenitor.

On the other hand, the suppression of the CPSU and the RCP gave a powerful stimulus to battle on the part of the ideologically committed minority in the former communist ranks. Even some who viewed the CPSU more than a little critically considered it immoral to break with the party under conditions of its suppression. Plainly this was not only a problem of moral or even political choice. After all, since 1917 the CPSU had become not just a party but an all-penetrating state institution that was the pivot of the Soviet state and the all-embracing organizational pinnacle of Soviet society. Thus many saw the ban of the CPSU as a blow to the state itself, as a move to expunge seventy years of history. This feeling only intensified after the signing of the Belovezhskie agreements in December 1991, which formally dissolved the U.S.S.R. The protest against the suppression of the CPSU thus became simultaneously a protest against the destruction of the Soviet state.

At the same time, as astutely observed by Sergei F. Cherniakhovskii, one of the leading younger activists in the Russian neocommunist movement, Yeltsin's decrees "presented, as it were, all members of the CPSU with a test of their reliability."[4] Although only a minority were prepared to remain in the communist ranks, those who chose to do so were not simply "true believers" convinced of their ideological probity but also politically militant, ready in word and deed to defend their views under extremely unfavorable conditions.

While these political and moral-psychological factors were certainly significant, perhaps even more important was an organizational consideration. In a word, the rapid rebirth of the communist movement in Russia was made possible thanks to the "proto-party structures" that had already been created in the formally monolithic CPSU during the last years of the Gorbachev era.

Proto-Parties Within the CPSU During the Last Years of the *Ancien Regime*

As the core ruling institution in Soviet society, the CPSU had inevitably attracted into its ranks people holding the most varied political views and theoretical convictions. And this does not even include the multitude who were ideologically indifferent and only hoped, thanks to membership in the communist party, to improve their careers and social status. In the traditional Leninist party-state system, however, these ideological and political differences were in no way openly manifested and the party projected an image of "monolithic unity."

The reforms begun by Gorbachev quickly and radically changed the socio-political conditions in which the CPSU operated. The policy of *glasnost* launched in 1986–1987, the first partially competitive national elections in 1989, the growth of social activism and informal associations, and the emergence of the rudiments of a multi-party system within the CPSU itself led to the creation in the U.S.S.R. of spheres of public politics outside the CPSU leadership's control. In the Soviet all-union elections of 1989 and the Russian elections of 1990 the party was already only one of several political players, a situation for which it was not prepared. The combined result of the accumulated socio-economic problems, the denunciations of the party-state elite (the *nomenklatura*) for corruption and abuses of power, and the ever more searing criticism of Soviet history created around the CPSU a zone of political alienation. Moreover, the gradual withdrawal of the full-time communist party functionaries (the *apparatchiki*) from immediate direction of the economy and polity meant that the CPSU was losing its much vaunted "leading role" in society, and this placed in doubt the very meaning of its existence.

In essence, during the years of *perestroika* the communist party threw down the gauntlet to itself. Once having initiated vast changes in Soviet society, it found itself facing the choice of (1) accommodating to the new "democratic rules of the game," for which it would be necessary to change the very nature of the party and its ingrained political culture; (2) reversing the reforms and returning to a party of an earlier type (Stalinist? Leninist?—the question remained open); or (3) ending its existence as a united political organization. The internal party debates over these options acquired a bitter and divisive character. They soon burst forth into the public arena, which led to their radicalization, on the one hand, and intensified society's doubts regarding the party's capacity for self-reformation on the other. The higher party leadership, under these conditions of deep internal party crisis, was rendered ineffective.

The consequence of this crisis was the emergence within the CPSU's ranks of different ideological tendencies that quickly acquired political and organizational forms. These ideological and political factions, in turn, still further aggravated the unhealthy state of the party.

However, the first new communist organizations arose not inside the CPSU but outside it. This was related to the fact that for orthodox communists the holiest of holies remained the Leninist prohibition against the creation of factions inside the party. The CPSU *apparat*'s control, moreover, still remained rather strict until the late 1980s. Thus several attempts were made to create movements outside the party that had a communist character but included non-party members as well. Their purpose was two-fold: first, to oppose the newly emerging democratic forces in Soviet society; and second, to bring pressure to bear on the CPSU leadership to compel it to resume its traditional "leading role."

The All-Union Society "Unity for Leninism and Communist Ideals"

The undisputed leader and ideological inspiration of the first organization of this orthodox but amorphous type was one of the most notorious critics of *perestroika*, Nina A. Andreeva. This ordinary teacher of chemistry from Leningrad acquired almost global fame after the March 13, 1988, publication in *Sovetskaia Rossiia* of her letter, "I Cannot Give Up My Principles." Dubbed the "manifesto of the anti-*perestroika* forces," the letter called for a halt to the reform of the country and a return to the Stalinist model of organization of society and the party.[5]

Although Andreeva had an unquestionably negative reputation, the wide publicity made her the center of attraction for various Soviet Stalinists. Thus May 1989 saw the founding conference in Moscow of a new organization which called itself the All-Union Society "Unity for Leninism and Communist Ideals." Andreeva, of course, was elected its leader. At first the group viewed its purpose as resistance to the widespread anti-Stalinist exposés that *glasnost* had unleashed by the late 1980s. Its members argued that all the U.S.S.R.'s misfortunes began only *after* the death of Stalin and the 20th CPSU Congress. They called Gorbachev and his supporters "revisionists" and "traitors to socialism." The Society consistently spoke out against any form of private property or market; its economic platform was based upon Stalin's 1952 work, *Economic Problems of Socialism in the USSR*. "Unity" was also convinced of the necessity of reestablishing the CPSU's dictatorship.[6]

The new organization declared that it possessed the only correct ideology and called for the recreation of "true Bolshevism," counterposing it to the "revisionism" allegedly prevailing in the communist party. After a second conference in April 1990, "Unity" called for the "Bolshevization of the CPSU." At this conference as well as the next one, in October 1990, there was a sharp debate about whether to recreate the Stalin-era All-Union Communist Party of Bolsheviks as a separate and authentically Marxist-Leninist party. However, such a step was judged to be premature: for the time being it was decided not to break with the "born again" CPSU but to continue to struggle against "revisionism" in its ranks. At the same time, "Unity" declared its readiness to replace the CPSU in case of its dissolution or outright rejection of communist ideals.

The October 1990 conference resolved to create a Bolshevik Platform within the CPSU (on the pattern of the already existing Democratic and Marxist platforms, about which more will be said below), which was supposed to institutionalize the interests of "Unity's" supporters and conquer a political bridge-head within the structure of the CPSU itself. "Unity" thus rejected its previous political strategy of pressuring the CPSU from without, and was now decisively bent upon moving the center of the political struggle into the very ranks of the party. This step made some sense: since many democratically oriented party members were by then abandoning the CPSU, the influence of orthodoxy within it could more easily be strengthened. The actual establishment of the Bolshevik Platform took place at a July 1991 conference.

In spite of the extremely orthodox and even reactionary character of "Unity," during 1990–1991 it enjoyed a certain limited influence. The organization's conferences were attended by representatives from both Russia and other Soviet republics. Local branches of the society existed in 68 regions of the former U.S.S.R., and its membership consisted of several thousand people. These were primarily pensioners, teachers, and instructors of the formerly required courses in "scientific socialism" in the institutions of higher education.

The United Front of Labor

Another attempt to counterpose a mass organization of a communist bent to the growing democratic movement was the creation of the United Front of Labor (UFL). The initiative for its formation came from a group of traditionalist party intellectuals who set out, in good Leninist fashion, to inculcate their view of "scientific socialism" in the workers' movement. They were supported by some working-class activists. In effect, the UFL could be seen as an effort under Soviet conditions to emulate Poland's "Solidarity," but with a diametrically opposed ideological purpose. A candidate for the role of the "Russian Lech Walesa" was even found in the person of one Veniamin A. Yarin, a worker from the Nizhnetagilskii Metallurgical Combine and member of the Supreme Soviet of the U.S.S.R.

While the UFL first emerged as a Soviet entity, with its founding congress in Leningrad in July 1989, its all-union structure existed only nominally. The UFL of Russia, founded in Sverdlovsk September 8–9, 1989, was a more effective organization. It was created with an eye on the forthcoming competitive elections for the Russian Congress of People's Deputies, the new legislative body patterned after the recently created Soviet Congress of People's Deputies. Indeed, the second UFL congress, which took place in January 1990, was specifically devoted to the organization's strategy and tactics in the elections to be held that March.[7]

As already indicated, among the leaders of the UFL were both industrial workers and members of the intelligentsia. The organization's ideologists were party intellectuals of an orthodox bent such as Richard I. Kosolapov, a professor of Marxist-Leninist philosophy who had been editor-in-chief of the CPSU's flagship theoretical journal, *Kommunist*, from March 1976 until

February 1986. The militant Victor I. Anpilov, subsequently one of the most striking leaders of the neocommunist movement in Russia, began his political career in the ranks of the UFL.

In spite of the fact that quite a few academic types entered the organization, its program was distinguished not by intellectual novelty but by an uncommon dogmatism. The UFL fought for the rebirth of Soviet power and revival of communist party activity on the basis of fundamentalist Leninist principles. The organization demanded the restoration of the leading role of the working class and to this end it proposed conducting elections based on both territorial and production districts. While it did not question the CPSU's monopoly on power, the UFL insisted that the party leadership, even the Politburo, should include more industrial workers.

In the opinion of the UFL ideologists, the reasons for the crisis in Soviet society were inherent in the partial economic reforms of the mid-1960s, of which Gorbachev's *perestroika* was seen as a direct continuation. The organization's economic platform embraced corresponding views: an absolute rejection of any kind of market, a strictly centralized and planned economy, and a harsh struggle against the emerging Soviet "shadow economy," beginning with a confiscatory monetary reform.

The programs of the UFL and "Unity" might seem, if not identical, then extremely close, all the more so since "Unity" was a collective member of the UFL. All the same, they had serious ideological differences. "Unity" was an unconditional supporter of cross-cultural albeit hardline internationalist positions. The UFL, on the other hand, tried to blend Soviet Marxism-Leninism with Russian nationalism and was thus more an organization of the national-Bolshevik type, similar in outlook to the post–World War II Stalinist regime. Above all, the UFL adopted what was then the major slogan of the Russian nationalists: safeguarding the full sovereignty of Russia. It thus advanced a series of proposals for the defense of the Russian and Russian-speaking population in other Soviet republics and demanded the creation of a separate Russian Communist Party within the framework of the all-union CPSU. Typologically, "Unity" embodied an early, internationalist Stalinism and the UFL its later national-Bolshevik version.

The UFL's appeal to the working class went unheeded, however. Its popularity even among highly qualified workers did not exceed thirteen percent.[8] The Bloc of Social-Patriotic Organizations of Russia (a coalition of Russian nationalists and neo-Stalinists supported by part of the party *apparat*), in which the UFL participated in the R.S.F.S.R. parliamentary elections of March 1990, suffered a crushing defeat. Given this failure to mobilize broad political support (its membership did not exceed a few thousand), the UFL, as had "Unity," decided to carry the political struggle into the ranks of the CPSU. There the UFL managed at least to achieve a real if temporary success, for it founded the Communist Initiative Movement, which, in turn, gave a powerful impetus to the creation of the Russian Communist Party as a distinct organization in mid-1990.[9]

Meanwhile, by 1990 the CPSU had entered a new stage of internal crisis. As already noted, factions—in fact, proto-party structures—began to take shape within the organization. Officially they called themselves platforms rather than factions, probably because of the particularly negative connotation of the latter term in the CPSU lexicon (the party statutes in fact forbid both). However, the boundary between platform and faction was extremely vague. A platform was supposed to unite ideologically like-minded individuals, while a faction had an organizational structure that counterposed itself to the party as a whole. In actuality, of course, association according to ideological affinity inevitably led to the emergence of organizational ties.

Broadly speaking, the emergence of platforms *qua* factions was the result of the influence upon the party of the democratization process in Soviet society at large. But more concretely, the forthcoming 28th CPSU Congress scheduled for the summer of 1990 gave a powerful stimulus to their formation at the beginning of that year. The presence of platforms provided the opportunity for their adherents to institutionalize their positions in the CPSU, to propose to the congress their own versions of party programs and rules, and to try to get their representatives into the top party leadership.

The Democratic Platform in the CPSU

The Democratic Platform (DP) had its beginnings in a series of party clubs—informal organizations uniting CPSU intellectuals of a social-democratic and moderate Marxist slant. The DP was founded at a first All-Union Conference of party clubs and organizations in January 1990. One of its best known leaders was the rector of the Moscow higher party school, Viacheslav N. Shostakovskii.

As Graeme Gill has aptly noted, "The main focus of the Democratic Platform was the internal structure and operating procedures of the party itself."[10] In other words, the DP put more emphasis on internal party problems than on general political questions. It sought the transformation of the CPSU into a party of a social-democratic parliamentary type, calling upon it to repudiate its monopoly on power and accommodate itself to the "democratic rules of the game." To this end, the DP called for the following measures: a ban on party committees in production units and other social organizations; the rejection of democratic centralism; the abolition of the system of *nomenklatura* and *apparat* privileges; a shift from a unitary structure to a federated party; and the purge of party leaders guilty of corruption as well as ideologists of a conservative, dogmatic bent.

The strategy for achieving these goals was discussed at the second conference of the Democratic Platform in June 1990. It was decided to propose the democratization of the party at the 28th CPSU Congress, and upon re-

jection of this motion (which all the participants in the discussion anticipated) to leave the CPSU and create a new party based on the DP.

Although the overall membership of the Democratic Platform consisted,
according to several sources, of approximately 100,000 communists, only
about 100 of the 5,000 delegates to the 28th CPSU Congress considered
themselves its supporters.[11] Twenty-four DP members followed the lead of
Yeltsin in demonstratively leaving the party at the congress. Among them
was Shostakovskii, who announced that the DP would soon abandon the
CPSU. In the meantime, he called upon its members to register as supporters of the Democratic Platform in the CPSU so as to have a basis for claiming a portion of the party property at the time of their departure.

Some of the DP members did not agree with Shostakovskii's decision and
chose to continue to struggle for the reform of the CPSU. In November
1990 two organizational steps occurred simultaneously. The proponents of
leaving the CPSU proclaimed the creation of a new party—the Republican
Party of the Russian Federation (RPRF), whose program bore a social-
democratic character. This was the first case of an organized, mass resignation from the CPSU. Those who strove to achieve the democratization of
the CPSU from within established the Democratic Movement of Communists, one of whose leaders was Vasilii S. Lipitskii, a scholar at the CPSU
Central Committee's Institute of Marxism-Leninism.[12]

The Marxist Platform in the CPSU

Like the Democratic Platform, the Marxist Platform (MP) traced its organizational roots to informal groups of party intellectuals. Composed primarily
of academics, researchers, and members of the technocratic intelligentsia, its
founders and supporters were committed to Marxist-Leninist rather than social-democratic views. Although their ideological spectrum was rather broad,
ranging from moderate orthodoxy to reform communism, they started out
as a fairly unified group. At the All-Union Conference of party clubs and organizations in January 1990, these Marxist circles did not agree with the
DP's social-democratic course and decided to create their own structure.
They thus established the Marxist Platform in April 1990, led by Aleksandr
V. Buzgalin, Aleksei A. Prigarin, and Anatolii V. Kriuchkov, the latter two of
whom would become important in the post-Soviet period as the leaders of
separate neocommunist formations.

According to Graeme Gill, the Marxist Platform, in contrast to the Democratic Platform, concentrated not on organizational, internal party problems but "sought to offer a Marxist solution to the crisis facing the country
as an alternative to what it perceived to be the inadequate response of the
party leadership."[13] Accordingly, the second conference of the Marxist Platform, in July 1990, approved the draft of a program that it intended to propose to the 28th CPSU Congress. This early MP draft program supported

the transition to a market economy but insisted that this be done in the interests of labor. It considered the views of the Workers' Opposition of the early 1920s (the Shliapnikov-Kollontai group) as still relevant and deemed its suppression at the Tenth CPSU Congress in 1921 a fatal mistake. For resolving the present crisis, the MP proposed a modernized "workers' opposition" program that would emphasize the role of workers' control over production as well as over the process of economic reform in general. The MP also stood for the transformation of soviets into organs of real power. While it opposed a multi-party system, it wanted to see broad democratization within the CPSU and an end to the *apparat*'s absolute power and bureaucratic centralism.

The Marxist Platform's political activism before and during the 28th CPSU Congress brought some results. At the congress three of its supporters, including Buzgalin and Prigarin, were elected members of the CPSU Central Committee. However, as already noted, from the start the MP brought together rather different ideological tendencies. One wing, headed by Prigarin and Sergei B. Skvortsov, held moderately orthodox views and considered the UFL and Communist Initiative Movement their political allies. The Buzgalin group, in contrast, stood for political democracy, accepted a market economy, and was receptive to an alliance with social democrats. After the Prigarin line prevailed in the MP, the Marxist reformers, while not leaving the organization, created within it the faction "Marxism-XXI."

From the beginning of 1991 the Marxist Platform began to prepare for the creation of a new communist party based on its positions in the event that the CPSU, at its next congress, should reject the basic principles worked out in the MP's draft party program. The author of that draft was Prigarin.[14]

The Communist Initiative Movement

This was the most powerful and influential of all the factional tendencies existing inside the CPSU. The prime mover behind the creation of the Communist Initiative Movement (CIM) was the United Front of Labor, which at its second congress in January 1990 had put forth the idea of convening an initiative congress for the formation of a separate Russian Communist Party within the CPSU. It was assumed that such a body would be able to seize the commanding positions in the CPSU and deliver a rebuff to the "revisionist and capitulationist policies" of its leadership.

The CIM's organizational nucleus was located in Leningrad and included middle- and lower-level party functionaries as well as grassroots activists and orthodox Marxist-Leninist intellectuals. The first stage of the initiative congress for a separate Russian Communist Party took place in April 1990 and the second in June of that year. In essence the initiative congress delivered an ultimatum to Gorbachev, who had been adamantly resisting the emergence of a distinct Russian Communist Party both because of the anti-reformism of its proponents and because of the threat it posed to the separatist impulses already gaining momentum in the Baltics, Georgia, and elsewhere in the Soviet Union. The gist of the ultimatum was that if a Russian CP was not formed and its leading organs created by the time of the 28th CPSU Congress, then the organizers of the initiative congress would take upon themselves this task. The threat was all the more serious inasmuch as the delegates to the initiative congress represented, according to some sources, as many as one and a half million communists in the R.S.F.S.R.

The CIM's program was a carbon copy of the national-Bolshevik program of the United Front of Labor. This was not surprising considering the genesis of the movement and the composition of its intellectual nucleus, which consisted primarily of UFL theoreticians. The CIM defended the leading role of the working class in the direction of society, maintained that the function of the dictatorship of the proletariat had not been exhausted, demanded the creation of workers' councils in economic enterprises, and insisted on the suppression of the "sprouts of capitalist restoration." It rejected outright the idea of a market and denounced the CPSU leadership for betraying communist principles and conducting policies that ran counter to the interests of the people. At the same time, it advanced the thesis of the unique, autochthonous character of communism in Russia.

In a formal sense the "initiators" were successful. For a Conference of Russian Communists consisting of the R.S.F.S.R. delegates to the upcoming 28th CPSU Congress transformed itself into the founding congress of the Russian Communist Party in June 1990. The details of this seminal development will be related in Chapter 3.

On the other hand, a third stage of the initiative congress, in October 1990, negatively evaluated the results of the 28th CPSU Congress and the first actions of the RCP. The "initiators" declared that the new Russian Communist Party had not become a bulwark against "the next dangerous social experiment—the mindless involvement of the country in a capitalist market." Moreover, the RCP's ranks included an alleged "anti-communist liquidationist tendency."[15] This marked the beginning of the formation of a separate Movement for a Communist Initiative as a faction within the RCP. In April and June 1991 this new group held a congress in two stages which demanded the convening in early autumn of an extraordinary congress of the CPSU and approved a draft party program worked out by a group of theoreticians headed by Richard Kosolapov. And in due course the CPSU Central Committee, at its July 1991 plenum, scheduled the 29th CPSU Congress for the following October.

The Democratic Party of Communists of Russia

Paradoxically, the establishment in mid-1990 of the Russian Communist Party facilitated the creation of the Democratic Party of Communists of

Russia (DPCR) in mid-1991. The RCP's orthodox style and leadership elicited protests and a feeling of estrangement among an ever larger number of communists, some of whom were prone to declare, "I am a member of the CPSU but not the RCP." Many of them sought political self-definition within the framework of a leftist perspective but not within the Russian Communist Party or even the CPSU, inasmuch as they had lost their illusions regarding the possibility of the latter's self-reformation. The DPCR had, moreover, a number of attractive qualities. First, the initiative for its creation came from a group of Russian parliamentary deputies, which significantly strengthened the position of the new organization and endowed it with respectability. Secondly, it had a charismatic leader in Aleksandr V. Rutskoi, all the more so since he was soon to become vice president of Russia, running with Boris Yeltsin in the June 1991 presidential election.

Rutskoi announced at the Third Russian Congress of People's Deputies (March–April 1991) the creation of a new parliamentary fraction, Communists for Democracy. This came as a bomb shell, particularly because precisely at this congress the more orthodox communists were bent upon dumping Yeltsin from his post as chairman of the R.S.F.S.R. Supreme Soviet. The new fraction announced its opposition to the anti-Yeltsin Communists of Russia fraction, and declared its support for the chairman personally and for the process of radical political and economic reforms he advocated. Rutskoi received the backing of both democratically oriented communists and anti-communist democrats, the latter seeing in his initiative the possibility of splitting the CPSU from within.[16]

Thereafter work on the creation of the new political party began, with the active participation of Vasilii Lipitskii's Democratic Movement of Communists. In early August 1991 the official establishment of the Democratic Party of Communists of Russia took place, and immediately afterwards its leaders—Rutskoi and Lipitskii—were expelled from the Central Committee of the recently created Russian Communist Party as well as from the CPSU.[17]

The DPCR program leaned toward the right wing of social democracy. The designation "communist" in its name did not correspond to its political and ideological profile but was intended to reassure would-be members and supporters from among the communists. The new party's potential drawing power appeared at the time to be rather significant. However, the failed putsch of August 1991 fundamentally changed the political situation throughout the Soviet Union and deprived the DPCR of the original reason for its existence.

The Neocommunist Spectrum After the Bans

The political self-assertion of the disparate ideological tendencies that had proliferated within the CPSU in 1990–1991 occurred during the very first days after the August 1991 putsch and Yeltsin's subsequent ban on the communist parties. Already on August 20 the DPCR leadership announced its party's withdrawal from the CPSU, and it soon explicitly repudiated its Marxist heritage. At its first congress in October 1991 the organization adopted the name People's Party Free Russia (PPFR). Although its programmatic documents made wide use of social-democratic phraseology, very little remained of leftist principles.

No less immediate was the reaction of the more orthodox communist groups as they began the process of transforming themselves into independent political parties. On August 26 the staff of the Movement for a Communist Initiative addressed a call to its party organizations to hold the founding congress of the Russian Communist Workers' Party in November 1991. The Bolshevik Platform and its progenitor, the "Unity" group, also planned the founding congress of the All-Union Communist Party of Bolsheviks for November 1991. In September the Marxist Platform split, and organizational groups were formed for the creation of two parties. Aleksei Prigarin headed the first, the organizational committee of the Union of Communists, and Anatolii Kriuchkov and others the second, the organizational committee of the Russian Party of Communists. The more moderate section of the Marxist Platform, the "Marxism XXI" group of Aleksandr Buzgalin, along with several other circles and trade unions of a leftist bent, launched plans to create the Party of Labor.

In chronological terms, however, the first new communist-led political party was formed not by orthodox party types but by representatives of the moderate, social-democratic tendency within the CPSU.

The Socialist Labor Party

The rapid formation of this moderate neocommunist group was possible thanks to the individuals who were its early supporters. On the one hand, they were well known and respected in society at large as well as in the communist milieu, and, on the other hand, some of them were Soviet or R.S.F.S.R. people's deputies, which enabled them to use their parliamentary connections to build the new political organization.

In the first days of autumn 1991 they issued an appeal declaring that the CPSU had exhausted its purpose and calling for the creation of a new party of socialist orientation as the successor to the CPSU. The authors of this document were the Soviet people's deputies and CPSU Central Committee members Anatolii A. Denisov and Roy A. Medvedev (the former dissident and supporter of "socialism with a human face"); the Russian people's deputies Ivan P. Rybkin (one of the leaders of the Communists of Russia fraction and later the first speaker of the Russian State Duma) and cosmonaut Vitalii I. Sevastianov; and also a group of deputies from local soviets. The Gorbachev team's mid-1991 draft of a new CPSU program was proposed as the ideological basis of the Socialist Labor Party (SLP). Its founders proclaimed their commitment to the principles of political pluralism and parliamentary democracy, defended the concept of a mixed economy, and recognized the right to entrepreneurial activity and owner-operated private firms.[18]

In essence, the creation of the SLP was an attempt to transfer onto Russian soil the model of successor communist parties developing in post-communist East-Central Europe. And although its program was categorically unacceptable to the orthodox Marxist-Leninist groups, it seemed in those first post-putsch days that a center-left reformist party really could become the main, if not the only, successor to the CPSU. Indeed, at its founding conference on October 26, 1991, there were representatives of practically all the former CPSU's left-wing factions, perhaps because they hoped to turn its proceedings to their own benefit.

The debate over the party's name—a significant number of delegates insisted that it include the word "communist"—had the effect of putting an end to any plausible effort at unity. The representatives of the Movement for a Communist Initiative walked out of the conference, while the Prigarin section of the Marxist Platform refused to enter the new party. Somewhat later the Kriuchkov group also left the SLP, disappointed by its failure to "communize" the new organization. In this way the very founding of the SLP hastened the crystallization of communist parties of a more Marxist-Leninist slant.

In November 1991 the SLP was officially registered, which indicated the conciliatory attitude of the Yeltsin government toward the moderate successor communists. At the same time, the very act of registration, which legalized its political activity, attracted to the SLP's ranks a sizable number of new members, including some former local CPSU functionaries.

In December 1991 the first congress of the SLP adopted a program that reflected the relatively moderate views of its original organizers. It also elected seven co-chairmen, from among whom the actual party leader gradually emerged as Liudmila S. Vartazarova, an economist by training and a secretary of the CPSU's Moscow city committee on the eve of the August putsch. The SLP's main political trump card was its connection to the left-wing parliamentary fractions, for thirty-one Russian Congress people's deputies were SLP members.

Thanks to its legal status, parliamentary access, and the inclusion in its ranks of a large number of former party functionaries, the SLP succeeded in quickly developing its organizational structures. By the beginning of 1993 SLP sections existed in almost all regions of Russia, and its membership reached, according to some estimates, as many as 100,000. At the same time, an important segment of the rank-and-file members and also functionaries who had joined the SLP because of its legal status held far more traditional communist views than the leadership. Indeed, there are indications that a number of them hoped to transform the SLP into their own successor organization should the Constitutional Court uphold the president's ban on the Soviet-era communist parties.[19]

During 1992, in the conflict that emerged between Yeltsin and the Russian Congress of People's Deputies over economic "shock therapy" and the division of powers between the executive and legislative branches of government, the SLP consistently took the side of parliament. However, its position was far from the radicalism of the "irreconcilable" opposition that will be discussed below. Beginning in November 1992, it came out in support of the idea of a social compact as a mechanism for reaching agreement among the political forces battling over the question of how to reform Russian society. In short, the SLP tried, unsuccessfully as it would turn out, to form a moderate left-wing opposition movement as an alternative to the increasingly vocal neocommunist and nationalist radicals.

Also during 1992 a heated discussion flared up within the neocommunist movement itself over the question of whether to reestablish the CPSU. The SLP leadership came out in favor of the restoration of the RCP, not the CPSU. This was due partly to its focus on exclusively legal and parliamentary methods of work but also to the good personal relations and ideological affinity between the SLP leadership and the organizers of the projected second congress of the still-banned RCP. However, the eventual reconstitution of the RCP as the Communist Party of the Russian Federation (CPRF) in February 1993, for which the SLP had worked so hard, led to a profound crisis in the latter. For a majority of the SLP's rank-and-file members as well as entire local sections joined the new CPRF. Two of its co-chairmen, Rybkin and Mikhail I. Lapshin (who would later in 1993 form the Agrarian Party of Russia), chose this same path. And by June 1993 the SLP's membership had declined by a factor of ten. The remaining leadership, supported by a number of regional units, decided to preserve the party as an independent organization. Now, however, the accent was placed on the identification of the SLP as a *non-communist* party of center-leftist bent which renounced any continuity with the legacy of the CPSU.

This orientation was embodied in the party program approved at the SLP's fourth congress in February 1994. Rejecting traditional Marxist-Leninist ideology, the SLP proclaimed its commitment to political democracy, the rule of law, a socially oriented market economy, mixed forms of property with social ownership playing the leading role, and a peaceful parliamentary path of development.[20] There was thus little to differentiate it from the many other small social-democratic formations that had begun to take shape in Russia from May 1990 onward.

The All-Union Communist Party of Bolsheviks

Rooted in the CPSU's Bolshevik Platform faction, the founding congress of the All-Union Communist Party of Bolsheviks (ACPB) took place in

Leningrad on November 8, 1991. In the course of its preparations and proceedings, the original Bolshevik Platform (BP) split three ways. Some of its
supporters threw in their lot with the soon to be formed Russian Communist Workers' Party. The group around Tatiana M. Khabarova, author of the
BP's economic program, insisted on the restoration of the CPSU, not the
creation of a new party, and preferred to keep its previous name, Bolshevik
Platform. The remaining members of the BP and its precursor, "Unity,"
proclaimed the creation of the new party and elected Nina Andreeva its general secretary.

The ACPB was the most dogmatic of all the emerging neocommunist formations. It believed that the rebirth of socialism and revival of the U.S.S.R.
were possible only through a second edition of the Great October Socialist
Revolution. The fierce proponent of a narrowly defined class legitimacy, it dismissed parliamentary democracy and insisted instead on the restoration of the
dictatorship of the proletariat. It categorically rejected all market elements and
any kind of private property. Contemptuous of the CPSU for having sold out
to "bourgeois illusions," it upheld the North Korean regime of the late Kim Il
Sung as the model for a revived Soviet Union.[21]

The Andreeva party demonstratively refused official registration, prefer-
ring semi-clandestine methods of work. While welcoming in words the unity
of all communist forces, it opposed in practice efforts to recreate either the
CPSU or the RCP. With the exception of the Russian Communist Workers'
Party, the ACPB leaders denounced all communist organizations for revisionism or other forms of deviationism. Because of its extremely unappealing
program and exclusionary tactics, the ACPB was in fact transformed into a
political sect numbering only a few thousand which enjoyed no influence in
Russian society and little authority in the communist movement.

The Union of Communists

At a meeting on September 7–8, 1991, the coordinating council of the
Marxist Platform resolved that the creation of a new communist party was
"the only possible path to the rebirth of the communist movement on an
authentically Marxist-Leninist basis." However, as previously noted, a number of ideological and programmatic differences among the MP members
led to the emergence of two organizational committees.[22]

On November 16–17, 1991, the MP group led by Aleksei Prigarin held
the founding conference of their new party, the Union of Communists
(UC), in Zheleznodorozhnii. The first congress of the UC took place the
following April in Moscow, and the party was registered in September 1992.
As for its program, the UC proclaimed the necessity of returning the country "to the path of socialist development," advanced the slogan of the
reestablishment of the U.S.S.R., and demanded a return to a planned economy. On the other hand, while rejecting the use of hired labor, it condoned

owner-operated private property. More importantly, the UC stood for the transfer of the full economic jurisdiction of enterprises to workers' collectives and the establishment of industrial self-management (again bringing to mind the goals of the Workers' Opposition in the early 1920s). In the political sphere the UC defended the soviets as the true form of democracy but called for deputies to be elected from both territorial districts and workplaces.[23]

Above all, the Union of Communists consistently aimed at the reestablishment of the CPSU. It declared its own primary organizations to be those of the CPSU in Russia and, as will be related in Chapter 5, it took an active role in the recreation of the CPSU as the Union of Communist Parties–CPSU in late March 1993.

As a whole, the UC's ideological-political profile can be classified as moderately orthodox, in contrast to the reactionary orthodoxy of the All-Union Communist Party of Bolsheviks. If Andreeva's party was oriented toward the Stalinist model of socialism, the Union of Communists looked to an earlier, albeit idealized, Leninist model. During 1992 its membership numbered about 10,000, but declined to some five to seven thousand after the founding of the Communist Party of the Russian Federation in February 1993.[24]

Prigarin, one of the moving spirits behind the UC's formation, soon became its first secretary. Born in 1930 in the Kaluga region, he was the son of a functionary in the People's Commissariat of Trade who got caught up in Stalin's Great Purge and perished in 1938. His mother taught middle school in Moscow, where Prigarin completed undergraduate and graduate studies at the Moscow State Economic Institute. After working as an economist in several capacities, he served for 15 years as the director of the Center for Scientific Organization of Labor and Management of the Russian Ministry of Radio Communications, becoming director of the corresponding Soviet body from 1983 until March 1991. Although a CPSU member since 1956, his politically active life started only in 1989. He first joined the informal association Communists for *Perestroika*, and then helped found the Marxist Platform in early 1990, later co-authoring many of its programmatic documents.[25] Still vigorous and articulate, upon his retirement in 1991 he devoted himself to full-time political activism.

The Russian Communist Workers' Party

This was one of the most influential and militant neocommunist organizations in 1992–1993. It originated in the Movement for a Communist Initiative, and its founding congress took place in two stages. At the first, held in Yekaterinburg November 23–24, 1991, a programmatic declaration was approved based on the relatively orthodox draft CPSU program worked out earlier by the Marxist-Leninist scholar Richard Kosolapov. Soon thereafter, in January 1992, the Russian Communist Workers' Party (RCWP) was registered. However, a more radical wing soon got the upper hand. As a result, during the second stage of the RCWP congress, held in Cheliabinsk December 5–6, 1992, a more extremist draft put together by the party's Leningrad branch was adopted as the new program. Meanwhile, the best known leaders of the party became Viktor A.Tiulkin, the first secretary based in Leningrad/St. Petersburg, and Viktor Anpilov, head of the Moscow branch.

In the RCWP's view, the roots of the crisis that had struck the country and the party were to be found in the Khrushchev-era reforms. The upshot was the "social-democratic degeneration of the CPSU leadership" and, ultimately, the usurpation of power by "bourgeois forces" led by Gorbachev and Yeltsin. The RCWP categorically rejected parliamentary democracy, dubbing it merely a form of "dictatorship of the bourgeoisie." Its program called for the return to a planned economy and rejected private property, the market, and privatization. The forcible reestablishment of the U.S.S.R. was one of its programmatic priorities. Above all, the RCWP proclaimed itself to be the "vanguard of the working class." The working-class character of the party was emphasized not only in its name but also in its rules, which stipulated that manual laborers comprise no less than fifty-one percent of the party membership.[26]

The nationalist accent that was apparent in the Movement for a Communist Initiative and its precursor, the United Front of Labor, was not particularly noticeable in the RCWP's programmatic documents. Possibly this was because the party intended to compete with the soon to be reconstituted Communist Party of the Russian Federation, among whose proponents Russian nationalist thinking was gaining strength. All the same, in their oral agitation RCWP activists made wide use of one of the main ideas of the Russian nationalists—the notion of a "Zionist-Masonic conspiracy" to take over the world. Indeed, the then head of the ideological commission of the RCWP's Moscow organization argued in June 1994 that the real threat of world domination came from Zionism, with its headquarters in the International Monetary Fund.[27]

With regard to ideology and program, the RCWP occupied an intermediate position between the All-Union Communist Party of Bolsheviks and the Union of Communists. Three features distinguished it from these latter two formations. First of all, the RCWP's emphasis upon recruiting blue collar workers contrasted sharply with the predominant role of people with technocratic, bureaucratic, or professional backgrounds in the other neocommunist groups. Secondly, the RCWP had many more members than the ACPB or UC, partly because it could rely on the organizational structures cultivated by the earlier Movement for a Communist Initiative and also use the printing facilities inherited from it. Thus, at the peak of its popularity it had, according to some estimates, 80,000 members while its numbers also included, during 1992–1993, six Russian people's deputies. But by late 1994 its ranks had fallen to 40,000, representing fifty-one regions,[28] in an apparent reflection of the bandwagoning effect of the Communist Party of the Russian Federation's growth and stature after February 1993.

A third distinctive feature of the Russian Communist Workers' Party was its aggressive, neo-Leninist activism. From autumn 1991 on, a radical grass-roots organization bent upon direct action in the streets began to emerge from the former ranks of the United Front of Labor. Named Toiling Russia, its strategy was to unleash an urban revolution by acting as a battering-ram in the struggle against the Yeltsin regime. As such, it became the center of attraction not only for communists but for practically all activist opposition forces. As will be discussed in Chapter 4, Toiling Russia was one of the chief organizers of the regular street actions that brought together some tens of thousands, and at times more than 100,000, people. Some of these, for example the demonstrations of February 23, 1992, and May 1, 1993, ended in clashes with the police and bloodshed. What is important here is that, while uniting activists from almost all neocommunist groups, the actual head of both Toiling Russia and its subsidiary, Toiling Moscow, was the RCWP's dynamic Moscow leader, Anpilov.

Anpilov was born in 1945 in the Krasnodar region. His father was a potter, his mother a peasant, and he himself (the youngest of six children) was trained as a metalworker. Still, he finished a middle school for working youth and, after serving three years in the Soviet Strategic Rocket Forces, he was able to study journalism and international affairs at Moscow State University. His subsequent employment included a brief stint as an interpreter in Cuba, a longer period as a reporter for a local Moscow paper, and twelve years with the Soviet State Committee for Television and Radio beginning in 1978. While there, he focused on Latin America and visited Nicaragua as a foreign correspondent. Turning to full-time political work in 1990, he founded the leftist newspaper *Molniia* (lightning) which first expressed the views of the United Front of Labor and the Movement for a Communist Initiative and later became the official organ of the RCWP Central Committee. Anpilov actively participated in the establishment of the new party, and in December 1991 he became the secretary in charge of the Moscow organization.[29]

The Russian Party of Communists (RPC)

The smallest of the neocommunist formations, this party was created by the Marxist Platform centrists identified with Anatolii Kriuchkov. As already indicated, the Kriuchkov group took part in the founding conference of the Socialist Labor Party and even announced that it would join it as a "platform of laborer-communists." But several days later Kriuchkov disavowed this position and began building an independent party.

In November 1991, after joining with a Moscow group led by Boris F. Slavin and a Leningrad group led by Yurii P. Belov, an organizational committee was set up to create the new party. Its founding conference took place

December 14–15, 1991, in Zheleznodorozhnii outside of Moscow. Kriuchkov, who assumed leadership responsibilities from the start, became the party chairman at a meeting of the RPC's central executive committee in May 1992. The party was registered in March 1992, and the following December it held its first congress.[30]

The draft program discussed at the congress placed the RPC somewhere between the Union of Communists and the Socialist Labor Party. While classifying itself unconditionally as a Marxist-Leninist party, the RPC—in contrast to the more dogmatic communist parties—was extremely negative toward Stalinism. In its view, Stalinism was a "course distortion of Marxism in the interests of the party-state bureaucracy," and the party-state bureaucratic system set up in the 1930s was one of the main reasons for the crisis of Soviet society. The political section of the RPC's program was very close to that of its more leftist neighbors on the neocommunist political spectrum: the highest form of democracy was the soviet system, in which elections should be held according to the mixed residence-workplace principle. However, in its economic platform the RPC differed substantially from the others. It called for an updated version of Lenin's New Economic Policy, a planned market economy in which some state-regulated private enterprise and private use (though not ownership) of land would exist for the foreseeable future. Unlike the other neocommunist groups, moreover, the RPC's draft program looked positively upon the reforms of the Khrushchev years as well as those of the early Gorbachev era.[31]

In what was deemed a scandal at the time, Kriuchkov himself abstained during the final vote on the program described above, which had been drafted by Boris Slavin. One point on which Kriuchkov disagreed was the evaluation of Khrushchev, whom he considered an "adventurer" who opened the U.S.S.R. to Western influence too quickly, thereby initiating the "bourgeoisification" of the *nomenklatura*, or upper echelons of the party-state bureaucracy.[32] Another bone of contention between the two leaders was their difference of opinion on the RPC's role in the soon–to–be–formed Communist Party of the Russian Federation. As will be discussed in Chapter 3, Kriuchkov wanted the RPC to retain its organizational autonomy, while Slavin chose to join the CPRF in order to influence its program from within. In doing so, he took two-thirds of the RPC's members, including Leningrad leader Yurii Belov, with him.[33] If this left the party with a much-reduced membership (according to some sources, its ranks thereafter numbered only in the hundreds), it also left Kriuchkov as its undisputed head.

Kriuchkov, an imposing figure with a persuasive manner and a sharp analytical mind, may be considered a self-made man in the post–World War II Russian context. He was born in 1944 in the Riazan region, the son of collective farmers, and he was educated at the Riazan railway trade school. While working at various blue collar jobs and then as a police inspector, he completed law school by correspondence. He was thus able to study at the Graduate Academy of the Soviet Ministry of Internal Affairs and to become a senior researcher at the ministry's All-Union Scientific Research Institute from 1983 until February 1992, when he retired to undertake full-time party work. Elected a member of the central committee of the newly formed Russian Communist Party in September 1990, he actively participated in the preparations for reconstituting the RCP as the Communist Party of the Russian Federation in 1992.[34]

The Elusive Quest for Unity

The total membership of the new communist parties, in comparison with the CPSU, was not impressive. According to the sometimes overstated figures released by their leaders, by the spring of 1992 their ranks counted altogether 200,000 to 300,000 people, of which 15,000 to 20,000 were in Moscow. This constituted only two percent of the membership of the former CPSU in the Russian Federation. At the same time, according to sociological surveys carried out by erstwhile communist functionaries in Moscow in September 1991, that is, at the peak of the post-putsch anti-communist hysteria, as many as twenty-five percent of former party members were ready to remain in the CPSU.[35] Even assuming that this figure was strongly inflated, it seems that a significant number of rank-and-file communists really wanted to retain their communist affiliation but were not drawn to any of the neocommunist organizations.

If none of the new communist parties enjoyed legitimacy in the eyes of the former rank-and-file loyalists, this may have been partly because the latter, who were often not well versed in theoretical niceties, simply became confused by the multiplicity of new parties and did not understand the substantive differences among them. Moreover, many may have feared the extremely orthodox programs, radical rhetoric, and lack of political flexibility among some of the new parties. But above all, those still active at the grassroots urged the creation of a single, united communist organization.

The differences among the various neocommunist parties were thus largely confined to the leaderships. At the lower level, especially in the Russian regions, these formations were either weak or nonexistent. De facto communist unity was initially achieved in joint street demonstrations, which attracted the participation of all communist activists and frequently all opposition organizations in general. The first such experience occurred during the preparations and conduct of the November 7, 1991, manifestation. Although Toiling Russia was the cover for this coordinated action and the ringleaders were members of the RCWP, it included practically all communist groups. But there were also other forms of grassroots unity: for example, the widespread practice of dual or even triple party membership, when the same individuals were simultaneously members of several communist organizations.

Among Russian communist leadership circles, there were three positions on the question of a successor to the CPSU.[36] The first one opposed the recreation of the old party and emphasized the activity of the neocommunist parties. This point of view was held above all by the RCWP. It considered itself the only ideological heir to the CPSU and, being one of the largest (in 1992) and most militant of the neocommunist formations, entertained the possibility of unification only on its own ideological platform. The RCWP leadership also took a much more negative position toward former higher party functionaries than did most of the other post-Soviet Russian communists. It thus flatly refused cooperation with any of them. At the same time, a significant number of rank-and-file members of the RCWP did not share this hardline position and were ready to take part in some kind of unification process.

Andreeva's All-Union Communist Party of Bolsheviks also took an absolutely irreconcilable position on the reestablishment of the CPSU, with the one difference that it saw *itself* as the true guardian of ideological purity. The ACPB thus categorically forbade its members to take any part in the recreation of the "opportunist Gorbachevist CPSU" (which subsequently led to a schism in its ranks).

The second tendency backed the reestablishment of the CPSU independently of whether the official ban on its activity continued or was removed. From the very beginning this was the adamant position of at least two of the neocommunist groups, Prigarin's Union of Communists and Khabarova's Bolshevik Platform. They were supported by a number of regional party organizations as well as some of the communist parties in the other former Soviet republics.

As for the third position, its representatives were committed to the view that it was necessary to act absolutely legally, within the framework of the law, and therefore it was better to wait for the decision of the Constitutional Court on the legality of Yeltsin's ban on communist activity. They included part of the former higher-level party bureaucracy, and they could be found in substantial numbers within the Socialist Labor Party and, to a lesser extent of course, in the Russian parliament.

The Union of Communists took upon itself the role of coordinating the forces supporting the rebirth of the CPSU. In January 1992 some of its members from the former CPSU Central Committee formed an initiative group to convene a central committee plenum. A month later, in February, a meeting of UC supporters from the former CPSU Moscow city committee and secretaries of several primary organizations founded the Information Bureau of the Moscow city committee, which assumed the function of a revived CPSU city committee office. The first congress of the Union of Communists, in April 1992, also proclaimed the formation of an International Union of Communists, uniting communists from a number of other former Soviet republics.

By summer 1992 this activism began to bear its first concrete results. In June a self-proclaimed plenum of the CPSU Central Committee, which was technically illegal, took place. It expelled Gorbachev from the party, dissolved the former Politburo and Secretariat, and formed an organizational committee for the preparation of a Twentieth All-Union Party Conference. It called upon former party members to ignore the ban on the CPSU, to convene meetings, and to reestablish the CPSU's primary and regional organizations. The basic organizational work for the preparation of the party conference was undertaken by activists from the Union of Communists and the Bolshevik Platform, supported by some highly placed figures from the former CPSU Central Committee.

At the same time, the reestablishment of the CPSU was intertwined with the question of the fate of the Russian Communist Party. In view of the fact that the U.S.S.R. had disintegrated, many communist loyalists viewed the idea of recreating the CPSU as either unattainable or an extremely distant prospect. On the other hand, the former RCP structures represented a significant organizational, human, and political potential. Disagreements emerged, however, over how to reestablish the RCP, over the leadership of this organizational process, and over the political program of the reconstituted party.

At a meeting of communist leaders and activists from Russia and the former Soviet republics on August 8–9, 1992, Kriuchkov proposed the creation of a Russian political consultative council (*Roskomsovet*).[37] Representatives of both the neocommunist parties and the banned RCP Central Committee joined it, and the last RCP first secretary, Valentin A. Kuptsov, headed it. Four options for the reestablishment of an all-Russian communist party were discussed: (1) to unify solely on the ideological basis of the RCWP; (2) to hold a unification congress of all Russian communist parties but with the preservation of their autonomy and *without* the participation of the old party leadership organs (the point of view of Kriuchkov's RPC); (3) to rebuild the party around the former RCP Central Committee and its leaders but separately from the CPSU and only with the permission of the Constitutional Court (Kuptsov's preference); and (4) to reestablish the Russian Communist Party as a section of the CPSU and regardless of the Constitutional Court's decision (the variant insisted upon by the Union of Communists, the Bolshevik Platform, and the organizational committee of the rump CPSU Central Committee). In the end, the second option of a consultative unification congress open to all but led by none of the banned party leaderships was chosen as a compromise. In late October 1992, the *Roskomsovet* set up an organizational committee for this purpose, headed by Kuptsov. The RCWP and the Andreeva group refused to take part in this "social-democratic" body and announced their intention to conduct an ideological struggle against it.[38]

Somewhat earlier in October, on the other hand, the projected Twentieth CPSU Conference took place, again flaunting the ban on its activities, with the presence of delegations from 13 former Soviet republics. The conference, organized by Prigarin's associates, adopted a series of notably orthodox documents, and it proceeded to schedule a *29th CPSU Congress* for late March 1993. In doing so it made no decision whatsoever about an RCP congress, thereby tacitly implying that the latter would be created subsequently as a section of the CPSU.

The Constitutional Court's
Verdict on the "CPSU Case"

All the above convoluted arrangements were swept away by the Constitutional Court's November 30, 1992, verdict on the "CPSU case." As mentioned at the beginning of this chapter, from a purely legal point of view the presidential decrees to ban the CPSU and the RCP had looked extremely doubtful. Accordingly, the petition to declare the decrees unconstitutional, which a group of former communist leaders and parliamentary deputies brought before the Constitutional Court in February 1992, emphasized precisely the legal rather than the political side of the issue. The opening of the trial was delayed, counter-charges were made, but on July 7 hearings on the case began and continued, with interruptions, until the end of November 1992.

The communists' position was very strong, largely due to the efforts of those who organized their defense, about which more will be said in the next chapter. Among other things, the petitioners demonstrated considerable political flexibility in their argumentation. They pointed out that their suit before the Constitutional Court was not an effort at confrontation with the president but a "struggle for the purity of presidential power."[39] They also had recourse to what was for them a rather uncharacteristic argument, namely, that the president had violated the constitutional guarantees on property.[40]

At first glance, the final verdict had a halfway, compromise character: Yeltsin's decrees on the suppression of the communist party structures were declared unconstitutional but only insofar as they concerned the *primary organizations of the RCP*.[41] In fact, however, this was both a political and a moral victory for the RCP supporters. From then on they could legally both create new organizations and reestablish the old ones. By the same token, the question of building a new unified Russian communist party automatically went by the board, for it was far easier to reestablish the old one.

But, as always, the devil lies in the details. The decision of the court was subject to a dual interpretation. On the one hand, it could be understood as granting permission *only* for the primary organizations of the RCP, not for CPSU activity. On the other hand, since according to the CPSU statutes the primary organizations of the RCP were at one and the same time the primary organizations of the CPSU in Russia, the verdict could also be taken as permitting the primary organizations of the CPSU.

Thus, while the court's verdict gave a powerful boost to the reconstitution of the Russian Communist Party, its ambiguity intensified the already strained relations in the communist movement in general and contributed to the beginning of a second, more serious round of infighting. At first the chief protagonists were, on one side, those who wanted to recreate the RCP independently of the CPSU and, on the other, the supporters of the establishment of a single, all-embracing CPSU in which the RCP would be simply an integral, constituent part. All too soon, however, the conflict was transformed into an open confrontation between the more orthodox *neocommunist* parties and the reconstituted but relatively more moderate former Russian Communist Party. The reestablishment of the RCP as the Communist Party of the Russian Federation will be the focal point of the next chapter, while the internecine battles within the communist movement as a whole will be addressed in Chapter 5.

Notes

1. On the conduct of the leadership of the Russian Communist Party right after the August putsch, see the illuminating if not disinterested comments in Sergei F. Cherniakhovskii, "Kommunisticheskoe dvizhenie v eltsinskoi Rossii: Ot raspada k konsolidatsii," *Rossiia XXI*, No. 1–2 (1994), p. 76.

2. For the legal arguments for and against the decrees, see *KPSS vne zakona?! Konstitutsionnyi sud v Moskve* (Moscow: Baikalskaia akademiia, 1992).

3. For details, see Graeme Gill, *The Collapse of a Single-Party System: The Disintegration of the CPSU* (Cambridge: Cambridge University Press, 1994).

4. Cherniakhovskii, "Kommunisticheskoe dvizhenie v eltsinskoi Rossii," p. 80.

5. For an analysis of the Andreeva affair, see Robert G. Kaiser, *Why Gorbachev Happened: His Triumph and His Failure* (New York: Simon and Schuster, 1991), pp. 204–214.

6. For details on "Unity" and the Bolshevik Platform, see *Politicheskie partii sovremennoi Rossii: Informatsionnye i analiticheskie materialy ob obshcherossiiskikh partiiakh i obshchestvennykh dvizheniiakh (1990–1993)*, first ed. (Moscow: Izdatelstvo "Rossiiskaia politicheskaia entsiklopediia" [ROSSPEN], 1993), pp. 343–344; and Vladimir Pribylovskii, *Slovar novykh politicheskikh partii i organizatsii Rossii* (Moscow: Informatsionno-ekspertnaia gruppa "Panorama," 1992), p. 27.

7. See *Pervyi (Uchreditelnyi) sezd Obedinennogo fronta trudiashchikhsia Rossii: Dokumenty i materialy* (Sverdlovsk: 1989); also *Vybory: programmy, kontseptsii, Platforma Obedinennogo fronta trudiashchikhsia*, typescript, December 1989.

8. John Dunlop, *The Rise of Russia and the Fall of the Soviet Empire* (Princeton: Princeton University Press, 1993), pp. 135–136.

9. Also on the UFL, see *Politicheskie partii sovremennoi Rossii*, pp. 339–343; and Pribylovskii, *Slovar*, pp. 68–69.

10. Gill, *The Collapse of a Single-Party System*, p. 122.

11. Ibid., p. 124.

12. On the Democratic Platform, see also ibid., pp. 122–124, 142, 144–145; and Pribylovskii, *Slovar*, p. 91.

13. Gill, *The Collapse of a Single-Party System*, p. 122.

14. On the Marxist Platform, see also ibid., pp. 124–125; and Pribylovskii, *Slovar*, pp. 45–46.

15. See *Rossiia: partii, assotsiatsii, soiuzy, kluby: Sbornik materialov*, 10 vols. (Moscow: "RAU-Press," 1992–1993), Vol. 1, p. 130.

16. On the Democratic Party of Communists of Russia, see Nikolai Gulbinskii and Marina Shakina, *Afganistan . . . Kreml . . . "Lefortovo": Episody politicheskoi biografii Aleksandra Rutskogo* (Moscow: Lada, 1994), pp. 59–84; also Pribylovskii, *Slovar*, pp. 55–56; Dunlop, *The Rise of Russia*, p. 65; Gill, *The Collapse*, pp. 147–148.

17. "Results of Plenum Detailed," Moscow TASS International Service, August 6, 1991; trans. *Federal Broadcast Information Service–Soviet Union* (henceforth *FBIS-SOV*), No. 152, August 7, 1991, p. 62.

18. *Politicheskie partii sovremennoi Rossii*, pp. 283–285; for the information that follows, see also ibid., pp. 279–283; Ia. G. Ermakov, T. V. Shashukova, and V. V. Iakunechkin, "Kommunisticheskoe dvizhenie v Rossii v period zapreta: ot KPSS k KPRF," *Kentavr*, No. 3 (1993), pp. 72 and 78; Pribylovskii, *Slovar*, pp. 125–126; and *Kto est chto: Politicheskaia Moskva 1994*, Vol. 1 (Moscow: Pushchinskii nauchnyi tsentr RAN, 1994), pp. 463–471. For further information on all the neocommunist parties discussed in this section, see *Rossiia: partii, assotsiatsii, soiuzy, kluby*, passim.

19. Information gleaned by the authors from personal conversations with current CPRF members.

20. *Sotsialisticheskaia partiia trudiashchikhsia (Programmnye dokumenty i materialy IV sezda partii)*, unpublished documents, March 1994.

21. *Politicheskie partii sovremennoi Rossii*, pp. 343–349. See also Ermakov et al., "Kommunisticheskoe dvizhenie," p. 74; Pribylovskii, *Slovar*, pp. 5 and 10; *Kto est chto*, pp. 57–66; and N. A. Andreeva, "Krizis burzhuaznogo restavratorstva v SSSR i puti obnovleniia kommunisticheskogo dvizheniia strany," *Bolshevik* (Saransk), No. 17 (1994), p. 1.

22. See the interviews with MP member Aleksandr Buzgalin in *Rossiiskaia gazeta*, September 14, 1991, p. 4, and *Pravda*, September 20, 1991, p. 2.

23. *Politicheskie partii sovremennoi Rossii*, pp. 313–317; see also Ermakov et al., "Kommunisticheskoe dvizhenie," pp. 72–73; Pribylovskii, *Slovar*, p. 134; and Aleksei A. Prigarin, "Put' Rossii k sotsializmu (Proekt tezisov)," *Golos kommunista*, No. 9 (September 1994), p. 3.

24. Authors' interview with Aleksei A. Prigarin in his Moscow apartment, November 3, 1994.

25. *100 partiinykh liderov Rossii: Prilozhenie k informatsionno-analiticheskomu sborniku "Obozrevatel"* (Moscow: Rau-Corporation, 1993), pp. 53–54.

26. *Programma i ustav Rossiiskoi kommunisticheskoi rabochei partii* (Leningrad, 1993); see also Ermakov et al., "Kommunisticheskoe dvizhenie," pp. 73–74 and 78; *Politicheskie partii sovremennoi Rossii*, pp. 349–352 and 338; Pribylovskii, *Slovar*, pp. 95–96 and 140–141; and *Kto est chto*, pp. 301–308.

27. Authors' interview with Valerii A. Podguzov at the Institute of History of the Russian Academy of Sciences on June 2, 1994. Podguzov also upheld the communist regime of North Korea as the ideal to which his party aspired.

28. *Pravda*, December 21, 1994.

29. *100 partiinykh liderov Rossii*, pp. 12–14.

30. On the RPC see Ermakov et al., "Kommunisticheskoe dvizhenie," pp. 72–73; *Politicheskie partii sovremennoi Rossii*, pp. 319–321 and 338; Pribylovskii, *Slovar*, pp. 98–99; and *Kto est chto*, pp. 315–322.

31. "Programma Rossiiskoi partii kommunistov," in *Rossiiskaia pravda* (special edition), No. 5–6 (1993), pp. 1–6.

32. J. B. Urban's interview with Anatolii V. Kriuchkov in the editorial offices of his party's newspaper, *Mysl*, on May 23, 1995.

33. J. B. Urban's interview with Boris F. Slavin in the editorial offices of *Pravda*, May 16, 1995. Ironically, Slavin and Belov would assume diametrically opposed political positions within the CPRF, with Slavin supporting Marxist internationalist reformism and Belov pro-Stalin Russian nationalism.

34. *100 partiinykh liderov Rossii*, p. 36.

35. Cherniakhovskii, "*Kommunisticheskoe dvizhenie v eltsinskoi Rossii*," p. 79.

36. On the three positions, see ibid., pp. 81–85; and Ermakov et al., "Kommunisticheskoe dvizhenie," p. 74.

37. *100 partiinykh liderov Rossii*, p. 36.

38. On this whole reestablishment process, see Ermakov et al., "Kommunisticheskoe dvizhenie," pp. 76–78; and Cherniakhovskii, "Kommunisticheskoe dvizhenie v eltsinskoi Rossii," pp. 81 and 85–86.

39. *KPSS vne zakona?! Konstitutsionnyi sud v Moskve*, p. 22.

40. Ibid., p. 26.

41. See the commentary of Otto Latsis in *Izvestiia*, December 2, 1992, pp. 1–2.

3

Unity in Diversity: The Founding of the Communist Party of the Russian Federation

The Communist Party of the Russian Federation (CPRF) was quickly to become the leading communist organization in post-Soviet Russia. Technically an outgrowth of the Communist Party of the R.S.F.S.R., or Russian Communist Party (RCP) as it was normally called, the CPRF was formally established under the leadership of Gennadii A. Ziuganov at a so-called "revival-unification congress" in mid-February 1993. The RCP itself had been a rather amorphous and not particularly effective force during its short-lived existence from June 1990 through late August 1991, while Ziuganov was only a second-tier party functionary in the vast CPSU Central Committee bureaucracy from 1983 until late 1990. By 1993, however, he had proven himself to be a shrewd political organizer and adept propagandist who managed to consolidate the ranks of the CPRF and to cultivate a personal image of political moderation and deep Russian patriotism.

Nevertheless, multiple political-ideological tendencies quickly surfaced within the newly created CPRF. These groupings, all-important for understanding this leading post-Soviet communist formation as well as for comprehending the later jousting by the party as a whole with the radical leftist neocommunist parties, cannot be adequately understood without taking a look back at the RCP's origins and initial political profile.

The Russian Communist Party: Its Fleeting Life and Leadership

In June 1990 the Russian Communist Party emerged as a potential organizational vehicle for those Russian Communists who actively opposed Gorbachev's increasingly far-reaching reformism. While all CPSU members from the R.S.F.S.R. were automatically also members of the RCP, the political profile of the latter's republic-level *apparat* of some 150 persons[1] was distinctly "conservative" in terms of being opposed to further democratization and proposals for radical economic reform. In contrast to the central organs of the CPSU, where individual views ran the gamut from Brezhnev-era traditionalism to market-based social democracy, the RCP activists included militant neo-Leninists, orthodox Marxist-Leninists, "Russia firsters" of many stripes, but few radical reformers.

In February 1990 the CPSU Central Committee resolved to give up the monopoly on power accorded it under article six of the 1977 Soviet Constitution. Shortly thereafter, in March 1990, competitive elections were held in the R.S.F.S.R. for a two-tiered Russian Congress of People's Deputies patterned after the Soviet Congress of People's Deputies elected the previous spring. That is, in each case the popularly elected congress chose from among its members a smaller body, the Supreme Soviet, to conduct ongoing business when the congress was not in session. Both the end to the CPSU's monopoly on power and the election of a Russian Congress of People's Deputies made the creation of a separate Russian Communist Party all but inevitable. While the CPSU's relinquishment of monopoly status legally opened the door in principle to a multi-party system, the election of a widely diversified Russian parliament showed that such a system was already taking embryonic shape. Gorbachev had long opposed the creation of a distinct R.S.F.S.R. communist party on the ground that such a step would exacerbate the escalating separatist tendencies in the U.S.S.R. Now, however, he was obliged to recognize that to continue such opposition no longer made political sense. The presence of a Russian Communist Party would be needed to offset the influence of the emerging anti-communist forces elected to the new Russian parliament.

The existence of a reformist-conservative communist split in the Russian Congress of People's Deputies was highlighted by the bitterly contested vote for the new body's chairman, or speaker, in late May 1990. Boris Yeltsin, by this time Gorbachev's chief rival with his base in the democratic camp, had been elected a deputy from his hometown of Yekaterinburg (then Sverdlovsk) with 84 percent of the vote. In the contest for chairman of the parliament, he could count on the support of the radical Democratic Russia bloc that won over 20 percent of the republic-wide vote as well as on a number of more centrist reformers. His chief opponent was Ivan P. Polozkov, the relatively conservative first secretary of the Krasnodar CP organization, while behind the scenes Gorbachev urged the election of R.S.F.S.R. prime minister Aleksandr Vlasov. With an absolute majority of 531 votes needed for election, on May 28 Yeltsin bested Polozkov by 497 votes to 473 in the first round and 503 votes to 458 in the second round. The following day

Polozkov withdrew in favor of Gorbachev's personal favorite, Vlasov, whom Yeltsin defeated by 535 votes to 467.[2]

The original impetus for the formation of a separate Russian Communist Party came from the militant neo-Leninists grouped around the United Front of Labor and the Communist Initiative Movement (CIM). Intransigently opposed to the multi-party and market-oriented reforms broached by Gorbachev and later implemented by Yeltsin, they would ultimately establish the activist, street-wise Russian Communist Workers' Party. In early 1990, however, they placed their hopes for the salvation of Leninist-style socialism in the creation of a Communist Party of the R.S.F.S.R., for which they lobbied during their initiative congress in the spring of that year. Ironically, their cause was now abetted by the May 29, 1990, victory of Yeltsin as chairman (or speaker) of the popularly elected Russian Congress of People's Deputies.

A step in the direction of forming a separate Russian CP was taken when the CPSU Central Committee, at its March 1990 plenum, agreed to hold a conference of Russian communists at which local and regional party organizations would be represented by the delegates they were soon to elect to the 28th CPSU Congress planned for mid-summer.[3] Soon thereafter, on April 3, 1990, a meeting of the CPSU CC's Russian Bureau chaired by Gorbachev created a Russian party conference preparatory committee.[4] Nevertheless, probably as a result of continuing reservations on the part of the Gorbachev leadership, roadblocks were still put in the way of the efficient functioning of the preparatory committee as well as coverage about its work in the party press.[5]

According to Viktor A. Tiulkin, arrangements for the Russian party conference began in earnest only the very last week in May. Tiulkin, a member of both the preparatory committee and the organizational bureau of the CIM's initiative congress (which took place in Leningrad in two stages during April and June 1990), testified on June 5 that "our preparatory committee started working at full speed literally last week, when it became clear to everyone that there really was to be a Russian Communist Party."[6] As suggested above, Yeltsin's election as chairman of the Russian Congress of People's Deputies had galvanized support for the creation of a Russian Communist Party even among the Gorbachev reformers. A few days later, on June 9, a joint session of the preparatory committee and the CPSU's Russian Bureau, again chaired by Gorbachev, confirmed that the Russian party conference by then scheduled to open June 19 would indeed become the founding congress of the Communist Party of the R.S.F.S.R. Not only that, but Gorbachev would be the keynote speaker.[7]

The conference, which took place June 19–23, 1990, formally constituted itself as the founding congress of the R.S.F.S.R. Communist Party on June 21. If Gorbachev had hoped to place his stamp upon the new body, however, he was to be sorely disappointed. Of the 2,768 delegates chosen by local party organizations to attend both the Russian party conference and the forthcoming 28th CPSU Congress, 42.3 percent were paid party workers.[8] As a group, these lower-level party functionaries along with grassroots activists such as Tiulkin were gripped by an anti-reformist mood and were, ironically, determined to use the expanding pluralism within the CPSU to rein in the Gorbachev team. Indeed, this all-Russian gathering provided a glimpse of what was in store at the coming 28th CPSU Congress.

One *Izvestiia* reporter described the tenor of the proceedings of this first RCP gathering as unprecedented:

> I think this is the first time, here in the Palace of Congresses, that we have heard such sharply worded criticism addressed to the top party leadership and the general secretary personally; moreover, this criticism from the conference podium is being greeted with noisy, unconcealed approval by some participants.[9]

It was hardly surprising, therefore, that on June 23 Polozkov, so recently outvoted by Yeltsin's supporters in the contest for chairman of the Russian parliament, was elected the new RCP's first secretary by a count of 1,396 yeas to 1,251 nays.[10] In subsequent speeches, Polozkov would caution against any transition to market relations that did not protect the interests of the "working people." He would likewise oppose the division of Soviet society into rich and poor and support the dominant role in the economy of state control and ownership.[11]

Meanwhile, other organizational matters relating to the RCP's formation were tabled until a second stage of the constituent congress, to be held after the CPSU's congress. The full central committee as well as the leadership organs and party program were to be determined only at that later date.

The 28th CPSU Congress, which opened July 2, 1990, and lasted for more than a week, further exposed to the world the fissures that were tearing apart the political fabric of that once "monolithic" Leninist structure. As detailed in Chapter 2, the starkly opposing views on the CPSU's shape and role in society had already crystallized into competing platforms and groups poised to do battle for their respective agendas on the floor of the congress itself. As an alternative to outright schism in the wake of furious debates and searing personal recriminations, Gorbachev was reelected general secretary, albeit with only 3,411 votes in his favor and an unprecedented 1,116 "cancellations" of ballots. But the Politburo was transformed into an unwieldy and virtually powerless 24-member body that included the heads of the communist parties in all fifteen Soviet republics, including of course Polozkov. And the public proceedings culminated in Yeltsin's dramatic announcement from the congress podium that he was resigning from the CPSU.[12]

The second stage of the RCP's constituent congress, which took place September 4–6, 1990, was a bit of an anti-climax to the two preceding conclaves. After an intense, often polemical discussion about the draft of a pro-gram specifically formulated for the RCP, consensus was deemed beyond reach and the decisions of the 28th CPSU Congress had to be adopted for the time being.[13] Indeed, one member of the party's newly elected Central Committee, General Aleksandr I. Lebed, later reported that he was appalled by the "petty bickering and screaming" he witnessed on this occasion.[14] Nevertheless, the assembled 2,584 delegates (down almost two hundred from the June session) did elect 125 additional members to the RCP Central Committee, bringing the total—including those designated in June—to 272.[15] And when the congress adjourned, the Central Committee elected an eighteen-member Politburo and a six-member Secretariat (by secret ballot).

As the Russian communist movement evolved over the next five years, however, only one of the top RCP leaders elected in September 1990 was to play a central role: Gennadii Ziuganov. Named to both the Politburo and the Secretariat, Ziuganov assumed responsibility for ideological work and contacts with the media and the intelligentsia. By 1995 only three other members of the RCP's 1990 Politburo and/or Secretariat would even be-long to the *Central Committee* of the successor Communist Party of the Russian Federation. One of them was Ziuganov's close associate, Valentin V. Chikin, editor-in-chief of *Sovetskaia Rossiia* and later number four on the CPRF's central party list for the 1995 elections to the State Duma, the post-1993 successor to the Russian Congress of People's Deputies. Another was Aleksandr S. Sokolov, who would also be a victorious CPRF candidate in 1995 and then serve as chairman of the Duma's Committee on Tourism and Sports. The third was Vladimir I. Kashin, who would be put in charge of the CPRF's commission on agrarian policy in March 1995.[16]

During the period between the mid-1990 communist congresses and the failed hardline coup of August 19–21, 1991, the political face of the Soviet Union changed beyond recognition. Nationalist separatism gained momen-tum, culminating in a bloody crackdown by Soviet security forces in Lithua-nia in January 1991. Non-communist political parties proliferated. Popular disenchantment with Gorbachev and the party he led intensified. And in di-rect elections for the R.S.F.S.R. president on June 12, 1991, Yeltsin won the race with 57.3 percent of the votes cast in a field of six candidates.[17]

Meanwhile, Gorbachev tacked to the anti-reformist right in autumn 1990 and then back to the radical reformers in April 1991, desperately trying to preserve the cohesion of the Soviet Union and his own hold on power. A de-cisive break in the stalemate between reform and reaction came in late March 1991 when a special session of the R.S.F.S.R. Congress of People's Deputies was convened by its conservative anti-reform members for the pur-pose of removing Yeltsin from the chairmanship of that body. The Demo-cratic Russia movement called for a mass demonstration in support of Yeltsin to be held in Red Square on March 28, the day the session was to open.

Whereupon Gorbachev responded by hastily decreeing a ban on all public rallies and ordering 50,000 troops into the center of Moscow to enforce it. In a stunning evocation of the Red Army's march into Prague some twenty-three years earlier, knots of civilian passers-by gathered around military personnel carriers to protest their presence, while hefty matrons brushed aside equally hefty officers to breach the barricades leading to the Kremlin.[18] Unlike the situation in Prague, however, push never came to shove. The Congress of People's Deputies suspended its proceedings while Yeltsin's personal emissary, first deputy speaker Ruslan I. Khasbulatov, successfully negotiated with Gorbachev for the withdrawal of the troops in return for a shift in the venue of the demonstration to a point several kilometers from the center of the capital.

Dramatic as these street scenes were, they triggered two more portentous developments. The Russian Congress deputies, called into session by an anti-Yeltsin minority, were transformed into a "Russia first" majority now united in their opposition to the all-union authorities in the Kremlin and prepared to schedule a direct popular election for the post of Russian president. And Gorbachev, unwilling to make common cause in the long run with the communist conservatives, shifted back to the side of reform. Less than one month later, he invited Yeltsin along with the heads of the other Soviet republics to a meeting in a government *dacha* in the Moscow suburb of Novo-Ogarevo where they agreed to join forces on behalf of the democratization, marketization, and genuine federalization of the U.S.S.R.[19] From then on the staging of a hardline anti-reform coup was merely a matter of time.

By summer 1991 the overall center of political gravity in Russia had shifted in the direction of democratic and market-oriented reform, and this in turn influenced the Russian Communist Party's leadership. Since its formation a year earlier, the party's top echelons had crystallized into three tendencies, all of them Marxist but each with its own specific character. There was the group associated with RCP first secretary Polozkov which was generally orthodox Marxist-Leninist. This tendency included RCP central committee members such as Tiulkin and Anatolii V. Kriuchkov as well as Aleksei A. Prigarin, who had entered the CPSU Central Committee in July 1990 but who also headed the Political Analysis and Forecasting Center of the RCP's *apparat*. Tiulkin, Kriuchkov, and Prigarin, as discussed in Chapter 2, would later head, respectively, the Russian Communist Workers' Party, the Russian Party of Communists, and the Union of Communists.

A second tendency, moderately reformist in orientation, was grouped around Valentin A. Kuptsov. Born into a peasant family in the Vologda region in 1937, Kuptsov was trained as a metallurgist and then worked his way up in the ranks of the local CPSU *apparat*, becoming regional first party secretary from Vologda in 1985. He was elevated to the CPSU Central Committee in 1986, elected to the Soviet Congress of People's Deputies in a competitive race in 1989, and assigned to the CPSU's Russian Communist Party Bureau in 1989–1990. In April 1990 he became chief of the CPSU Central Committee's department dealing with mass organizations, and at the 28th Congress in July he was advanced to the post of CPSU secretary with similar duties.[20] In other words, he was representative of the many party functionaries who initially backed wide-ranging political and economic reform but who drew the line at systemic transformation. This was underscored in an article by Kuptsov in the May 1991 issue of the CPSU Central Committee's news bulletin in which he attacked the "so-called democrats" for their denial of socialist values.[21]

The third tendency included individuals more attuned to Russian nationalist thinking. Relatively new but rapidly growing in influence, its views were most notably articulated by Gennadii Ziuganov. The child and grandchild of village school-teachers, Ziuganov was born in 1944 in the Orel region. His study in the faculty of physics and mathematics at the Orel Pedagogical Institute was interrupted by military service from 1963 through 1966 when he was drafted into a special army unit for nuclear and chemical weapons reconnaissance and also joined the CPSU. After reportedly participating in the clean-up of a nuclear accident near the city of Cheliabinsk in the southern Urals, he was assigned to a chemical intelligence unit with the Soviet Group of Armed Forces in East Germany.[22] Ziuganov's tour of duty in East Germany, on top of his upbringing in an area occupied by Nazi troops during World War II, may have contributed to his virulent brand of Russian nationalism. It may have also played a role in his unquestioning approval of the Soviet invasion of Czechoslovakia in 1968, a stance at odds with that of many Russians of his age at that time, although such attitudes did not become public knowledge until the Gorbachev era.[23]

From 1969 until 1974 Ziuganov taught math at the Orel Pedagogical Institute and also actively participated in Komsomol work. In 1974, during what we might call the apogee of the Brezhnev era, he began his full-time career as a party functionary. From the start he is said by colleagues to have displayed a preference for ideological work rather than party organization. His rise through the ranks of the local *apparat* thus included graduate training in philosophy at the CPSU's Academy of Social Sciences in Moscow (1978–1980) and part-time teaching of Marxism-Leninism when he returned to Orel.[24]

In 1983 Ziuganov began to work in the Moscow bureaucracy of the CPSU Central Committee, where he remained until his election in 1990 to the RCP's Politburo and Secretariat. During this period, 1983 through mid-1990, he worked in the CPSU Central Committee's Department for Ideology and is reported to have been appointed one of its deputy directors toward the end of the decade.[25] But there is evidence that he was also associated with the Soviet intelligence services. As Ziuganov himself stated in his closing speech to the Third CPRF Congress in January 1995, "I was involved for five years with the state security services, the law enforcement organs, the militia, and all the rest. All [their] methods and technology . . . are well known to me (besides which I now also have advisers who spent their whole professional life in such work)." However, these particular remarks, which were prompted by Ziuganov's anger at the Yeltsin regime's surveillance of *him*, appeared only in the CPRF's internal information bulletin.[26] They were omitted from the version of the above-quoted talk which appeared in the official account of the congress proceedings. Also omitted was Ziuganov's parting shot on this subject, namely, that those involved in the current internal security forces should bear in mind "the fate that befell Yezhov, Beria, Yagoda [Stalin's secret police chiefs], and all the rest."[27] It is perhaps not accidental that the start of Ziuganov's work in Moscow coincided with former KGB chief Yurii V. Andropov's brief tenure as CPSU General Secretary. According to a former college chum, Ziuganov held Andropov in great esteem and was deeply upset at his untimely death.[28]

Ziuganov first made headlines with the publication on May 7, 1991, of a blistering attack against Gorbachev's close adviser, Aleksandr N. Yakovlev, in the ever more nationalist party daily, *Sovetskaia Rossiia*. Entitled "Architect Amid the Ruins: An Open Letter to A. N. Yakovlev Concerning His Recent Statements and Not Only That," the article included many themes that would characterize Ziuganov's later political profile as head of the Communist Party of the Russian Federation. Among these were the comparison of the current Soviet economic decline and internecine warfare to the damage wrought by the "invasion by Hitlerite fascism," fury at the "unpardonable historical lies and moral ugliness" unleashed by *glasnost*, despair at the transformation of Moscow into a "hotbed of filth and immorality," revulsion at the degradation of Russian youth whom *perestroika* was turning into "hard currency hookers and pimps," and a curious blending of Marxism-Leninism with profound Russian nationalism. As Ziuganov put it, Yakovlev's call for the U.S.S.R.'s "return to world civilization" opened the way to carving up "the unique living organism—formed over not just decades but centuries—of Soviet, of Russian society and statehood" and grafting onto it managerial, political, and cultural notions "picked up in a Western flea market."[29]

Ideas such as these explained why Ziuganov had taken part the previous February in organizing an RCP-sponsored conference of left- and right-wing nationalists and also co-chaired the coordinating council of the People's-Patriotic Forces of Russia movement created on that occasion. They also explained the inclusion of Ziuganov's name among the twelve signatories of a passionate hardline nationalist manifesto, "A Word to the People," published in *Sovetskaia Rossiia* on July 23, 1991.[30] That document called, in a nutshell, for the overthrow of the "evil and pompous rulers" (plainly Gorbachev, Yeltsin, and their supporters) who were plundering the national wealth and betraying Soviet Russia to "all-powerful neighbors." Not coincidentally, the appeal was also signed by three leaders of the August putsch that was then just weeks away (General Valentin I. Varennikov, Vasilii A. Starodubtsev, and Aleksandr I. Tiziakov). At the time Ziuganov maintained that he had signed the manifesto not in his capacity as an RCP Central Committee secretary but as an ordinary citizen.[31] Be that as it may, he later disclosed that he had actually co-authored the document with his good friend Aleksandr A. Prokhanov, editor-in-chief of the right-wing nationalist news journal *Den* (renamed *Zavtra* after the autumn 1993 constitutional crisis).[32]

Ziuganov's nationalist views were sufficiently well received among some of the party's more radical activists for him to be nominated to succeed Polozkov as first secretary at an RCP Central Committee plenum on August 6, 1991.[33] On that occasion Tiulkin's Communist Initiative Movement faction even agreed to support his candidacy, an ironic twist given the deep antipathy that would eventually develop between the two men.[34] At issue, however, was the danger that the alternative successor to Polozkov would be Kuptsov, who was Gorbachev's personal choice for the post and thus guilty by association, as it were, with the General Secretary's reformist agenda.

The August 6 plenum met to assess developments in the aftermath of the Russian Federation's presidential election. The RCP's candidate, former Soviet prime minister Nikolai I. Ryzhkov, had come in a poor second with some 16.85 percent of the vote. As Kuptsov bluntly put it, "Our candidate got nowhere."[35] Polozkov thereupon resigned from the post of first secretary, and Ziuganov, Kuptsov, and Yurii A. Prokofiev, first secretary of the Moscow city party organization, as well as CPSU Politburo member, were nominated to succeed him. However, both Prokofiev and Ziuganov withdrew their candidacies, the former because of his commitment to the Moscow city party organization, and Ziuganov, reportedly, out of deference to Kuptsov's superior knowledge of economic matters and industrial production.[36] Tiulkin later recalled that Ziuganov, in announcing his withdrawal, blushed, averted his eyes, and was unusually agitated.[37] This may have been due to the fact that on the eve of the August 6 plenum Ziuganov and two other RCP secretaries, Ivan I. Antonovich and one A. N. Ilin, had actually asked Kuptsov to accept the position of RCP first secretary.[38] Evidently, by mid-1991 Ziuganov felt closer to Kuptsov's views, at least on economic policy, than to those of the ultra-leftist Marxist-Leninists.

What transpired thereafter was recounted by Kuptsov over Moscow Central Television on August 15: "I was left alone on the secret ballot paper. The procedure went ahead, and out of 185 members of the RCP Central Committee, 150 voted for me and 35 against."[39] In the same interview the new first secretary vowed to cooperate with Yeltsin (with whom he claimed to have already had a constructive meeting) in solving the whole range of problems confronting Russian society.

The numbers cited above by Kuptsov were highly significant. Of the 272 members elected to the RCP Central Committee in June/September 1990, almost one-third failed to attend the August 6, 1991, plenum. Among the absentees were presumably the supporters of Aleksandr V. Rutskoi and Vasilii S. Lipitskii, whom the plenum voted unanimously to expel from its ranks because of their creation of the Democratic Party of Communists of Russia just days earlier.[40] Others may have simply "tuned out" politically or have become preoccupied with personal matters, disoriented by the kaleidoscopic course of political developments during that last summer of the U.S.S.R.'s existence. At the same time, thirty-five members, or over one-fifth of those present, took advantage of the secret ballot to oppose the election of the relatively moderate Kuptsov. It may be assumed that they constituted the more orthodox Marxist-Leninist tendency in the RCP, those individuals who would rapidly move in the autumn of 1991 to establish the neocommunist formations headed by Tiulkin, Kriuchkov, and Prigarin, all three of whom would eventually take an openly hostile position toward the RCP's successor, the Communist Party of the Russian Federation.

From the RCP's Ban to the CPRF's February 1993 Founding Congress

Yeltsin's post-putsch suspension of communist activities and his November 6, 1991, ban on the RCP (and the CPSU on Russian territory) affected the party's three main tendencies in significantly different ways. As detailed in Chapter 2, many Marxist reformers whose views were similar to those of Kuptsov joined the Socialist Labor Party (SLP) of Roy A. Medvedev and Liudmila S. Vartazarova, but they concentrated their attention on opposition activity in the Russian Congress of People's Deputies. The more radical Marxist-Leninists, shunning cooperation with the SLP and contemptuous of parliamentary activity, quickly established their own successor communist parties. Ziuganov, maintaining a certain public distance from all these neocommunist formations, became involved with a number of nationalist organizations, pending the outcome of the Constitutional Court's verdict on the legality of Yeltsin's ban on the RCP.

Ivan P. Rybkin served as a vital link between the more moderate former RCP activists and the Communists of Russia group in the Russian parliament. Rybkin, a graduate student and then instructor at the Volgograd Agricultural Institute from 1970 until 1987, became a full-time party functionary only in the late 1980s, the heyday of *perestroika*, when he occupied important posts in the CPSU organization in the Volgograd region. Elected a people's deputy to the Russian parliament, he joined the Communists of Russia fraction in May 1990. Although Rybkin was reportedly opposed to the creation of a separate Russian CP for the same reasons as Gorbachev, he nonetheless became head of the RCP Central Committee's department for contacts with lower-level soviets of people's deputies in early 1991.[41] He was thus well positioned in September 1991 to become co-leader of the Russian parliament's communist fraction as well as an intermediary between the latter and the activists working for the RCP's reestablishment.

During the two years following the failed August 1991 coup only sixty-seven of some 1,050 or so national-level people's deputies remained committed to the communist cause. Nevertheless, they had the satisfaction of seeing their early intransigent opposition to the Yeltsin team's radical economic reforms eventually become the majority position.[42] Their status as deputies in the Russian Congress also enabled them to retain some measure of public visibility even during the official ban and—in the case of Rybkin and others—to hone their skills as a parliamentary opposition. All the same, they initially projected a very low profile. This was so much the case that the communist deputies in the Supreme Soviet of the Russian Congress for the most part backed Yeltsin's policies in December 1991. As Ziuganov later conceded to the reform-oriented but anti-Yeltsin economist and politician, Grigorii A. Yavlinskii, during a debate published verbatim in *Moskovskii Komsomolets* on November 29, 1995,

> You are right on one point, that [the] members of the CPSU who were in the Supreme Soviet were fooled. . . . They voted for presidentialism. . . . They voted additional powers for Yeltsin. . . . They voted for the Belovezhskie putsch.

During the Fifth Congress of People's Deputies, in late October–early November 1991, Vladivostok lawyer Svetlana P. Goriacheva was one of the few exceptions to this pattern of conciliatory conduct. A deputy chairman of the Supreme Soviet since spring 1990, she was one of only thirteen legislators to vote against the declaration of Russian sovereignty passed by the Congress of People's Deputies on June 12, 1990.[43] She soon turned openly against Yeltsin, reading aloud to the Supreme Soviet on February 21, 1991, the so-called "Statement of six" opposition deputies which denounced him for "authoritarianism" and called for convening the extraordinary Third Congress of People's Deputies in late March 1991 to repudiate him. Finally, on October 31, 1991, she registered her disapproval of Yeltsin's ever more radical reform agenda by asking to be relieved of her position as deputy chairman of the Supreme Soviet; her request was approved by a vote of 774 to 109, with 28 abstentions.[44]

Meanwhile, Ziuganov developed the public image of a would-be unifier of oppositionists, communist and nationalist, leftist and rightist. To cite just a few of his activities during this period, in January 1992 he was elected chairman of a revived coordinating council of People's-Patriotic Forces of Russia; the following June he took part in the first congress of former KGB major-general Aleksandr N. Sterligov's right-wing Russian National Assembly, becoming one of its co-chairmen; and in October 1992 he was directly involved in the founding of the National Salvation Front, co-authoring its "Appeal to the Citizens of Russia" published in *Sovetskaia Rossiia* on October 1, 1992, and serving as one of its nine co-chairmen. At the same time, he became a leading adviser to the opposition bloc, Russian Unity, in the Congress of People's Deputies. As Veljko Vujacic has persuasively argued, during the course of 1992 "both ideologically and organizationally Ziuganov's activity pointed in one direction: a new national-socialism."[45]

All the while, the future of the Russian Communist Party hinged on the outcome of the Constitutional Court's deliberations on the "CPSU case." As related in Chapter 2, hearings were held during the summer and fall of 1992 which culminated in the November 30, 1992, verdict that the RCP's primary party organizations could legally resume their activity. The chief witnesses in defense of the CPSU/RCP were Ziuganov, Kuptsov, Rybkin, Vladimir A. Ivashko, who had been elected deputy general secretary of the CPSU at the 1990 congress, and Ivan I. Melnikov, the young leader of the CPSU party organization of Moscow State University from 1988 through 1991 and member of the last CPSU Secretariat. Ziuganov did not play a particularly important role, given his many other activities during this period. Rather, the primary burden of organizing the defense was assumed by Kuptsov, Melnikov, and a group of SLP leaders. Nevertheless, the basic line of argument presented by both Ziuganov and Kuptsov was the same. On the one hand, it was absurd to accuse the party that had created the Soviet governmental system of unconstitutionality and illegitimacy in trying to preserve it. On the other hand, the CPSU had been responsible for all the achievements of the Soviet era, not to mention the victory in World War II and the transformation of the Soviet Union into a superpower.[46]

Ziuganov conceded that the CPSU was at fault for maintaining a monopoly on power, which caused it to lose sight of the real situation in the country and the support of the masses. But at the same time, he was especially outspoken in his condemnation of the "traitors" Gorbachev and Yakovlev. Most notably, he articulated a conspiracy theory regarding the collapse of the U.S.S.R. Referring to certain secret documents that he did not submit to the Court, he argued that the West led by the United States had engineered the deformation of the Soviet economy, the surge in nationalist separatism, and the transformation of the Soviet mass media into an anti-communist weapon.[47] These were themes to which he would repeatedly return in his later writings and official addresses at communist party functions.

Immediately after the Constitutional Court's verdict, an Initiative Committee to organize the "Second Extraordinary Congress" of the RCP's successor organization, the Communist Party of the Russian Federation, was formed which included not only Ziuganov and Kuptsov from the former

RCP leadership and a number of representatives from the SLP (of which Rybkin was a co-chairman) but also at least the nominal cooperation of Prigarin's Union of Communists (UC) and Kriuchkov's Russian Party of Communists (RPC). As Kuptsov announced on December 7, at a joint press conference with the Russian parliament's Communists of Russia fraction, primary party organizations had already begun to function with very simple admission procedures: "A communist merely has to show his party card."[48] Significantly, formal registration for membership in the reestablished party would take place only after the congress. Initial participation was thus open to all interested members of the former RCP/CPSU.

An appeal by the Initiative Committee for grassroots support, published in *Pravda* and *Sovetskaia Rossiia*, specified that the congress itself would determine the political profile of the reactivated party of Russian communists.[49] As already discussed in Chapter 2, by autumn 1992 there were a number of conflicting views on this question: the insistence of the Russian Communist Workers' Party (RCWP) on its own program, the RPC's preference for an entirely new political formation, and the UC's call for the reestablishment of the CPSU. But the Initiative Committee's leaders were determined to control the program and structure of the revived RCP and to ensure its preeminence as the exclusive Russian successor to the CPSU. As Prigarin's group later publicly charged, Kuptsov, Ziuganov, and Rybkin did everything in their power to thwart the call for convening a 29th CPSU Congress in late March 1993.[50] A first step to thwart it was the decision to hold the constituent congress of the CPRF on February 13–14, 1993, that is, a month and a half before the already scheduled 29th CPSU Congress.

The CPRF's "revival-unification congress" (so named by its organizers) took place in a semi-clandestine atmosphere exacerbated by media controversy regarding its legality and political profile. Its location in a rest home outside Moscow was publicly announced only at the last minute, evidently because of fear of judicial or political harassment. And the character of its proceedings, newly elected leadership, and program was distorted by both the Russian and Western press. Perhaps due to a certain time lag in the publication of reliable information, the new CPRF was generally described as a throwback to the old CPSU in its pre-*perestroika* days.[51]

In actuality, the diversity of views expressed by both guests and delegates and the controversy over the list of central committee members proposed by the organizers were remarkable by traditional CPSU standards. This was hardly surprising, given the presence of the neocommunist parties' leaders (Tiulkin, Kriuchkov, and Prigarin, among others) as well as the uncertain political outlook of the 805 delegates representing some 450,000 members of local communist organizations. The number of delegates far exceeded the planned quota of 693, thus suggesting a lack of control from above and considerable grassroots spontaneity. According to the official CPRF account, twenty-six regional organizations sent a larger number of delegates than that to which they were entitled. While "such deviations" were in principle unacceptable, it was decided that on this occasion the 112 extra delegates would be given a consultative vote and permitted to attend all the proceedings. Specifically, at regional conferences where there had been a split vote on key issues, those delegates representing the majority were given a deliberative vote. In other cases, the regional delegations themselves had to decide by the close of the first day of the congress who among them would receive a deliberative and who a consultative voice.[52]

The specific steps taken by local RCP/CPSU organizations to reconstitute themselves is a subject for future systematic field research. But preliminary soundings suggest that this was in many areas a largely spontaneous process. Not only that, but in a number of regions the initiative was taken by rank-and-file loyalists rather than by former paid party functionaries. Once the ban was lifted and the February 1993 congress scheduled, however, members of the Communists of Russia fraction in the Congress of People's Deputies constituted a major point of contact between the localities and the congress organizers.[53]

Dissension developed from the very opening of the founding congress of the Communist Party of the Russian Federation on February 13, 1993. Tiulkin proposed that the agenda be amended to include a report by the RCP Central Committee on its activities since August 1991, to which Kuptsov replied, "There is nothing to report on." Plainly Tiulkin sought to embarrass the congress organizers by forcing them to admit either to passivity or to behind-the-scenes maneuvers during the period of the official ban. Kriuchkov next objected to the fact that the congress's first item of business was to constitute itself as the linear successor to the RCP, to designate itself as the "second congress" of that body under the new name, Communist Party of the Russian Federation. When the original agenda item to this effect was put to a vote, however, only seventeen delegates opposed it and three abstained.[54]

Immediately after these exchanges, Kuptsov delivered his report on the CPRF's tasks under current Russian socio-political conditions.[55] He began by saying that the present congress was the most difficult since the creation of the party at the turn of the century because of the pressing need to figure out what had gone wrong. In order to know what to do now, the communists first had to analyze the reasons for the defeat of state socialism in the Soviet Union and Eastern Europe. That having been said, Kuptsov was far more explicit on what the reconstituted CPRF should *avoid* than on what it should undertake. For a start, he cautioned that those who thought of the reestablishment of the CPSU and the U.S.S.R. immediately after coming to power were "either fools or adventurers." He went on to warn against dogmatism, in particular "the absolutization of force," as well as against "bureaucratic centralism" and "unthinking discipline." As he put it, "The sub-mission of the minority to the majority should be accompanied by respect for the opinion of the minority."

On the other hand, Kuptsov was notably vague on how the party might return to the "socialist path," calling for aid to science and education, re-spect for servicemen, attention to the "healthy forces" among the youth, and defense of the Russian parliament in its mounting confrontation with President Yeltsin. While this last point may have an equivocal ring in light of the subsequent October 1993 bloodshed, in his February report Kuptsov in-sisted on avoiding even "the threat of civil war."

He also appealed for unity among the "five newly formed" communist par-ties (evidently including in their number Andreeva's group and the Socialist Labor Party), and deplored the way in which their quarrels and attacks on one another objectively aided their mutual enemies, including the regime's secu-rity services. In response to Kriuchkov's proposal for a coalition of communist parties rather than a single united organization, Kuptsov pointed to the CPRF's draft statute permitting dual party membership. And he remarked that internal party "platforms" and "factions" were "inevitable," adding that "on this question V. I. Lenin in a different age thought differently."[56]

Kuptsov's conciliatory approach to disagreements within the communist movement found an echo in his call for potential allies beyond the commu-nist camp. He thus envisaged the possibility of a CPRF alliance with the cen-trist Civic Union of industrialist Arkadii I. Volskii and others (which showed some political promise at the time of its formation in mid-1992 although it soon faded from the scene). And he insisted on the necessity of eliminating conflicts between communists in general and the many emergent social-democratic groups, thereby facilitating the creation of a "united party of cre-ative Marxism."[57] The allusion to "creative Marxism" was an interesting throwback to the reformist terminology associated with the rule of Nikita S. Khrushchev.

Kuptsov's strictures against "bureaucratic centralism" and "unthinking discipline" found concrete expression in the CPRF's draft statutes, which were presented to the congress by people's deputy Viktor I. Zorkaltsev. Born in 1936 in the Tomsk region where he was educated as a construction engineer, Zorkaltsev began full-time party work in 1964. Like Kuptsov, his career blossomed during the Gorbachev era, when he became first secretary of the Tomsk regional party organization and a member of the CPSU Cen-tral Committee as well. After Yeltsin's ban on the communists, Zorkaltsev joined the Socialist Labor Party.

In his report to the February 1993 CPRF Congress, Zorkaltsev empha-sized that the new party rules were designed to overcome the "administra-tive-command legacy" of the CPSU. To this end there was to be a redistri-bution of power between the leadership and the base in favor of the primary party organizations, with safeguards to prevent the party as a whole from becoming the "hostage" of its central organs. The draft statutes stipulated, moreover, that there should be no *apparat* of paid party functionaries.[58] Implicit in these comments was the view shared by all the post-Soviet Russian communist groups that the higher echelons of the former CPSU *apparat* had at the very least lost touch with the party masses.

Following the formal reports of Kuptsov and Zorkaltsev, the congress was addressed by the four left-wing neocommunist leaders present: Tiulkin, Prigarin, Kriuchkov, and Richard I. Kosolapov, until that time head of the "Leninist Platform" in Tiulkin's RCWP.[59] Tiulkin's speech was the most extreme. As the official account of the proceedings paraphrased it, "We are for unity, but we will not unite with social democrats and opportunists"— plainly a slur against the CPRF's organizers. Kosolapov was a bit more balanced. After rejecting as a model the militant RCWP, the moderate SLP, and the CPSU during its last twenty years, he went on to declare that the chief danger to the CPRF came from the right: "The party, having purged itself of opportunists, should now purge itself of semi-opportunists."

Prigarin, in contrast to the RCWP representatives, insisted on the reestablishment of the CPSU. Inasmuch as this had been the position of his Union of Communists from the start, he took exception to Kuptsov's remark that "only fools and adventurers" could contemplate such a step. He also claimed credit for the reactivization of local party organizations in Russia, saying that this had occurred in connection with the preparations for the purported Twentieth CPSU Conference, which his party had organized the previous October. In a preview of the jousting soon to come between the CPRF and the organizers of the 29th CPSU Congress scheduled for the last days of March 1993, he emphasized that local party units in Russia were simultaneously organizations of both the CPRF and the CPSU.

For his part, Kriuchkov cautioned against any attempt at communist unification for the time being. Given the existing ideological and political disagreements, he declared, this should instead be a gradual step-by-step process.

Following the statements of the neocommunist leaders, Ziuganov and two of his fervently nationalist associates, Yurii P. Belov, representing the CPRF's organization in the Leningrad region, and Tamara V. Pletneva from the Tambov region, took the floor.[60] Ziuganov, who was introduced to the assembly as a co-chairman of the National Salvation Front, focused on two themes: the need to promote the strengthening of the Russian state and the need to protect the interests of science, education, and technology. As Ziuganov put it with regard to the second theme, "Our party must be the party of intellect." But his basic message, one with which he would become ever more closely identified, was that the search for allies in support of the revival of Russia was the chief "strategic and tactical task" of the moment. Pletneva echoed this, arguing that disagreement among the regime's opponents only played into the hands of their common enemies, "that small group of renegades" who were riding roughshod over the interests of the people and the nation.

Belov took a somewhat broader tack. He urged the party to draw the necessary lessons from both the CPSU's defeat and Lenin's New Economic Policy, recommending the latter to those who maintained that "socialism and the market are altogether incompatible." At the same time, he also stressed the "Russian question," a code-word for belief in the uniqueness and greatness of Russia through the ages. To those who equated this with national chauvinism, he replied that Russian culture was multinational, even global in character. Belov concluded with an appeal for the "unity of socialism and patriotism." Here it bears recalling that Belov was, along with Boris F. Slavin, a leading figure in Kriuchkov's Russian Party of Communists during 1991–1992. However, whereas Belov aligned himself with the CPRF's Russian nationalist tendency, Slavin was a reform-oriented internationalist.

To sum up what had thus far transpired at the congress, it opened with presentations in quick succession by spokesmen of all three tendencies that had made up the Russian Communist Party activists back in 1990–1991: the Marxist reformers, the orthodox Marxist-Leninists, and the "progressive" nationalists. While the reports of Kuptsov and Zorkaltsev embodied the ideas of the Marxist reformers, the last three speakers cited above represented the nationalist wing of the Russian communists. The irony of the situation was that the orthodox Marxist-Leninists who had spearheaded the creation of the original R.S.F.S.R. Communist Party were now outsiders. To be sure, they were invited to join the reconstituted CPRF and encouraged to do so through the mechanism of temporary dual party membership. However, their ideological orthodoxy, political intransigence, and neo-Leninist vision of a communist party's organization and role in society were spurned by both the Marxist reformers and the communist nationalists.

The February 13 session concluded with several discourses reflecting an even wider range of views. Omar O. Begov of Dagestan, editor of a local newspaper called *For the Homeland, for Stalin!*, declared that the communist party and Stalin "were indivisible." To this, erstwhile RPC member Slavin retorted that it might still be worthwhile to analyze Stalin's personality but "there can be no return to Stalinism."[61] Oleg S. Shenin, soon to become the leader of the reconstituted CPSU at its 29th congress, evidently tried to win support for this venture from everybody. For he asserted that what the communist movement now needed was a new form of socialism, but one with "Russian specifications" which would refuse "to live by the borrowed wits of Western social democracy."[62] Anatolii I. Lukianov, former chairman of the U.S.S.R.'s Supreme Soviet and the last speaker of the day, cautioned that communists in the provinces were fed up with the divisions among their national leaders and wanted only to see the party reestablished.⁶³

The second day of the congress was devoted to a discussion of the Kuptsov and Zorkaltsev reports and the election of an 89-member (later enlarged to a 124-member) Central Executive Committee.⁶⁴ There were reportedly some "very sharp" questions put to Kuptsov and Zorkaltsev, although their content was not spelled out. More significantly, the selection of the Central Executive Committee did not proceed smoothly. According to the published account, "there was a lively, at times very sharp, discussion" of some forty names on the list of nominees proposed by the congress organizers. This, in turn, led to a number of rejections, withdrawals, and additions.

Several years later Rybkin recalled in an interview with Slavin that at the February 1993 congress the "leadership of the so-called parliamentary group of communists" was to a large extent forced out. "You surely remember," commented Rybkin, "how at the congress they 'took shots at' such people as [Gennadii I.] Skliar, [Aleksandr N.] Maltsev, [Roy A.] Medvedev, those who therefore declined to join the CPRF and today belong to the SLP"⁶⁵ All three individuals cited by Rybkin were among the original organizers of the SLP and also actively participated in the Initiative Committee to reconstitute the CPRF.⁶⁶ In other words, the more social democratically oriented former CPSU members were from the start excluded from the CPRF. They were, in effect, punished for their previous ties to Gorbachev.

According to the published reports on the proceedings of the Second CPRF Congress, on February 14, 1993, the newly designated Central Executive Committee (CEC) also met to elect a Presidium composed of a chairman and six deputy chairmen. Ziuganov was chosen for the top post "by an absolute majority" (albeit not by secret ballot, in contrast to Kuptsov's election in 1991),⁶⁷ reportedly with only one vote against him and one abstention. There was, however, more to it than this sparse account suggests. Delegates to the congress were divided on whether to choose Kuptsov or Ziuganov as party leader. At one point General Albert M. Makashov spoke up against the candidacy of Kuptsov, accusing him of "conciliationism and Gorbachevism."⁶⁸ The radical leftist Makashov supported Ziuganov instead, moving that the delegates as a body take a vote on this question. His motion failed to pass. But in fact already on the eve of the congress Kuptsov had withdrawn his candidacy, and the decision to designate Ziuganov the new CPRF chairman had been reached by the four key organizers of the congress: Kuptsov, Rybkin, Lukianov, and Ziuganov himself. The situation was thus the reverse of what it had been in early August 1991 when, at the last RCP plenum, Ziuganov withdrew his candidacy in favor of Kuptsov.

The explanation for this turn of events varies. Some of those involved claim that Kuptsov was simply "too tired" to take on the CPRF leadership. Others argue that there was a mutually understood division of responsibility between Kuptsov and Ziuganov. According to this second line of reasoning, Kuptsov was the skilled party organizer content to tend to the network of cadres behind the scenes, while Ziuganov was the more decisive, energetic, and innovative public figure capable of enhancing the CPRF's national stature and broadening its electoral appeal.[69] Whatever the case, Ziuganov and Kuptsov pursued their respective roles without perceptible friction for the next three years.

Meanwhile, before the Second CPRF Congress adjourned on February 14, the party statutes were reviewed, amended, and approved. However, the finalization of the programmatic declaration was postponed, ostensibly to permit some "finishing touches."

The Emerging Political Tendencies Within the CPRF

The composition of the new CPRF Presidium[70] and the contents of the programmatic declaration finally published on March 2, 1993, suggest that a deal had been struck between the Marxist reformers and the communist nationalists, with the orthodox Marxist-Leninists for the most part left out in the cold. The gist of the arrangement was that Ziuganov, leader of the nationalist wing, became CPRF chairman, while the programmatic declaration was weighted much more in the direction of Marxist reformism than Russian nationalism. The political profile of the six deputy chairmen lends support to this conjecture. Only two were identified with Ziuganov's position: the Leningrad region's CPRF leader, Belov, and the former deputy speaker of the Supreme Soviet, Goriacheva. Among the remaining four were Kuptsov and Zorkaltsev, on the one hand, and Rybkin and Mikhail I. Lapshin, coordinator of the Agrarian Union fraction in the Russian parliament, on the other. The latter pair would be instrumental in creating the Agrarian Party of Russia later in 1993, and Rybkin, as speaker of the post-1993 State Duma, would turn out to be much more moderate than Kuptsov and Zorkaltsev.

Evidently, Ziuganov was seen by all tendencies on the Central Executive Committee as the most effective CPRF standard-bearer at a time when public support was growing for the restoration of Russian national pride but the communist past was still very much under a cloud. Given these circumstances, Ziuganov's ability to build bridges between the reconstituted CPRF and the erstwhile anti-communist right-wing nationalists, those whose views were articulated by the news journal *Den/Zavtra*, was seen as a distinct asset. Ziuganov himself, moreover, had displayed impressive organizational skills in the course of his involvement with the various "red-brown" opposition groups during 1991–1992. An additional point in his favor was the positive impression he had made on the more orthodox communist activists as a result of his impassioned denunciation of Gorbachev's key adviser, Yakovlev, in May 1991.

The "Programmatic Declaration," which was considered an interim document pending the adoption of a fully developed program at the next regular party congress, contained six sections.[71] The first was devoted to what had gone wrong in the Soviet party-state. A major miscalculation was the failure to adapt to the "global technological revolution of the 1960s and 1970s," i.e., the computer age, and thus the inability to bring to fruition the economic possibilities of socialism. Additional mistakes of the past included a flawed nationalities policy, the "bureaucratization" of the soviets, and the CPSU's faulty cadres policy. The latter led, in turn, to the "degeneration of the party elite," its abuse of power and double moral standard at both the central and local levels of the party bureaucracy. "The betrayal by . . . Gorbachev and his associates completed the process." Here we should emphasize that while this initial CPRF programmatic document, in contrast to the orthodox neocommunist programs, avoided any reference to developments before the Brezhnev era, it shared their animosity toward the CPSU *apparat* in general and Gorbachev in particular.

The second section, entitled "The Fatherland Is in Danger," also echoed the neocommunists' fury at the impoverishment and social degradation wrought by the economic reforms of the Yeltsin regime. But its rhetoric recalled that of Ziuganov, as did the solution it prescribed for overcoming Russia's humiliation, namely, "the consolidation of all genuinely democratic and patriotic forces united by the idea of the salvation of the Fatherland."

Next came a section on the CPRF's "chief goals and principles," which reflected the views of the Marxist reformers. It spoke of Russia's "voluntary" return to socialism as well as "freedom of speech and association in political parties and social organizations."[72] Yet all the while it professed to be guided by "Marxist-Leninist teaching" and committed to the interests of the working class and all laborers.

Section four dealt primarily with economic policy. While it too articulated the ideas of the Marxist reformers, evidence mounted over the next few years that Ziuganov agreed with their economic views.[73] This section called for the formation of a "planned-market, socially oriented, ecologically safe economy" in which the state sector would be the basis of a "mixed economy" that permitted various forms of property (albeit not private ownership of land, aside from family gardens). And it flatly opposed a return to the "former bureaucratic system of economic management." Tacked on to the end of this section, however, was a part that again echoed the preoccupations of Ziuganov's right-wing nationalist colleagues. It lamented the spiritual degradation and cultural-scientific impoverishment of Russia, voiced respect for the "selfless patriotic activity of eminent representatives of the

Russian Orthodox Church,"[74] and warned against the "total commercialization and Americanization of the spiritual sphere."

If the foregoing sections on political and economic policy embraced views that were largely unacceptable to the more radical neocommunist groups, the same can also be said of the next section which dealt with the Soviet Union's dissolution. On the one hand, the CPRF declaration deplored the destruction of the U.S.S.R.; but on the other hand, it refrained from calling for its restoration. Instead, it proposed the gradual "integration" of the new independent states in a manner that resembled more the European Union than the old Soviet order.

The last section focused on questions of party organization and conduct. The declaration affirmed that the CPRF would operate according to the Leninist principles of "broad democracy and conscious discipline." At the same time, it insisted that it would not tolerate either careerists in its ranks or "*nomenklatura*-bureaucratic distortions" of its structure. As for its political conduct, it would engage in parliamentary and extra-parliamentary activity, use all available legal and constitutional means, and develop as broad an alliance strategy as possible to bring down the Yeltsin regime. Meanwhile, the CPRF would also seek to establish ties with the communist and socialist parties in the "near abroad," with the aim of creating a "firm union of communist parties."

The new CPRF statutes provided a number of safeguards against the kind of "bureaucratic centralism" which Kuptsov had denounced in his report to the congress.[75] While the "principle of democratic centralism" was affirmed, its operational thrust was substantially tempered. The right of members to "criticize any party organ or [individual] communist" was guaranteed. "Openness" in all party proceedings was required. Above all, members were permitted to form "associations based on platforms" (albeit not factions) which could, in turn, request a hearing on specific issues or offer alternative reports at meetings of their respective executive organs.

CPRF membership, moreover, did not preclude concurrent (but temporary) affiliation with other "social organizations and movements," e.g., neocommunist groups, while members of the latter could join the CPRF simply on the basis of "an application and presentation of a party membership card." If the first of these provisions would lead to the phenomenon of dual party membership, the second would facilitate the rapid influx into the CPRF of former members of one or another neocommunist organization. As related in Chapter 2, two-thirds of Kriuchkov's Russian Party of Communists followed Slavin into the CPRF, while the SLP's membership declined by a factor of ten as a result of a similar shift in allegiance. Indeed, two of the new deputy chairmen of the CPRF, Lapshin and Rybkin, had been co-chairmen of the SLP.

Competition for members among the existing pool of communist activists was, however, just one of the consequences of the CPRF's entry into the communist playing field. Another had to do with the maneuvers by various leadership groups to enhance their respective parties' appeal to new constituencies. One such action on the part of the CPRF leadership occurred behind the scenes in the aftermath of the February 1993 "Revival-Unification" Congress.

According to Boris P. Kurashvili, a prominent legal scholar who represented the banned communist parties before the Constitutional Court in 1992 and also participated in the Second CPRF Congress, the Program Declaration published in early March was a "falsified" version of the document actually approved by the congress delegates. Whereas the original had rejected any form of property which entailed the "exploitation of man by man," the published declaration deleted the latter phrase and endorsed the idea of a "mixed economy" (*mnogoukladnost*). The purpose of this revisionist "falsification," Kurashvili argued, was to facilitate a united front between the reconstituted CPRF and the non-communist "national bourgeoisie" against the Yeltsin reformers and their Western capitalist backers.[76] A committee of four, comprising Ziuganov, Belov, Slavin, and Aleksandr K. Frolov, was charged with editing the Program Declaration, but the final revisions were made by Belov.[77]

Kurashvili's basic contention that the CPRF leadership was more moderate, or "conciliationist" to use his term, than the assembled delegates was entirely plausible. This is particularly so if one compares the 1993 program document to the far more doctrinaire, indeed Marxist-Leninist, party program that would eventually be approved by the Third CPRF Congress in January 1995, after a wide-ranging discussion of multiple drafts at all levels of the party. The details regarding the formulation of the January 1995 program will be discussed in Chapter 6.

Meanwhile, from an analytical point of view Kurashvili's revelations are important because they underscore the fact that the range of distinctive political positions within the Russian communist movement was becoming more complex and nuanced. As before, "orthodox Marxism-Leninism," which stood at one end of the communist spectrum, comprised both extreme orthodoxy (of the neo-Stalinist Andreeva and neo-Leninist Tiulkin-Anpilov variety) and more moderate orthodoxy (Prigarin and Kriuchkov). At the opposite end of the spectrum was Ziuganov's "progressive" nationalism. In the middle were the Marxist reformers. But by 1993 the earlier catch-all category of "orthodox Marxist-Leninists" was further subdividing.

In addition to the two types of orthodox neocommunist parties mentioned above, there was yet a third constellation that we shall designate as "Marxist-Leninist modernizers." By way of illustration, Kurashvili, a senior researcher at the Institute of State and Law of the Academy of Sciences since 1972, was a Marxist-Leninist modernizer.[78] So, too, was Kosolapov, a Moscow State University professor of philosophy as well as former editor-in-chief of the CPSU's theoretical journal *Kommunist*, who moved his "Leninist Platform" group from the RCWP to the CPRF at the time of the February 1993 congress. The Marxist-Leninist modernizers, in other words, represented the left wing of the CPRF's upper echelons.

On the other hand, as we have already seen, Kuptsov and Zorkaltsev can be better characterized as Marxist reformers on the basis of their reports to the February 1993 congress. The same was true of the CPRF's March 1993 Program Declaration. In these latter cases, the support for a mixed market economy, associational pluralism, and minority rights within the communist party were reminiscent of both the Gorbachev era circa 1988 and the Prague Spring of 1968. Individuals associated with the Marxist reformer group also tended to be progressive internationalists, that is, they believed in genuine cross-cultural solidarity based on class-based identity rather than ethnic origin. In this respect they also differed from the Marxist-Leninist modernizers for whom, as in the case of Kosolapov, "proletarian internationalism" was more often than not simply a code-word for a Soviet-dominated socialist community and world communist movement.

As for the members of the CPRF's nationalist tendency, the elaboration of their views, above all those of Ziuganov himself, will be a focal point of the following chapters. While they might share the Marxist reformers' ideas on a mixed economy and even to some extent on political pluralism, they were plainly unreceptive to progressive internationalism. And they agreed with the hardline variant of internationalism only insofar as it presupposed the preeminence of Russia within the Soviet Union.

All the while, the resurgent rank-and-file CPRF, which grew from a reported 450,000 members in February 1993 to some 600,000 three years later, embraced a considerably broader political spectrum. If elderly demonstrators in the center of Moscow were frequently seen bearing portraits of Stalin, there were also progressive internationalists in the provinces who had welcomed Khrushchev's destalinization policies and who viewed peoples around the world as brothers and sisters divided only by the Marxist tenets of class struggle, not by ethnic or national particularities. Individuals in their forties, moreover, were as likely as pensioners in their sixties to be repelled by the inequities of economic "shock therapy" or to yearn for the certainties of the Soviet era. And college students in the hard sciences were more apt than those in the humanities and social sciences to be receptive to the CPRF's promises of renewed funding of basic research. Above all, whatever their specific political preferences, genuine ideological commitment rather than opportunistic careerism was a common defining characteristic of the

CPRF's grassroots activists. These considerations as well as the new leadership's programmatic cleavages were to shape the party's evolution over the
next few years.

Notes

1. This figure of 150 is cited in Gennadii A. Ziuganov, *Drama vlasti: Stranitsy
politicheskoi avtobiografii* (Moscow: Paleia, 1993), p. 18.
2. For the specific voting results, see John B. Dunlop, *The Rise of Russia and the
Fall of the Soviet Empire* (Princeton, NJ: Princeton University Press, 1993), pp.
24–26. Dunlop coined the felicitous term "Russia firsters."
3. See the report by G. M. Khodyrev, chairman of the Russian party conference
credentials commission, in *Sovetskaia Rossiia*, June 21, 1990, p. 2.
4. See the report by Ivan P. Osadchii on the work of the Russian party conference
preparatory committee in *Sovetskaia Rossiia*, June 20, 1990, p. 3.
5. Ibid.
6. A. Gamov, "Eto—put k edineniiu," *Sovetskaia Rossiia*, June 5, 1990, p. 5.
7. *Pravda*, June 10, 1990, p. 1.
8. Khodyrev report, credentials commission, *Sovetskaia Rossiia*, June 21, 1990, p. 2.
9. P. Gutiontov, *Izvestiia*, June 21, 1990, pp. 1–2; cf. the description of the congress in Robert G. Kaiser, *Why Gorbachev Happened: His Triumphs & His Failure*
(New York: Simon & Schuster, 1991), pp. 336–339. On the formation of the RCP,
see also Graeme Gill, *The Collapse of a Single-Party System* (Cambridge: Cambridge
University Press, 1994), pp. 126–130.
10. The runner-up was Oleg I. Lobov, with 1,066 yeas and 1,581 nays; see *Sovetskaia Rossiia*, June 24, 1990, p. 2.
11. Stephen White, *After Gorbachev* (Cambridge: Cambridge University Press,
1994), p. 236.
12. For a trenchant analysis of the proceedings, see Giulietto Chiesa, "The 28th
Congress of the CPSU," *Problems of Communism*, Vol. XXXIX (July-August 1990),
pp. 24–38.
13. "Informatsionnoe soobshchenie," *Sovetskaia Rossiia*, September 7, 1990, p. 1.
14. See Lebed's comments in an interview with *The Washington Post*, October 21,
1995, p. A21. In another interview, Lebed commented, with regard to his impres-
sions as a delegate to the 28th CPSU Congress, "And when I saw all the geriatrics
there close to, I realized that we would collapse"; *Komsomolskaia Pravda*, March 19,
1996, trans. in *Federal Broadcast Information Service—Soviet Union* (henceforth
FBIS-SOV), No. 57, March 22, 1996, p. 25. The authors would like to thank Ed-
ward T. Coffey for calling their attention to these interviews.
15. N. Andreev and V. Vyzhutovich, "Na sezde Kompartii RSFSR," *Izvestiia*, September 7, 1990, p. 2; see *Sovetskaia Rossiia*, September 7, 1990, p. 1, for a complete
list of the RCP Central Committee members.
16. See "Pervyi plenum TsK Kompartii RSFSR," *Sovetskaia Rossiia*, September 8,
1990, p. 1. For their later CPRF roles, see *Pravda Rossii*, No. 16 (30), September 7,
1995, p. 1; *Segodnia*, January 20, 1996, p. 1; and *Pravda Rossii*, No. 2 (16), March
30, 1995, p. 1.

17. Of the other candidates, Nikolai I. Ryzhkov received 16.85% of the vote, Vladimir V. Zhirinovskii 7.81%, Aman G. Tuleev 6.81%, General Albert M. Makashov 3.74%, and Vadim V. Bakatin 3.42%.

18. Authors' personal observations of these events in Moscow, March 28, 1991.

19. Boris Yeltsin, *The Struggle for Russia* (New York: Random House, 1994), pp. 26–27.

20. "TASS Profiles New Leader Kuptsov," Moscow TASS in English, August 6, 1991, in *FBIS-SOV*, No. 152, August 7, 1991, pp. 60–61.

21. V. A. Kuptsov, "KPSS otkryta dlia sotrudnichestva," *Izvestiia TsK KPSS*, No. 5 (May 1991), pp. 4–9.

22. *100 partiinykh liderov Rossii: Prilozhenie k informatsionno-analiticheskomu sborniku "Obozrevatel"* (Moscow: RAU-Corporation, 1993), pp. 28–29. Ziuganov's confidant, Aleksei I. Podberezkin, was president of the RAU (Russian-American University) Corporation when this directory was published. See also David Hoffman, "Ex-Foot Soldier Zyuganov Vies To Lead Russia," *The Washington Post*, June 2, 1996, p. A27.

23. Ziuganov's attitude toward the crushing of the "Prague Spring" was described to David Hoffman by a college friend of the CPRF leader; see ibid., p. A1. Author J. B. Urban discovered in the early 1990s that numerous scholars at her Russian host institute, which was in 1968 a part of the Soviet Academy of Sciences, systematically compared *Pravda*'s reports on developments during the Prague Spring with news accounts in the Czechoslovak press, to which they had ready access. In this way they were able to accurately assess the situation.

24. For a sensitive investigation into Ziuganov's personal background, see also Alessandra Stanley, "The Hacks Are Back," *The New York Times Magazine*, May 26, 1996, pp. 26ff.

25. See, for example, *100 partiinykh liderov Rossii*, pp. 28–29.

26. *Informatsionnyi biulleten*, No. 2 (14), February 1, 1995, p. 25.

27. *III Sezd Kommunisticheskoi partii Rossiiskoi Federatsii (Materialy i dokumenty)* (Moscow: "Informpechat," 1995), p. 66.

28. Hoffman, "Ex-Foot Soldier," *The Washington Post*, June 2, 1996, p. A27.

29. Text in Ziuganov, *Drama vlasti*, pp. 17–23.

30. Text in ibid., pp. 41–44.

31. T. Zamiatina, "Press-konferentsiia posle Plenuma: Gotovy rasshiriat sotrudnichestvo," *Sovetskaia Rossiia*, August 8, 1991, p. 1.

32. Ziuganov, *Drama vlasti*, p. 53; see also the interview with Ziuganov in *Zavtra*, No. 40, 1994, p. 2. The authors would like to thank Robert Otto for these references.

33. Ziuganov was nominated by the writer Yurii V. Bondarev and one G. G. Gusev; see *100 partiinykh liderov Rossii*, p. 29.

34. V. Tiulkin, "Osobaia papka Gennadiia Ziuganova," *Trudovaia Rossiia* (St. Petersburg), No. 2 (April-May 1994), p. 2.

35. *Pravda*, August 8, 1991, p. 2.

36. Interview with Ziuganov, Moscow All-Union Radio Mayak in Russian, August 7, 1991, trans. *FBIS-SOV*, No. 153, August 8, 1991, pp. 57–58.

37. Tiulkin, "Osobaia papka," p. 2.

38. Anatolii Salutskii, "President ili gensek," *Pravda: ezhenedelnaia gazeta*, No. 18 (May 17–24, 1996), p. 1.

39. Moscow Central Television First Program Network in Russian, August 15, 1991, trans. *FBIS-SOV*, No. 159, August 16, 1991, pp. 37–38.

40. See Chapter 2, p. 20.

41. *100 partiinykh liderov Rossii*, pp. 58–59.

42. For an overview of voting alignments in the Russian Congress of People's Deputies, see Thomas F. Remington, Steven S. Smith, D. Roderick Kiewiet, and Moshe Haspel, "Transitional Institutions and Parliamentary Alignments in Russia, 1990–1993," in *Parliaments in Transition*, ed. Thomas F. Remington (Boulder, CO: Westview Press, 1994), pp. 159–180.

43. J. B. Urban's interview with Svetlana P. Goriacheva in her Duma office, June 4, 1996.

44. See text of the February 21, 1991, "statement of six" in *FBIS-SOV*, No. 36, February 22, 1991, pp. 90–91; also, "Russian Congress Stenographic Report," *Rossiiskaia Gazeta*, October 30–31 and November 1, 2, 5, 6, 7, 9, 13, 14, 1991, trans. *FBIS-USR*, No. 11, February 7, 1992, p. 38.

45. See Vujacic's meticulously researched article, "Between the Soviet Left and the Russian Right: Russian Nationalism, Gennadii Ziuganov, and the Third Road," forthcoming in *Post-Soviet Studies*; cf. *100 partiinykh liderov Rossii*, p. 29.

46. *KPSS vne zakona?! Konstitutsionnyi sud v Moskve* (Moscow: Baikalskaia akademiia, 1992), pp. 34–35 and 40–41.

47. Ibid., pp. 42–44 and 137. See also Ziuganov, *Drama vlasti*, pp. 83–90. In this respect, as pointed out by Veljko Vujacic, Ziuganov's arguments were reminiscent of the "stab-in-the-back" theory articulated by "KGB chief Vladimir Kriuchkov at a closed session of the U.S.S.R. Supreme Soviet on June 17, 1991," based on a "confidential document prepared by Yurii Andropov in 1977"; see his "Between the Soviet Left and the Russian Right," note 21.

48. Quoted by Moscow ITAR-TASS, December 7, 1992, trans. *FBIS-SOV*, No. 236, December 8, 1992, pp. 18–19.

49. "Obshchimi usiliiami vozrodit nashy partiiu: Obrashchenie initsiativnogo Komiteta po sozyvu sezda kommunistov Rossiiskoi Federatsii," *Sovetskaia Rossiia*, December 3, 1992, pp. 1–2; the appeal named thirty-eight signatories, including a number of individuals noted in this and later chapters: Yurii P. Belov, Nikolai G. Bindiukov, Liudmila Vartazarova, Gennadii Ziuganov, Viktor I. Zorkaltsev, Valentin Kuptsov, Boris P. Kurashvili, Aleskandr N. Maltsev, Ivan Melnikov, Ivan Osadchii, and Ivan Rybkin.

50. "Zaiavlenie," *Golos kommunista*, No. 10 (1995), p. 3.

51. For details of this press coverage, see Wendy Slater, "Russian Communists Seek Salvation in Nationalist Alliance," *Radio Free Europe/Radio Liberty Research Report*, Vol. 2, No. 13 (March 26, 1993), pp. 8–13.

52. *II Chrezvychainyi Sezd Kompartii Rossiiskoi Federatsii* (Moscow: Paleia, n.d.), pp. 3–4. Here it should be mentioned that this official CPRF publication did not include any of the reports or discussion at the congress. For a detailed, albeit paraphrased, account of the actual proceedings of the Second CPRF Congress, see *Glasnost*, No. 7 (February 18–24, 1993), pp. 1–4. *Glasnost* was the most important communist newspaper from autumn 1991 through 1993 although it expressed the editorial viewpoint of those who sought to reestablish the CPSU.

53. Authors' in-depth interviews with CPRF leaders in the Ivanovo region, June 13, 1996. Our findings that grassroots loyalists played a more important role than former *apparatchiki* in reviving local party organizations there are similar to reports on what occurred in the Volgograd region; see Valerii Vyzhutovich, "Korni travy," *Isvestiia*, March 20, 1996, p. 5.

54. The account of these proceedings can be found in *Glasnost*, No. 7, 1993, p. 2.

55. Ibid.

56. Ibid.

57. See the excerpts from Kuptsov's report in *Politicheskie partii sovremennoi Rossii: Informatsionnye i analiticheskie materialy ob obshcherossiiskikh partiiakh i obshchestvennykh dvizheniiakh (1990–1993)*, Vol. 1 (Moscow: Izdatelstvo "Rossiiskaia politicheskaia entsiklopediia," 1993), pp. 324–325.

58. *Glasnost*, No. 7, 1993, p. 3. For the biographical data on Zorkaltsev, see A. S. Barsenkov et al., *Federalnoe Sobranie Rossii: Biograficheskii spravochnik* (Moscow: Fond "Foros," 1995), p. 345.

59. *Glasnost*, No. 7, 1993, p. 3.

60. Ibid.

61. Ibid.

62. Ibid., pp. 3–4.

63. Ibid., p. 4.

64. Ibid. According to the official account of the Second CPRF Congress, published some time later, the Central Executive Committee included 128 members and the Central Revision Commission 46 members; the additional members were apparently elected at a subsequent plenum. See *II Chrezvychainyi Sezd Kompartii Rossiiskoi Federatsii*, p. 3. On the other hand, CPRF functionaries gave the authors of this book a typed list of CEC members for the year 1993 which contained only 124 names.

65. Ivan Rybkin, "Eti vybory dadut neozhidannye resultaty," *Pravda*, December 5, 1995, p. 2.

66. See *100 partiinykh liderov Rossii*, pp. 44, 47, and 63. Maltsev did initially join the CPRF's Central Executive Committee, but evidently not for long as his name did not appear on the list received by the authors, cited in note 64.

67. *II Chrezvychainyi Sezd Kompartii Rossiiskoi Federatsii*, p. 32.

68. See *100 partiinykh liderov Rossii*, p. 43. For the substance of Makashov's objections to Kuptsov, see Gleb Cherkasov, "KPRF za dva mesiatsa do vyborov," *Segodnia*, April 23, 1996, p. 2.

69. See Salutskii, "Prezident ili gensek?," *Pravda: ezhenedelnaia gazeta*, No. 18 (1996), p. 5.

70. *Glasnost*, No. 7, 1993, p. 2.

71. "Politicheskoe Zaiavlenie: II Chrezvychainogo sezda Kommunisticheskoi partii Rossiiskoi Federatsii (vosstanovitelno-obedinitelnogo)," *Sovetskaia Rossiia*, March 2, 1993, pp. 1–2. Cf. *II Chrezvychainyi Sezd Kompartii Rossiiskoi Federatsii*, pp. 17–26.

72. Alessandra Stanley reports that, according to Kuptsov, he and some others—but not Ziuganov—took the lead on the issue of pluralism in discussions about the CPRF program, "coaxing and cajoling the Central Committee"; see "The Hacks Are Back," *The New York Times Magazine*, May 26, 1996, p. 46.

73. This was a point emphasized by Boris F. Slavin during J. B. Urban's interview with him, December 5, 1995.

74. Alessandra Stanley quotes Kuptsov as saying to her, "You can definitely credit Ziuganov for pushing religious freedom onto the party platform. . . . The party still has a lot of pure atheists, myself included." See "The Hacks Are Back," *The New York Times Magazine*, May 26, 1996, p. 45.

75. "Ustav Kommunisticheskoi partii Rossiiskoi Federatsii," *Pravda*, February 26, 1993, p. 2. Cf. *II Chrezvychainyi Sezd Kompartii Rossiiskoi Federatsii*, pp. 6–17.

76. Boris P. Kurashvili, *Kuda idet Rossiia?* (Moscow: "Prometei," 1994), pp. 41–48; according to Kurashvili, Kosolapov's "Leninist Platform" group found altogether twenty-four cases of "falsification" in the published text; see ibid., p. 48.

77. J. B. Urban's interview with Boris F. Slavin, December 5, 1995.

78. For Kurashvili's views during the late 1980s, see White, *After Gorbachev*, pp. 228–229.

4

The CPRF, the Radical CPs, and the Constitutional Crisis of 1993

The events of September–October 1993 and their bloody culmination, the attacks by armed mobs on the Moscow mayor's offices and the state-run Ostankino TV station followed by the Russian military's bombardment of the "White House," the seat of the Supreme Soviet of the Russian Congress of People's Deputies, were among the most dramatic pages in the brief history of post-Soviet Russia. They also represented the concluding phase of an intense political crisis that had been developing during the course of 1992 and 1993. Our purpose in this chapter is to analyze the political strategy of the various communist parties in this crisis, to explain the extent of their participation in it and the motives behind their involvement.

We begin with an overview of the worsening relationship between President Yeltsin and the Russian parliament, a confrontation that was triggered by disagreements over the advisability and impact of economic "shock therapy" and exacerbated by divergent interpretations of the respective powers of the executive and legislative branches of government. The second section picks up the story of the CPRF where Chapter 3 left off, that is, the proceedings of the party's "revival-unification" congress of February 1993 and the designation of Gennadii A. Ziuganov as party chairman. As we shall see, during the following spring and summer Ziuganov sought to superimpose his own political outlook upon the CPRF's ideological profile. We next discuss the reaction of the more radical Russian communist parties to the emerging executive-legislative gridlock that culminated in Yeltsin's dissolution of the Russian parliament on September 21, 1993. The chapter concludes with a discussion of the role of the CPRF and the other neocommunist formations during Moscow's "time of troubles" (*smuty*) in late September–early October 1993.

The Development of
Executive-Legislative Gridlock

One of the major reasons for the eventual confrontation between the new Yeltsin government and the Soviet-era Russian parliament was the forced-pace transition of Russia after August 1991 from the former communist political order and planned economy to an embryonic free-market, democratic, and mixed presidential-parliamentary system. Essentially what was at stake was a fundamental redistribution of property and political power, a radical transformation of the social structure of Russian society, and a break with established egalitarian values. However, while these far-reaching changes were more than enough to challenge any nascent institutional structures, they in no way signified the inevitability of armed civil conflict. Indeed, a similar transition to a new economic and political order was already being achieved in several of the former Soviet client states of Central and Eastern Europe without the development of such a harsh, uncompromising, and bloody confrontation.

Here it should be recalled that on the eve of the August 1991 putsch, two basic plans for a transition to a market economy were being considered in Russian leadership circles. While both sought to integrate Russia into the global "post-industrial" economy, the first might be called the "Chinese" model. It envisaged the relatively slow creation of market structures under the control of the government and with the preservation of the pivotal role of the state sector. The latter was to make the transition to market mechanisms only gradually, in tandem with the formation of the requisite infrastructure and changes in forms of property. This plan was backed by a powerful managerial lobby—in the first place, by the directors of the military-industrial complex and the machine-building industry, who focused on the Russian internal market. In the political arena their interests were represented by moderate technocratic reformers who later united in centrist coalitions such as the Civic Union of Arkadii I. Volskii.

The second plan for the transition to a market economy had a much more radical character and might well be called the "Polish" variant. This model was promoted by the liberal wing of the Russian political elite, above all by the associates of Yegor T. Gaidar and the Western *laissez-faire* economists who advised them. It represented the interests of the new financial-commercial structures which specialized primarily in wholesale trade and export-import operations. This plan, too, had both economic and political goals. But in sharp contrast to the "Chinese" model, it was aimed at the rapid formation of a viable free-market sector which was expected to create economic and social guarantees against the restoration of an authoritarian single-party system and centrally planned economy. Its basic elements included the replacement of the system of state distribution with a structure of commodity exchanges and wholesale firms; the denial of state financing for the greater part of industry, above all the military, which would lead to its forced integration into the market; the demonopolization of the fuel and energy complex; and the liquidation of the collectivized system of agriculture.[1]

The economic program of Grigorii A. Yavlinskii, on the other hand, occupied an intermediate position between the above two variants. To be sure, at one time he had envisaged the rapid transition to a market (in the course of the renowned "500 days" plan proposed in 1990). But, in contrast to the Gaidar program, in 1991–1992 Yavlinskii emphasized that first of all there should be de-monopolization, or privatization and the creation of a competitive market infrastructure, rather than immediate price liberalization, or so-called "shock therapy."[2]

Until August 1991 the radical version of the transition to a market had scarcely any serious chance of success. However, the abortive putsch not only dealt a crushing defeat to the more conservative wing of the Soviet political establishment; it also struck a simultaneous blow at the plans for a gradual "Chinese" approach to the market. Hence the political preconditions were suddenly created for the realization of the liberals' "Polish-style" reform program. President Yeltsin formed a new government in which Gaidar's circle of radical reformers was the dominant policymaking group. Not only that, but by a majority vote the Fifth Congress of People's Deputies (October–November 1991) granted Yeltsin the authority to rule by decree for one year, to designate his own prime minister (himself initially), and thus to implement radical economic reform in 1992.

Without going into detail, suffice it to say that the new reform program lacked certain very important political preconditions, namely, broad societal understanding of the hardships to come and the consensus of many elite groups. As a result, the first failures, problems, and inflationary costs of the reforms, which turned out to be much harsher and more prolonged than the reformers had suggested, led to a dangerous growth of social dissatisfaction and sharp criticism of the Yeltsin reform team's economic strategy. The government reformers found themselves in the position of a beleaguered minority who were able to implement their plans only thanks to the support of the president.[3]

The political crisis sparked by the economic reforms thus resulted in a bitter institutional confrontation between the executive and legislative branches of government, a conflict between the president and the parliament. At the same time, there is little ground for a widely held view in the West that the Russian Congress of People's Deputies was somehow automatically programmed for opposition to the president because it was elected under the old Soviet constitution. For, as already noted in Chapter 3, at the time of Yeltsin's election as chairman of the R.S.F.S.R. Supreme Soviet, in May 1990, more than half of the one thousand–odd Russian deputies voted for him. Not only that, but after Yeltsin was elected president of Russia in June 1991, his successor as chairman of the parliament, Ruslan I. Khasbulatov, was initially his close ally. Moreover, in the fall of 1991, when Yeltsin was at the peak of his popularity, he received his special decree powers with the consent of a significant majority of the deputies.

Even in 1993, when the confrontation between the parliament and the president was approaching the point of gridlock, the nucleus of the unbending anti-presidential opposition consisted of only about 300 deputies. At the same time, however, the number of Yeltsin's unconditional supporters on the eve of 1993 had sharply declined to only about 150 persons. Indeed, it came as an extremely unpleasant surprise to Yeltsin when, at the Seventh Congress of People's Deputies in December 1992, his appeal to his legislative supporters to walk out of the parliament was heeded by only about 120 deputies rather than the one-third that his advisers had anticipated in their misfired plan to deprive the congress of its necessary two-thirds quorum.[4] The suspicion thus arises that the president himself, through his seemingly unconditional approval of "shock therapy," significantly reduced the base of his own support in parliament and increased the number of his opponents.

Opposition between the legislative and executive branches of the Russian government was further heightened by the absence of a juridical basis and tested mechanisms for applying the principle of the division of powers. Indeed, the fundamental question of whether the post-Soviet Russian polity would evolve into a presidential system on, say, the French pattern or a parliamentary system on the British or German federal pattern had not yet been posed, let alone resolved. The situation was further complicated by the fact that the Soviet-era constitution still in effect (which was originally designed to give an aura of legitimacy to the monolithic single-party Soviet state) accorded ostensibly supreme authority to the legislature, giving it the legal advantage over the executive branch. Perhaps most important, as the political confrontation unfolded neither the president nor the parliament was prepared to concede supremacy to the other side.

The political and institutional conflict also acquired a highly personal character. This was a clash between politicians who were ambitious and not averse to risk-taking: President Yeltsin, on the one hand, and his one-time allies, Khasbulatov and Vice-President Aleksandr V. Rutskoi (whom Yeltsin had chosen as his running mate in 1991), on the other. The sense of personal betrayal in what was already a tense political conflict gave it an added element of obstinacy, harshness, and excess emotionalism.[5]

With regard to the intense animosity between Khasbulatov and Yeltsin, it most likely dated only from December 1992, the time of the Seventh Congress of People's Deputies, as will be elaborated below. Thereafter, however, its negative influence on Russian politics was exacerbated not only by the unclear division of powers and lack of experience in the democratic resolution of political conflicts but also by the transformation of the parliament into a focal point for the consolidation of all opposition to Yeltsin, both within and beyond the institution itself.

The situation was somewhat different in the case of Rutskoi, who early on was pushed by an irrepressible love of power in the direction of the political opposition. From the very beginning of his vice-presidency, he reacted negatively to the status accorded the institution of vice-president in the American political system. As Yeltsin himself has recalled,

> Rutskoi's main mistake—or more accurately, not a mistake but an organic characteristic—was his stubborn refusal to understand and accept his own status. From the very first day he considered the vice-president to be the . . . first deputy president.[6]

It was Rutskoi who first threw down the gauntlet to the president. In November 1991, during a trip through Siberia, the vice-president was sharply critical of Yeltsin's economic reform team. This was tantamount to criticism of Yeltsin himself. Relations between the president and vice-president noticeably cooled, and Yeltsin reportedly even stopped greeting Rutskoi. The latter was relieved of all his duties except for protocol functions.

According to well informed sources, during the winter of 1991–1992 Rutskoi's closest entourage hit upon the idea of turning him into the focal point of the nationalist forces opposing the president. Their goal was to dump Yeltsin and bring Rutskoi to power.[7] But for a number of reasons this scheme did not succeed. In the first place, the Russian nationalist opposition was still too weak and uncoordinated to serve Rutskoi as a springboard for seizing power. In the second place, Yeltsin was able to take steps to distract Rutskoi from active opposition. He entrusted him with supervising agrarian reform (in Russia this was a way to "sink" any politician) as well as with the leadership of an interagency commission for the struggle against corruption and organized crime.

The ambitions of the vice-president did not lessen, but for a time he was obliged to reject the strategy of a frontal assault and place his bets on a drawn-out siege. Rutskoi acquired a new political niche in the ranks of Volskii's Civic Union, a coalition of a moderate, centrist slant, which proclaimed itself a "third" force between the liberal reform democrats and the radical nationalist and communist opposition. The Civic Union represented the interests of moderate managers and technocratic reformers, the former proponents of the "Chinese" model, who sought a more gradual approach to a market economy, a serious readjustment in socio-economic policy, and changes in Yeltsin's cabinet.

Khasbulatov was a keener politician than Rutskoi. His position also looked much stronger because, in contrast to Rutskoi, he relied on the existing institution of representative power rather than on would-be or nascent political parties. In the first months of the post-communist era Khasbulatov's conduct was distinguished by shrewdness and caution as he tried to avoid even a hint of confrontation with the president. Indeed, thanks largely to his efforts, the Sixth Congress of People's Deputies (April 1992) ratified the treaty on the formation of the Commonwealth of Independent States in spite of powerful resistance to it by a recently formed opposition bloc of deputies, Russian Unity. Nevertheless, although Khasbulatov actively supported the new Yeltsin team in the autumn of 1991, already at the beginning of 1992 he criticized the economic course of the reformers. Perhaps this was related to the fact that at the end of 1991 he began to have serious clashes with the closest entourage of the president, especially with Gennadii E. Burbulis, who at that time, in his capacity as first deputy prime minister, monopolized the formulation of Russian policy and practically ran the government. But at the same time, Khasbulatov viewed Rutskoi's position just as Yeltsin did. As the parliament's chairman put it, "The president and vice-president ought to act as a single team . . . , and the vice-president . . . should not side with the parliament's criticism [of the president] but should be on the other side."[8]

For most of 1992 Khasbulatov thus conducted an intense behind-the-scenes struggle not so much against Yeltsin as for influence over him, trying to turn him against the radical reformers in the government and joining forces with those within the parliament who supported a slower paced version of economic reform. In April 1992 President Yeltsin was compelled to concede to the deputies' pressure and to remove their *bête noire*, Burbulis, from his post in the government. Thereupon several representatives of the industrial lobby whom the parliamentary opposition thought would moderate the pace of reforms, including Viktor S. Chernomyrdin and Vladimir F. Shumeiko, were appointed ministers in the president's cabinet. In June the president himself resigned his position as head of government, but at the same time he appointed his key economic reformer, Gaidar, as acting prime minister.

Pressure against the president continued to intensify as the economic crisis deepened. In the fall of 1992 the Supreme Soviet of the Congress of People's Deputies refused Yeltsin's request to postpone the Seventh Congress, scheduled for December, to a later date. It also announced that, in the absence of changes in the government's reform program and ministerial personnel, it would revoke the special decree powers it had granted the president in late 1991 and place before the congress the question of selecting a new cabinet and prime minister. Meanwhile, Khasbulatov, exercising the Supreme Soviet chairman's considerable patronage powers over committee and staff appointments as well as the distribution of such amenities as cars and apartments in Moscow, skillfully lubricated the process whereby the deputies bandwagoned to the side of the anti-Yeltsin opposition within parliament between April and December 1992.[9]

The president, however, flatly refused to consider any kind of strategic compromise with the parliament and the political opposition in general. Within Yeltsin's entourage the idea of reducing the parliament's powers (in violation of the existing constitution) began to take root almost a year before the events of September–October 1993.[10] And from the beginning of 1993, preparations to this end were undertaken in the international sphere as well. According to Yeltsin himself, during a meeting in Moscow in early 1993 he asked German Chancellor Helmut Kohl how the West would react to a "limitation on the activity of parliament." Kohl assured him that both he and the other leaders of the "seven" would (in Yeltsin's words) "look with understanding upon harsh but necessary measures for the stabilization of the situation in Russia."[11]

The Seventh Congress of People's Deputies in December 1992 constituted the turning point in the relationship between the presidential and parliamentary institutions of power as well as between Yeltsin and Khasbulatov on a personal level. By that time the oppositionists within the parliament had become numerous enough to thwart the president. Thus from December 1992 onward began the count-down in the irreconcilable political confrontation between the legislative and executive branches of government. The basic milestones in this process were the following: the December 1992 conflict at the Seventh Congress, during which Gaidar was removed as acting prime minister and replaced by Chernomyrdin; the March 1993 clash at the Eighth Congress over, among other things, the question of holding a popular referendum on the issues dividing the two branches of government; Yeltsin's March 20, 1993, threat to introduce a "special type of presidential rule" in the country; the abortive attempt to impeach the president at the Ninth Congress (also in March) in response to Yeltsin's threat; the April 25, 1993, referendum, the results of which, as we shall see, worked in the president's favor; and the summer 1993 struggle over the draft of a new constitution.[12] The attempts to reach a compromise that had been apparent in 1992 gradually fell by the wayside. The issue at hand was no longer the search for a mutually acceptable agreement between the two branches of government but the question of how one side might gain supremacy over the other, relegating it to a subordinate and dependent position.

During December 1992–April 1993, moreover, the parliament and Rutskoi formed a mutually beneficial political alliance. The presence of Rutskoi on the parliament's side gave an air of actuality to the threat of impeachment: a legitimate replacement for Yeltsin stood at the ready. The parliament, in turn, gave Rutskoi a political "cover" after his decisive break with the president.

Meanwhile, the president's strategists sought to mobilize support among the Russian people for possible extra-constitutional actions on the part of the president. It was precisely in this light that they interpreted the results of the April referendum, which asked the voters to indicate whether or not they supported Yeltsin personally as well as his socio-economic program (with about 63 percent voting, 58.7 percent said yes to the first question and 53 percent said yes to the second). Although the results of the referendum did not represent an unconditional victory for the president and had no legal force, they undermined the hopes of the opposition both within and beyond the parliament that Yeltsin might lose in an electoral showdown.

It was thus after the April referendum that Khasbulatov drew even closer to the opposition deputies, the so-called Russian Unity bloc, and the parliament's leadership in general began to show public solidarity with the extra-parliamentary radical nationalist and communist opposition. From spring 1993 onward the content of Khasbulatov's public addresses, interviews, and articles converged in many ways with the basic programmatic theses of the so-called "irreconcilable" opposition. In the eyes of both, the radical democrats (not the former communist system) were responsible for the collapse of the U.S.S.R. and the destruction of the Russian economy; the Soviet Union had been the historical successor of the pre-revolutionary Russian government; Russia bore overall responsibility for the territories of the former Soviet Union; and supreme authority rested in the soviets, or popularly elected parliamentary bodies, which had the right to establish and control the organs of executive power.[13] Such oppositionist positions ultimately led to the transformation of the Congress of People's Deputies into a center of attraction for all forces opposed to President Yeltsin.

By the end of the summer of 1993, the political confrontation had reached the point where both sides were acting according to the principle of "winner take all." Neither showed any inclination for concessions or compromise. In his speeches during this period, Yeltsin underscored more than once that August was the month of "preparation for battle" and September would see the showdown during which key political questions would be decided. The Supreme Soviet, in turn, passed one law after another directed against Yeltsin. Meanwhile, it planned to convene a full Congress of People's Deputies in November at which time the president would again be subjected to impeachment proceedings.

It may be that the parliament's chairman deliberately provoked the showdown predicted by the president. It is otherwise difficult to explain Khasbulatov's conduct on September 18, 1993, before the leaders of the regional soviets. After warning them of the possible establishment of a presidential dictatorship, the Supreme Soviet chairman pejoratively characterized Yeltsin with a flick of his fingers to his throat. In Russia this insulting gesture is used to describe a heavy drinker. In the opinion of some well informed observers, Khasbulatov's speech was the last straw that prompted Yeltsin to sign the already drafted Decree Number 1400 dissolving the Russian Congress of People's Deputies.[14] Both Khasbulatov and Rutskoi were well informed about the contents of the draft decree a full week before its actual issuance on September 21, 1993.[15] This suggests that they resolved to provoke Yeltsin into decisive action. The oppositionists who by then dominated the legislative branch needed the president to attack first so that their side would enjoy the moral advantage.

In the final analysis, the mounting confrontation between the parliament and the president was not so much a struggle between reformist and anti-reformist forces (within the parliament a majority also backed reforms, but of a more moderately paced type than the president) or between democratic and authoritarian-oligarchic tendencies. Rather, it was a struggle between antagonists with little experience in the art of political compromise who, through fate and circumstances, had become ensconced in the separate branches of the post-Soviet Russian government.

Ziuganov's National Front Strategy

During the late spring and summer of 1993, as the executive and legislative branches of the Russian government moved toward a showdown, Gennadii Ziuganov's influence over the political profile of the Communist Party of the Russian Federation became increasingly apparent. In effect, Ziuganov adapted to contemporary Russian conditions the CPSU's World War II national front strategy for the communist parties in Nazi-occupied Europe.

From late 1942 onward, Moscow had directed the European communist parties to form "national front" resistance movements embracing all political forces opposed to German military occupation. The initial calls for unity of action between communist and center-left forces, on the pattern of the Third Communist International's anti-fascist popular front strategy of the mid-1930s, was quickly broadened to include cooperation with Catholic groups, industrialists, monarchists, and even dissident fascists.[16] Ideological precepts quickly receded into the background. Indeed, the declared goal of the communist-supported national liberation movements was to create governments of national unity after the expulsion of the German occupation forces. And during the first week of April 1944, the increasingly powerful French and Italian communist parties publicly announced their readiness to participate as junior partners in post-fascist democratic coalition governments.[17] It was largely due to their broadly targeted nationalist appeals, resistance activism, and democratic rhetoric that the French and Italian communist parties experienced spectacular growth during World War II, the former increasing from some 340,000 in the late 1930s to 900,000 members after the war and the latter from some 5,000 clandestine activists in early 1943 to well over 1.5 million members by late 1945.[18]

Ziuganov, as a member of the CPSU Central Committee's staff dealing with propaganda and ideology, was surely familiar with Moscow's wartime national front strategy. In 1993 he altered it, however, to fit the circumstances of post-Soviet Russia. In place of armed resistance to military occupation, Ziuganov's speeches and CPRF documents called for "national liberation" by legal means from domination of the Russian state by Western "liberal-bourgeois cosmopolitanism" and its traitorous Russian agents. To this end, they urged communists to join forces with all patriotic groups, including local entrepreneurs. As one widely published CPRF statement put it, as though by way of justification, "state patriotism . . . permeated all communist activity during the years of the Great Patriotic War."[19]

Ziuganov's early personal commitment to unity of action between anti-reformist communists and Russian nationalists during the last months of the Soviet regime, as described in Chapter 3, suggested that such an approach was integral to his political mentality. It was thus hardly surprising that, after the dissolution of the U.S.S.R. and Yeltsin's consolidation of a pro-Western regime, Ziuganov promptly renewed his efforts to form a national front of anti-reformist communist and right-wing patriotic groups. In contrast to 1991, however, when he viewed the newly created Russian Communist Party as the nucleus of such joint activity, he now focused his attention on the nationalist organizations. Meanwhile, the neocommunist formations took a backseat role as a reservoir of mass support. The reason for this shift in emphasis was clear. The Russian Communist Party was officially banned, while communist ideology itself was experiencing a deep crisis as its influence in society dramatically declined.

In place of Marxism-Leninism, therefore, Ziuganov proposed the ideology of Russian state patriotism. Accordingly, in December 1991 Ziuganov and the Leningrad communist leader, Yurii P. Belov, addressed an open letter to the communists of Russia in which they argued that a "union of state-patriotic forces was the dictate of the times."[20] Ziuganov's purview included all the newly created organizations of a Russian nationalist orientation. To recapitulate what was said in Chapter 3, he entered into the leadership of Sergei N. Baburin's Russian All-People's Union (formed in December 1991) and the coordinating council of the movement "Native Land" (formed in January 1992). From January 1992 onward he led the coordinating council of the People's–Patriotic Forces of Russia movement and was a co-chairman of Aleksandr N. Sterligov's Russian National Assembly (formed in February–June 1992) as well as the National Salvation Front (formed in October 1992). But not one of these Russian nationalist opposition groups was able to become the catalyst of a unified national front, and the orthodox neocommunist parties were scarcely in a rush to support such a cause. Therefore, after the reconstitution of the CPRF and his election as party chairman, Ziuganov returned to his initial conception of the national front according to which the Russian communist party would be the nucleus around which Russian nationalists and left-wing statists would unite.

From approximately the middle of 1993 onward, the national front strategy and the idea of state patriotism thus became cornerstones of the CPRF's ideological-political outlook. They were all the more relevant since precisely at this time the party decisively staked its hopes on a peaceful electoral path out of the current political crisis. Until the April 1993 referendum the CPRF, in all likelihood, did not exclude the possibility that the regime might fall as the result of a spontaneous socio-political explosion. But after the referendum it repudiated this notion, although the radical neocommunist groups continued as before to anticipate a new revolution.

The CPRF's new strategic approach began to take shape at the Third Plenum of its Central Executive Committee on May 29, 1993. At the initiative of the Leningrad and Rostov party organizations, the plenum issued a declaration entitled "On the Danger of Political Extremism." This statement reflected not only the relatively pro-regime results of the April referendum but even more the shock elicited by the May 1, 1993, bloody street clashes in the center of Moscow. On the latter occasion, militiamen forcibly halted a communist May Day procession, leading to numerous casualties on both sides. The CPRF leadership concluded that any sign of communist extremism might provoke a government crackdown and that the party should thenceforth concentrate on legal means of resistance, including the call for early parliamentary and presidential elections. As the May 29 declaration spelled out,

> One must have the courage to recognize that political extremism has no place in the communist arena but is the expression of petty-bourgeois revolutionary activism with its inherent psychology that tomorrow we shall either conquer or perish.[21]

The CPRF's new approach was set forth in two documents published during the summer of 1993—the party's projected election platform and an open letter from the Presidium of the Central Executive Committee to all the communists of Russia. The former, which was initially discussed in draft form at the Third Plenum, was published in *Sovetskaia Rossiia* on July 22, 1993. The latter, which reflected the nationalist inclinations of both Ziuganov and Belov but was reportedly written by the latter, appeared about five weeks later in all the major communist publications: *Pravda*, *Glasnost*, and *Pravda Rossii*.[22] (At that time *Pravda Rossii* was the only specifically CPRF newspaper but it appeared only as a periodic insert in the more generically communist *Pravda*.)

Picking up where the Third Plenum's declaration against extremism left off, the party's platform called for early simultaneous elections for both the president and parliament as the best way of resolving the escalating constitutional crisis. And it proposed that the CPRF participate in the elections as a member of a broad national front coalition, "an electoral bloc of people's

state-patriotic forces."[23] The CPRF Presidium's open letter echoed these
themes, declaring its commitment to exclusively legal methods of struggle
against the ruling regime. It also underscored that the immediate order of
the day, so to speak, was not the proletarian revolution and a rapid return to
socialism but the creation of a "national-liberation and people's-democratic
movement."

The open letter proposed that the ideological basis of this movement be
the doctrine of "state patriotism," which it called the "ideology of the salvation and rebirth of Russia." What exactly did "state patriotism" entail? In the
first place, it looked upon the state as the inner thread of continuity in Russian history and the key factor in the development of the country. "The path
to socialism . . . is impossible without the salvation of the fatherland's statehood," proclaimed the open letter.[24] Secondly, state patriotism signified
recognition of the priority of state interests, especially at times of national
crisis, over the interests of the individual and all social, corporative, and ethnic groups, that is, society as a whole. In this sense the concept seemed alien
if not outright inimical to the ideas of civil society, liberalism, and democracy
in their generally accepted meanings. Thirdly, it viewed the Russian people
as the nucleus and cement of the Russian and Soviet state. With regard to
this last point, the open letter hastened to ward off charges of Russian nationalism by declaring, preemptively as it were, that "the internationalist
essence of our ideology is not opposed to patriotism that is free of national
separatism and chauvinism."[25] Fourthly, the open letter departed from the
traditional communist position on the contrast between the pre-1917 and
post–October Revolution periods in the country's history; instead, it accentuated the continuity in Russian-Soviet history, calling it a "single and indivisible history of the fatherland."[26]

Ziuganov's own books elaborated upon his understanding of state patriotism. In his 1993 volume of autobiographical ruminations, he spoke of the
replacement of the class approach to social analysis with the notion of *sobornost*, that is, the idea of the organic spiritual unity of the Russian people. According to this proposition, the Great October Revolution of 1917 turned
out to be not a triumph of communist ideology but an immense tragedy. Indeed, the undermining of *sobornost* at the beginning of the century "by the
emergence of class conflict almost led to catastrophe."[27] In his 1994 book,
Derzhava (Great Power), Ziuganov also sharply revised the traditional communist version of Soviet history. He maintained that during the Russian Civil
War both the "reds" and the "whites" were right, each in their own way. The
task of the present-day communists was thus to achieve a synthesis of the
"red" and "white" ideas by "reuniting [sic] the 'red' ideal of social justice . . .
and the 'white' ideal of nationally conceived statehood."[28] Needless to say, in
the eyes of the orthodox communists such an interpretation smacked of outright "counter-revolutionary thinking," as we will elaborate in Chapter 5.

In the summer of 1993, however, the official CPRF documents did not wholly embrace Ziuganov's historical-ideological revisionism. To be sure, the electoral platform stressed the need to strengthen spiritual values, the most important of which was "love of the Fatherland," and to propagate the historical contribution of ethnic Russians to the creation of the Russian/ Soviet "Great Power." The CPRF Presidium open letter, in turn, hailed the Russian tradition of *sobornost,* warning that a "dictatorship of any class in contemporary Russia would in the final analysis lead to a historical catastrophe," and it also deplored the "Americanization of the spiritual life of our society." But in other respects both documents were still attuned to the Marxist reformism of the February 1993 CPRF congress.

A case in point has to do with the threat of the collapse of the Russian Federation along the lines of the U.S.S.R.'s collapse, which was considered one of the country's most acute problems during 1992–1993. On this issue the CPRF displayed considerable political astuteness. Plainly, the preservation of Russian unity was an unconditional imperative for the communist statists. In contrast to the Russian nationalists, however, they deemed it best not to alienate the non-Russian ethnic groups and their elites, all the more so since the autonomous republics within the Russian Federation, such as those along the Volga and in the Northern Caucasus, were viewed as an important source of communist voters.[29] Therefore, the CPRF came out in favor of the federal principle as the mechanism most likely to secure the unity of the country. But at the same time, it was extremely important for the party not to spoil its relations with the numerically preponderant electorate from the ethnically undifferentiated regions, or *oblasti.* The latter, however, were demanding the same political and economic rights as those enjoyed by the autonomous republics. The CPRF thus proposed to resolve the conflict between the "Russian" and the autonomous ethnic units of the Russian Federation by raising the status of the former to the level of the latter.[30]

By the same token, the party platform spoke of the "immutability of the soviet form of statehood."[31] However, the CPRF in no way viewed the soviets in the traditional communist manner, as organs of the dictatorship of the proletariat. Rather, it saw them as the specific Russian form of democracy, as a manifestation of Russian national character and the embodiment of Russian traditions. As the CPRF Presidium open letter put it, the soviet type of state was the natural historical response to "the national traditions of *sobornost* and collectivism."[32]

If the interpretation of the soviets as the most desirable form of democratic representation was somewhat ambiguous, the CPRF's mid-1993 position on economic matters was much less so. Both the electoral platform and the open letter continued to endorse the idea of a mixed economy with a combination of state regulation and market methods of economic management. Indeed, the CPRF categorically rejected the possibility of a return to the former command economy. In the words of the open letter, "We consider it impossible for Russia to return to the super-centralized economy of bureaucratic-authoritarian socialism with the state's absolute monopoly on property."[33]

Meanwhile, the CPRF was compelled to make a concession to its critics on the left on at least one point, the issue of the reestablishment of the U.S.S.R. Both of the mid-1993 party documents put this on their agenda, albeit with significant qualifications. The reestablishment of a Union government would come about as the result of an "evolutionary," "step-by-step," and "voluntary" process. The end result of that process was thus relegated to the very distant future.

The Radical Communists Prepare for Confrontation

While all the left-wing political groups were sharply critical of the Yeltsin government, they expressed their opposition in different ways. The most radical position was assumed by the Russian Communist Workers' Party (RCWP). Its starting premise was that Yeltsin's "bourgeois regime" had no firm basis of support in Russian society and that the economic reforms it had launched would inevitably elicit a powerful movement of social protest which would sweep away the democrats. The RCWP's goal was thus to give this wave of indignation an organized character, to implement a Leninist revolutionary strategy—in short, to lead a mass uprising.

The militant grassroots movement, Toiling Russia (*Trudovaia Rossiia*), which was created under the aegis of the RCWP in late 1991, was to play the role of battering-ram against the Yeltsin regime. As described in Chapter 2, its nucleus was located in Moscow, where a subsidiary, Toiling Moscow, was formed in December 1991, and it included representatives of almost all the neocommunist organizations in the Russian capital. The militant leftist, Viktor I. Anpilov, was the ideological founder of both Toiling Moscow and Toiling Russia. Nevertheless, although a coordinating council and political executive committee were formally in charge of Toiling Russia, in practice the local organizations (not only Toiling Moscow but also Toiling Leningrad, Toiling Cheliabinsk, Toiling Voronezh, and so forth) were independent groups.

At the same time, Toiling Russia was little more than a weakly structured radical coalition group. This was due to the fact that while more often than not RCWP cells created the local organizations, their protest actions attracted the participation of other neocommunist parties and groups as well as non-party communist sympathizers. A series of small Russian nationalist organizations also participated in the Toiling Russia demonstrations. This ideological hodgepodge, coming on top of the sharp competition among the different communist groups, militated against the transformation of Toiling Russia into a disciplined political organization guided by a single leadership.[34]

Although Toiling Russia did not become the detonator of a social explosion, it nevertheless succeeded in organizing a number of mass protest actions which greatly contributed to the growth of political tension, especially in Moscow. Despite the fact that the number of its activists in the Russian capital was scarcely more than 300 people, its mobilizing capability was rather high. Some twenty to thirty thousand demonstrators regularly took part in Toiling Russia actions in Moscow. Moreover, on those occasions when the number of participants exceeded 100,000, it was usually a case of Toiling Russia organizing the demonstration in cooperation with other opposition forces.

At least three times—on February 23, 1992 (Soviet Armed Forces Day), on June 22, 1992 (after ten days of picketing of the Ostankino TV station), and on May 1, 1993—opposition activity led to direct clashes with the police and ended in bloodshed. And on May 9, 1993 (Victory Day), some 250,000 to 300,000 oppositionists marched in protest against the authorities' conduct during the May Day confrontation earlier that month.[35] This latter demonstration was evidence of a widely held public view that Anpilov and his comrades, despite their commitment to sparking an "urban revolution," were not the only ones to blame for the earlier violent encounters. Indeed, it appeared to many that the aggressive, militant style of Toiling Russia was often matched by the authorities' intent to "teach a lesson" to the communists.

The radicalization of Toiling Russia and its RCWP supporters intensified with the development of executive-legislative gridlock and the worsening of the country's socio-economic situation, including continuing *monthly* rates of double-digit inflation. After the clashes with the police, Toiling Russia moved to create "people's patrols" which were intended to preserve order during mass demonstrations but in fact began to look like a new edition of the Bolshevik Red Guards. The radicals' revolutionary fuse was also shortened by the fact that Toiling Russia had good relations with the Union of Officers, whose leader, Stanislav N. Terekhov, was a member of the Toiling Russia leadership. Terekhov's organization consisted mainly of retired or reserve officers, and its leaders were former political officers who had traditionally enjoyed little authority or respect among the ranks of the Soviet armed forces. Nevertheless, in the eyes of the communist radicals, blinded as they were by revolutionary enthusiasm, it may well have seemed that the army was coming over to their side. Plainly, during the course of 1992–1993 the conviction grew among a number of RCWP leaders and militants that the regime had lost all its bases of support and would come tumbling down if only one could give it a good shove.

The attitude of the other neocommunist parties to the revolutionary strategy of the RCWP and Toiling Russia was rather contradictory. On the one hand, as related in Chapter 2, they were also convinced of the instability of the new Russian government and wanted to precipitate its downfall. But at the same time, the other neocommunist leaders were angered by the pretensions of the RCWP's extremist wing to a monopoly of influence in the communist movement and Toiling Russia. There were also substantial differences of opinion on concrete political tactics. Aleksei A. Prigarin's Union of Communists and even part of the RCWP leadership opposed the isolationist course of the latter's radical wing. The neocommunists as a whole took an ever more guarded view of Anpilov's growing extremism, fearing that his tactics would condemn them to isolation in Russian society. Indeed, as a result of these disagreements, in November 1992 Toiling Russia split into two organizations with one and the same name: one was led by Boris Gunko and Prigarin and the other by Anpilov.[36]

The communist radicals defined their attitude toward the conflict between the parliament and the president only with some difficulty. At first they were highly suspicious of a Russian parliament which approved of shock therapy and the dissolution of the U.S.S.R. while also granting Yeltsin special decree powers. Beginning with the Sixth Congress of People's Deputies in April 1992, Toiling Russia began to regularly picket its sessions. The neocommunists' attitude toward the parliament changed for the better only as the executive-legislative confrontation intensified in early 1993.

At that time the parliament, in turn, entered into an unspoken alliance with the radical opposition, hoping thereby to mobilize mass support for its cause. Public indications of this political connection became apparent between May 1 and 9, 1993. Supreme Soviet chairman Khasbulatov sharply denounced the bloody May Day clashes, blaming them on the Moscow authorities and, indirectly, on the president. And the protest march on Victory Day, May 9, was organized under the aegis of the Supreme Soviet and led by Union of Officers' chief Terekhov.[37]

In supporting the parliament in its opposition to the president, the neocommunist radicals did not back off one iota from their strategy of a new socialist revolution and the establishment of the dictatorship of the proletariat. They were, so to speak, fully liberated from "petty bourgeois illusions" with regard to the Congress of People's Deputies and its Supreme Soviet. According to a declaration by the All-Union Communist Party of Bolsheviks (ACPB), for example, the conflict between the legislative and executive branches was caused by "political-mafia realignments among the different clans that have penetrated the power of the bourgeoisie," while the soviets represented merely a "form of bourgeois democracy."[38]

Meanwhile, as the political crisis intensified, one of the key goals of the radicals was the creation of a coalition of "rightists" and "leftists," of "reds"

and "whites," of neocommunists and Russian nationalists, that is, the formation of a broad based oppositionist national front. On March 1, 1992, hard
on the heels of the government's violent dispersal of the February Armed
Forces Day demonstration, the creation of a united opposition was announced. The founding declaration was signed both by the main Russian nationalist organizations and by all the neocommunist parties (including the
Socialist Labor Party) except the ACPB.[39] The demands of this united radical opposition, as published at the beginning of July 1992, included the resignation of the president's cabinet and the formation of a "government of
people's trust," the abrogation of the regime's economic privatization program, the preservation of collectivized agriculture, allocation to the opposition of one-third of the time on state television and radio, etc.[40] Soon,
moreover, these demands acquired a more irreconcilable character. In an
agreement signed on September 17, 1992, the united opposition proclaimed that its chief goal was "the removal from power of the ruling Yeltsin
team by means of impeachment of the President."[41] The opposition also refused to recognize the dissolution of the U.S.S.R. and considered the Soviet
Constitution of 1977, in its pre-*perestroika* form, to be still in force.[42]

Real unity of "leftists" and "rightists" occurred, however, only at the parliamentary level. In April 1992, on the eve of the Sixth Congress of People's Deputies, the Russian Unity bloc was formed, which included five parliamentary fractions, including the Communists of Russia group. The bloc
had about 300 members, that is, slightly less than a third of the total number of people's deputies. As has already been noted, its influence in the
Russian parliament steadily grew as the executive-legislative confrontation
unfolded.[43]

By way of contrast, the extra-parliamentary communists and nationalists
conspicuously failed to create a stable and well organized bloc. Ideological
and political disagreements as well as personal ambitions worked against
unity. Anpilov and his Toiling Russia supporters, not wishing to lose their
particular identity in an alliance with other opposition forces, left the ranks
of the united opposition in its early organizational stages. The RCWP, for its
part, sought to demarcate itself from all the other opposition groups to the
right of it at its February 1993 congress (which took place at the same time
as the CPRF's Second Congress). It also took a negative position toward the
National Salvation Front (NSF), which had been created in October 1992 as
an umbrella organization for both nationalist and communist opponents of
the Yeltsin regime. Those members of the RCWP leadership who insisted on
the necessity of a broad national front coalition and entered the NSF—for
example, Marxist-Leninist scholar Richard I. Kosolapov and retired general
Albert M. Makashov—were expelled from the RCWP Central Committee
and quit the party altogether, choosing to throw in their lot with the newly
reconstituted CPRF. Meanwhile, at a December 1992 plenum the Union of

Communists also endorsed the activity of the NSF and urged its members to work toward the formation of local front cells. The Russian Party of Communists took a similar position.[44]

The most ardent and steadfast proponent of a national front of leftist and rightist opposition forces was, however, the CPRF under the leadership of Ziuganov. As discussed in the previous section, during 1991–1992 Ziuganov took part in the formation and leadership organs of a series of united opposition groups, including the NSF. Where Ziuganov diverged from extremists of both a leftist and rightist orientation was in his public emphasis upon legal methods and non-violence. While this stance was consistent with his emphasis upon the integral unity of the Slavic peoples, it also had a more pragmatic basis. As Ziuganov bitterly commented at the beginning of June 1993,

> The opposition has disoriented itself and its supporters by betting on a rapid explosion of popular discontent and the downfall of the ruling regime. The assumptions that the regime did not have any kind of broad support among the masses were not adequately substantiated.[45]

Such practical considerations undergirded the CPRF's declaration "On the Danger of Political Extremism" which, as already noted, was approved at its Third Plenum in late May 1993.

One further development that occurred before the outbreak of the full-blown constitutional crisis remains to be discussed: the Congress of the Peoples of the U.S.S.R. which was held in Moscow on September 20, 1993. Despite the many and profound ideological, political, and personal disagreements among the Russian oppositionists, they all agreed on one point: non-recognition of the Belovezhskie agreements and the reestablishment of the Soviet Union (whether by force or a peaceful, evolutionary path). Thus, although the Congress of the Peoples of the U.S.S.R. was convened by the traditionalist Union of Communist Parties–CPSU (about which we will have more to say in Chapter 5), it was attended by almost the entire opposition spectrum—from the Anpilov extremists to the moderate centrists of the Civic Union. Many of the former union republics were also represented at the forum. The congress formally called upon all oppositionists to denounce the Belovezhskie agreements as "anti-constitutional."[46]

What was most striking about this occasion was that the leadership of the Russian Congress of People's Deputies expressed open solidarity with the congress participants. Not only was the Supreme Soviet's first deputy chairman, Yurii M. Voronin, a member of the conclave's presidium, but he also read a message to the congress from Khasbulatov in which the latter announced that he shared with the delegates the "weight of the loss of the great power—the Union of Soviet Socialist Republics."[47] The formation of an open political bloc between the parliament and the extra-parliamentary opposition, which had first become evident in early May 1993, had thus reached a new stage.

Moscow's "Time of Troubles," September 21–October 4, 1993

On September 21, 1993, President Yeltsin issued his famous decree Number 1400, which dissolved the Congress of People's Deputies and called for elections the following December to a new Russian parliament as well as a simultaneous referendum on a new constitution. However paradoxical it may seem, the intransigent opposition people's deputies (about 300 persons) greeted the news with something akin to exultation. According to eyewitness accounts, on the night of September 22 euphoria reigned in the House of Soviets, or White House, as it was popularly known.[48] The innermost if unstated hope of the president's parliamentary opponents had come true. Yeltsin had attacked first, making them look like the victims of tyranny. His removal from power should now be simply a matter of time. Apparently, the oppositionists assumed that the "miracle" of August 1991 would be repeated: the regime would fall during the course of several days if not hours. While they settled in to defend the White House, however, the building was cordoned off by policemen and barbed wire.

Practically all currents of the Russian opposition stood united in their denunciation of the presidential decree and their support for parliament. In the early morning of September 22, a joint declaration of Russian nationalists and leftists, signed by both the extremists and the less radical groups (including, for example, the leaders of the Socialist Labor Party), was disseminated which stated flatly that President Yeltsin had become "the leader of the anti-state and anti-constitutional forces" in the country.[49] Whereupon the opposition legislators turned White House defenders swore in Vice-President Rutskoi as Yeltsin's legitimate successor, and Rutskoi proceeded to select a new cabinet of ministers from among his supporters.

Although on September 21–22 the leftist parties all unanimously condemned the president's action as an attempted coup and took the side of the legislature, they nevertheless chose different political strategies during the course of the confrontation. As was to be expected, the most radical position was taken by the RCWP and its affiliates, Toiling Russia and Toiling Moscow. They promptly announced the beginning of the "proletarian revolution" and appealed to the Congress of People's Deputies to reinstitute the full functions of the local and regional soviets.[50] Consistent with their understanding of Lenin's strategy between February and October 1917, the RCWP activists aimed to stimulate the transformation of what they saw as the revolution's "people's-democratic" stage into the socialist stage.

In a mid-day interview on September 22, Anpilov announced the radical opposition's intention not to undertake any action except agitation, albeit also expressing the hope that the regime's opponents would be supported in the Russian regions.[51] However, that very evening the opposition deputies, who occupied the White House in defiance of Yeltsin's decree, passed a resolution demanding that the state-run Ostankino TV station as well as Russian Radio broadcast addresses by "President" Rutskoi and his newly appointed "Minister of Defense," the militant general Vladislav Achalov. In its attempt to break the regime's information blockade, the resolution further insisted that the Russian TV program "Parliament," which had expressed the viewpoint of the anti-Yeltsin deputies, be reinstated "without cuts." After the meeting Anpilov announced, "If these demands are not met, we will be forced to march on Ostankino together with fighting detachments of the Union of Officers."[52] Anpilov's threat not only evoked memories of the radicals' ten-day siege of the "empire of lies," as Ostankino was called in opposition circles, in June 1992; it also indicated that the march by armed rioters on Ostankino the evening of October 3, 1993, which ended in such terrible bloodshed, was not a spontaneous idea but had been maturing from at least the start of the September–October confrontation.

Even so, state-run television was not the extreme leftists' first object of attack. According to several sources, at that same White House meeting the evening of September 22, Anpilov called upon the participants to storm the building of the Ministry of Defense, insisting that for this about 100 men would be sufficient.[53] The following evening an attempt to seize the military headquarters of the Commonwealth of Independent States was undertaken by a group of armed fighters under the command of Union of Officers leader Terekhov. This action was coordinated with Anpilov, who summoned the occupiers of the White House to go to the aid of Terekhov. The deputy-defenders of the parliament building, however, proved to be more discerning and took Anpilov's appeal to be a provocation.[54]

After the failure of the armed assault, the communist radicals changed their tactics, even if they did not renounce the strategy of "heating up" the revolution. Since their hopes for the regions' active intervention on the parliament's side were quickly disappointed and they did not have enough strength for a direct armed clash with the regime, they shifted their attention to the creation of a multiplicity of hotbeds of tension in the center of Moscow. Apparently, the idea was to provoke a generalized urban rebellion in the Russian capital which would spark the "triumphant march of soviet power" throughout the whole country, on the pattern of 1917.

Both the RCWP, with its allies, and the Union of Communist Parties–CPSU (UCP-CPSU) were on the list of political parties and movements (of ultra-nationalist as well as leftist orientation) that would be banned by the Yeltsin government after the final showdown on October 4, 1993. In fact, the UCP-CPSU's organizational structures would be accused of direct participation in the later armed attacks on the Moscow mayor's offices and on the Ostankino TV station.[55] This, however, was hardly plausible. For although the UCP-CPSU did pass a resolution in support of the parliament on the evening of September 21, it did not have its own organizational network. Its leaders tried to influence the deputy-defenders of the White House simply through personal contacts. For instance, one of the associate heads of the UCP-CPSU was Aleksei Prigarin (also chairman of the separate Union of Communists), who spent day and night in the parliament building. Another link between the UCP-CPSU leadership and Khasbulatov was the latter's adviser, Sergei Kurginian, a well known political scientist and opposition intellectual, but he advocated a peaceful resolution of the confrontation. Indeed, this was so much the case that on September 30 Aleksandr P. Barkashov's band of Russian fascists took away Kurginian's work I.D. and evicted him from the White House.

On the other hand, even if the tactics of the UCP-CPSU were not as confrontational as those of the RCWP and Toiling Russia, they nonetheless embraced a similar concept of revolutionary development. In contrast to the Anpilov line of direct coercion and the instigation of "urban warfare," however, the UCP-CPSU placed its bets on attracting wide strata of Russian society into the conflict. On the evening of September 21 its leader, Oleg S. Shenin, addressed a letter to Rutskoi in which he advised him to announce a series of top priority measures capable of attracting mass sympathy with the parliament. He proposed, in particular, the immediate abrogation of the Belovezhskie agreements, the freezing of prices on basic food stuffs and consumer goods, the takeover of private banks, and so forth.[56] These ideas were in many ways consistent with Lenin's 1917 writings in which he set forth the strategy of the growth of the bourgeois-democratic revolution into the socialist revolution. In other words, although the UCP-CPSU line was relatively "moderate" in comparison with the extremism of Anpilov and his comrades, at its core lay the same notion of "heating up" the revolution, and the goal was likewise the revolutionary restoration of socialism.

In fact, the Shenin-Prigarin group and the RCWP circles were committed to the same strategy. The difference between them lay in tactics and can be explained by the fact that they took as their point of departure different elements of the Leninist legacy on revolution. The UCP-CPSU set its hopes on the "decisive role of the popular masses," Anpilov and company on the "proletarian vanguard." At the same time, the hardline, instigative tactics of the RCWP–Toiling Russia leaders, which were adapted both from Lenin's conduct in October 1917 and from contemporary new left theorists of "urban warfare," seemed more feasible than the UCP-CPSU scheme. In the first place, neither the opposition deputies nor their leaders were ready to undertake the radical steps proposed by the UCP-CPSU. Secondly, even if they had decided to announce such measures, the country would scarcely have heard them because of the regime's information blockade of the White House.

Meanwhile, the position of the ultra-leftist All-Union Communist Party of Bolsheviks (ACPB) proved to be extremely ambiguous during the crisis. On the one hand, the party declared that the country was being run by "state criminals who have violated the Constitution . . . and are striving to establish a single-man dictatorship of a fascist type," and it appealed for the organization of strikes, meetings, and a campaign of civil disobedience.[57] On the other hand, these incendiary formulations and appeals were to a large extent nullified by the following assertion: "[T]here is not . . . any kind of dual power in the country. Power lies in the hands of the bourgeoisie."[58] This implied abstention from any active role in the conflict. In effect, the ACPB neo-Stalinists took the position that the warring factions of the bourgeoisie should be left to destroy one another in an internecine struggle, thereby hastening the onset of the real socialist revolution.

Indirect evidence of the relative political passivity of the ACPB can be gleaned from the fact that, though it too was banned after October 4, the authorities assigned it to the second category of participation in the final clashes. To the first category belonged those political formations, such as the RCWP and UCP-CPSU, accused of participating in the armed conflict *in their capacity as political organizations*, while to the second category belonged those parties and movements whose members participated in the storming of the mayor's offices and Ostankino *in an individual capacity*.[59]

More importantly for our analysis, the CPRF was likewise included in the second category. The night of September 21–22, Ziuganov announced to journalists that "Khasbulatov and Rutskoi have burned their bridges, and there is now no other way [out of the crisis]."[60] On September 23 the CPRF Central Executive Committee published a declaration in which it called upon all strata of Russian society "to implement only the decisions of the Supreme Soviet and A. V. Rutskoi, who has legally assumed the responsibilities of president."[61] And in an appeal published that same day to military personnel, policemen, and government security forces, the CPRF underscored that law enforcement officers were "obliged to abide strictly by" the Constitution and that all power was now in the hands of the Supreme Soviet and the former vice-president.[62]

At the same time, however, the radical rhetoric of the CPRF leadership was not followed up by any corresponding political action by its network of activists. Although the largest political party in Russia, it did not organize a single meeting or mass protest in Moscow. At the beginning of the crisis, Ziuganov expressed the hope that a wave of strikes in support of the parliament might begin throughout the country,[63] but his party did not once publicly appeal to its organizations to help bring this about. And Ziuganov himself went home from the White House every evening, allegedly fearing an assault.[64] Such cautious ambiguity continued to characterize his conduct throughout the crisis, as we shall see below.

As for other more moderate leftist formations, a declaration by Mikhail Lapshin's newly formed Agrarian Party of Russia (APR) spoke of its readiness to use all means—peasant assemblies, meetings, pickets, strikes, the blocking of main arteries—in order to "put an end to the feeble efforts of the dictatorship."[65] But the APR did not lift a finger to translate its threat into action. Similarly, the Socialist Labor Party also loudly proclaimed its support for parliament and called upon "the citizens of Russia, independently of their political views and personal sympathies, to rebuff the dictatorship in this hour of supreme trial."[66] At the same time, the party refused to be drawn directly or indirectly into public involvement in the conflict, fearing that any sharpening of the confrontation "threatened to grow into civil war."[67] It chose to concentrate its efforts exclusively on the search for a peaceful resolution of the crisis.

Here it should be noted that both the parliament and the president's side seriously erred in their strategic calculations. The opposition deputies clearly overestimated the degree of their support in society, within the security and armed forces, and among the regional elites. Mass strikes did not occur, the army did not hasten to their side, and supporters in the regions confined themselves to making declarative statements rather than taking any kind of decisive action. Only the more extremist opposition groups with few members and little influence gave any substantial backing to the deputies occupying the White House. On September 25 Khasbulatov had a meeting with leaders of the nationalist and ultra-leftist parties during which they discussed forms and methods of cooperation between the opposition and the beleaguered parliament, with major attention being given to breaking the information blockade.[68] Through the efforts of some activists, the most important of whom were not communists but two Russian nationalist writers, the RCWP succeeded in setting up a small radio station in the White House.[69] However, given its limited range of transmission, the propaganda effect of its broadcasts was hardly noticeable.

By the same token, the president plainly underestimated the parliament's capacity for resistance and erred in assuming that its dissolution would meet with the approval of the Russian people. A tough bout of positional warfare began in which the initiative and all the advantages seemed to lie at first with the president. The opposition deputies well understood the danger to themselves of an armed confrontation and tried not to provoke one. The weapons belonging to the parliament's watchmen, which during the first two or three days of the siege were distributed to the defenders of the White House, were soon collected and placed in a securely locked storeroom, where they remained even on October 4, when the artillery assault on the parliament took place. The legislators' approach was instead to lock themselves up in their building and to demonstrate to the world what a mockery was being made of the legally elected legislative branch of government (the White House was fenced off by barbed wire and looked very much like a concentration camp set up in the center of the Russian capital). As a result, with each passing day their moral capital increased in the eyes of many citizens and the position of the president was weakened.

By the beginning of October the influence of moderating forces began to have some effect. The Russian Orthodox Church stepped in, and negotiations between the two sides began under its aegis. The regions also entered the fray, insisting on a "no-fault" solution (the abrogation of both the president's decree and the subsequent resolutions by the oppositionists in the parliament) as well as the holding of simultaneous early elections for both parliament and president. If this was not accepted, they threatened to bring political and economic pressure to bear upon the central authorities.[70] The Soviet of the Federation, an extra-constitutional body created by Yeltsin and scheduled to meet October 4, intended to present the president with an ultimatum to this effect. Although such a compromise formula would have saved society from the threat of civil war, it also would have been tantamount to a moral victory for the parliament. But the possibility of its realization was cut off by the outburst of violence in Moscow on October 3.

It is hard to say whether the major events of that day—the breaking of the White House blockade by armed supporters of the opposition deputies and their subsequent assault on the mayor's offices and attempt to storm Ostankino—were the result of the spontaneous development of the conflict or, as several authors maintain, a shrewd plot on the part of the executive branch to provoke the opposition into violent actions in order to have a cause and justification to deal mercilessly with it and the parliament.[71] If one gives credit to the latter proposition regarding a premeditated plan on the part of the regime, one must also contemplate the risks involved in such a game. For it is well known how difficult it was for Yeltsin to persuade the leadership of the Ministry of Defense to agree to use army units for the suppression of the opposition. October 3 was a day on which the outcome of the political confrontation hung in the balance for a certain time and the parliament seemed to be literally within a hair's breadth of victory.

It is more likely, however, that the transformation of the political confrontation into an armed clash was determined by the very dynamics of the conflict's development and by the irreconcilability of the positions of its major antagonists. If for the president's side a compromise was tantamount to defeat, the opposition deputy-defenders of the parliament (and here we are not even speaking of their ultra-leftist and ultra-rightist supporters) did not display any inclination to dialogue. Even some members of the moderate Socialist Labor Party, which supported the idea of simultaneous early elections of both parliament and president, insisted that the necessary precondition for the resolution of the political crisis was that Yeltsin relinquish all his power.[72] To a large extent these irreconcilable attitudes were exacerbated by the fact that the extra-parliamentary radicals' goal of inciting "urban warfare" was beginning to bear its first fruits.

From the evening of September 21 the parliament building had become the center of attraction for significant groups of the population, who were drawn there not so much from sympathy for the opposition deputies as hatred of the president. Among the defenders of the White House, first fiddle was played by extremists of all shades: from the Anpilov communist "reds" to the fascist "blacks" of Barkashov's Russian National Unity. Both ends of the political spectrum were far from the thought of defending democracy in the country. Indeed, they were moved by an entirely different goal—the instigation of revolution, whether social or national. The rightists assumed the function of armed guards in the parliament building, while the leftists tried to broaden the scope of conflict and attract the popular masses, organizing meetings and demonstrations in the center of Moscow. At an opposition conference on September 29, a Council of Patriotic Forces of Moscow was created, with operational leadership assigned to the headquarters of the National Salvation Front under the direction of Anatolii V. Kriuchkov (leader of the Russian Party of Communists). A program of protest actions was worked out, including both the holding of city-wide meetings and the initiation of multiple "spontaneous" gatherings in crowded localities.[73] The anxious mood of the city's inhabitants was well suited for the implementation of this tactic.

After the start of the blockade of the parliament building, which was cordoned off by policemen and internal security troops and also surrounded by barbed wire, a rapidly growing crowd of people wanting to break into the White House began to gather along its entire perimeter. Their aggressiveness grew in tandem with the harsh beatings of demonstrators by the Ministry of Interior's OMON forces (detachments of special purpose militia). A meeting called by Toiling Russia and the NSF, which took place Saturday, October 2, on Smolensk Square and drew about five thousand people, grew into a clash with OMON detachments. From the tribune Anpilov summoned the assembled participants to civil disobedience and open resistance to the forces of public order.[74]

But on that very same day the leaders of the largest left-wing parties simultaneously hastened to distance themselves from the extremism of their more radical comrades. APR leader Lapshin called off an all-Russian strike of agrarians planned for October 2 (although there is considerable doubt that it would have actually taken place). More importantly, the evening before, on October 1, Ziuganov went to the headquarters of Russian Television and asked to be given the opportunity to speak to the Russian viewers. Thus, on the news program "Vesti," he warned the public against violence, declaring that "we all have an interest in ensuring that in the coming days there are no clashes or conflicts and that no parties or movements call for violence and extremism."[75] It is hard to say whether these conciliatory declarations stemmed from fear of a bloody outcome capable of provoking civil war or from elementary political calculation, from fear of showing up "in the spotlight" at a moment when the outcome of the confrontation was still not fully clear. Ziuganov later maintained that when he met with Khasbulatov at the beginning of October, he warned him of the danger of provocation and proposed peaceful solutions to the crisis. And he placed responsibility for the bloody denouement on "ultra-revolutionary actors" (read leftist communist parties) who were carried away by impatience.[76] Whatever the case, at the time little depended on Ziuganov's call for caution, all the more so since his personal conduct had not been blameless. Violence was in the air, making it all but inevitable that there would be a bloody explosion.

Analysts are in agreement that the fatal mistake of the opposition deputies, or at least their leaders, was their encouragement of the crowds that broke through the blockade during the day of October 3 to storm the mayor's offices and march on Ostankino. Indeed, the call for the latter action was sounded by Rutskoi himself from the balcony of the White House. The more militarily competent defenders of the parliament immediately assessed both steps as a catastrophe.[77] In their view, had only the crowd remained in the White House, the opposition would more than likely have been able to celebrate its victory, claiming that the people had risen against the dictatorship of Yeltsin.

It is difficult to explain these acts that were so disastrous for the opposition. Did the fault lie with the excessive emotionalism of Rutskoi and the euphoria that seized the parliament's defenders? Khasbulatov rushed to declare to the deputies that once the mayor's office and Ostankino were taken the Kremlin would fall. Prigarin, leader of the Union of Communists and deputy head of the UCP-CPSU, called for "storming everything more quickly." Even the cautious Ziuganov, so moderate on the eve of the showdown, hastened the evening of October 3 to entrust the party's "golden pen" to Kosolapov so that he might write a declaration about the "victory of Soviet power."[78] Or did the fault lie with a crowd so gripped by enthusiasm that it no longer yielded to any side's control? Or did responsibility ultimately rest with the extremist rightists and leftists? A column of protesters led by Anpilov had set off for Ostankino directly from a gathering in October Square,[79] that is, before Rutskoi sounded his appeal and people headed to the television station from the White House in stolen cars and buses.

One must not absolutely exclude, moreover, the possibility of a conscious provocation from the president's side. According to many recollections of eye-witnesses, the immediate reason for the assault on the mayor's offices was shots fired from inside that building. In exactly the same way, as later became clear, the government troops defending the Ostankino TV station and not the oppositionist attackers opened fire first.

Whatever the ultimate truth, the outbreak of violence in the center of Moscow, which was blamed on the opposition, gave the president the grounds to retaliate with armed force. Although the army's high command vacillated literally until the last minute, on the morning of October 4 volleys of tank artillery fire put a bloody end to the one-and-a-half year political confrontation between the Russian parliament and president. According to official sources, over 150 people died during the armed clashes of October 3 and 4, almost all of them civilians.

The defeated opposition's political organizations and newspapers were immediately suspended. The government drew up a list of twenty-eight parties and movements which were divided into three categories according to the degree of their involvement in the events of October 3–4. The first category included fourteen formations which, according to the official list, were the most active and participated in the conflict in their capacity as organizations. Among the leftist parties and movements listed were the RCWP, the UCP-CPSU, the Union of Officers, Toiling Russia, Toiling Moscow, the Russian Party of Communists, and the United Labor Front. Anpilov was arrested and placed in the Lefortovo prison. The second category of groups, whose members participated in the armed confrontation as individuals, consisted of eight organizations, including the ACPB, the CPRF, the Union of Communists, and the All-Union Leninist Union of Communist Youth.[80] There was also a temporary ban on thirteen opposition publications, including the chief leftist newspapers, *Glasnost, Molniia, Pravda*, and *Sovetskaia Rossiia*.[81]

The ban on the CPRF along with the largest circulation leftist newspapers was dictated by electoral considerations as well as by their radical positions during Moscow's "time of troubles." The Yeltsin government rushed to remove potentially dangerous competitors on the eve of the December 12 elections for the new State Duma, the lower house of the successor Russian parliament. Although the ban on the CPRF was quickly lifted, the authorities probably calculated that during the few remaining weeks the party would not have time to mobilize its electorate, especially in the absence of nation-wide newspapers. Publication of *Sovetskaia Rossiia* resumed only after the elections. The ban on *Pravda* was lifted earlier, but because of financial difficulties and internal disputes among the newspaper's editors it came out for just a little over two weeks (from November 2 through 19), after which its publication again came to a halt and resumed only December 10.

These obstacles notwithstanding, however, the CPRF received almost thirteen percent of the party preference vote and some ten percent of the seats in the new State Duma, as will be discussed in the next chapter. When all is said and done, it may well be that the repressive measures against the left—coming as they did on top of the regime's bombardment of the White House—became one of the reasons for the CPRF's electoral success and its growing acceptance by the Russian public as a legitimate actor in the emerging post-Soviet political order.

Notes

1. For the conceptual foundations underlying this approach as well as a highly positive assessment of its implementation in post-Soviet Russia, see Anders Aslund, *How Russia Became a Market Economy* (Washington, DC: The Brookings Institution, 1995); as the author states in his "Acknowledgments," he was an economic adviser to the Yeltsin government from November 1991 to January 1994.

2. For a comprehensive analysis of Yavlinskii's views, see Deric Hetzel, "Grigory Yavlinskii, Russian Economist and Politician" (Washington, DC: unpublished manuscript, The Catholic University of America, May 1995). See also the series of articles by Yavlinskii in *Moscow News*, 1992–1993.

3. For a negative assessment of the Russian economic reforms which is based on extensive survey research data, see Lynn D. Nelson and Irina Y. Kuzes, *Radical Reform in Yeltsin's Russia: Political, Economic, and Social Dimensions* (Armonk: M.E. Sharpe, 1995).

4. Nikolai Gulbinskii and Marina Shakina, *Afganistan . . . Kreml . . . Lefortovo . . . ? Episody politicheskoi biografii Aleksandra Rutskogo* (Moscow: Lada, 1994), p. 301. For an overall analysis of this confrontation, see Lilia Shevtsova, "Parliament and the Political Crisis in Russia, 1991–1993," in Jeffrey W. Hahn, ed., *Democratization in Russia: The Development of Legislative Institutions* (Armonk: M.E. Sharpe, 1996), pp. 29–48.

5. See the interesting political-psychological portrait of Rutskoi in Gulbinskii and Shakina, *Afganistan . . . Kreml*, passim.

6. Boris Yeltsin, *Zapiski prezidenta* (Moscow: Izdatelstvo "Ogonek," 1994), p. 49. This autobiographical work was published in English as *The Struggle for Russia* (New York: Random House, 1994).

7. Gulbinskii and Shakina, *Afganistan . . . Kreml*, p. 174.

8. Ibid., p. 281.

9. See the superb analysis by Thomas F. Remington, "Menage à Trois: The End of Soviet Parliamentarism," in Hahn, ed., *Democratization in Russia*, pp. 106–139.

10. Gulbinskii and Shakina, *Afganistan . . . Kreml*, pp. 250–251.

11. Yeltsin, *Zapiski prezidenta*, pp. 176–177.

12. For a short chronology of the confrontation, see *Nezavisimaia gazeta*, September 21, 1993, pp. 1 and 3.

13. See, for example, *Nezavisimaia gazeta*, March 24, 1993, p. 2; *Rossiiskaia gazeta*, May 27, 1993, p. 3, July 13, 1993, p. 3, July 17, 1993, pp. 3–4; *Sovetskaia Rossiia*, June 19, 1993, pp. 1–2, June 22, 1993, p. 1; *Literaturnaia Rossiia*, No. 33 (September 10, 1993), pp. 2, 3, and 5. See also Ruslan I. Khasbulatov, *Vybor sudby: Stati, vystupleniia, interviu, ianvar-iiun 1993* (Moscow: 1993) as well as his autobiographical account, *The Struggle for Russia: Power and Change in the Democratic Revolution*, ed. by Richard Sakwa (London: Routledge, 1993), esp. Part III.

14. Gulbinskii and Shakina, *Afganistan . . . Kreml,* pp. 296–297.

15. Ibid., pp. 298–299.

16. Joan Barth Urban, *Moscow and the Italian Communist Party: From Togliatti to Berlinguer* (Ithaca, NY: Cornell University Press, 1986), pp. 154–161.

17. Ibid., p. 191.

18. Ibid., p. 189.

19. "Pismo Prezidiuma Tsik KPRF kommunistam Rossii: O meste Kommunisticheskoi partii Rossiiskoi Federatsii v politicheskoi zhizni sovremennoi Rossii," *Pravda,* August 28, 1993, p. 2. This open letter to the Russian communists was reprinted in *Glasnost,* No. 32, September 2–8, 1993, p. 4, and *Pravda Rossii,* special edition No. 4, September 7, 1993, p. 3.

20. Gennadii A. Ziuganov, *Drama vlasti: stranitsy politicheskoi avtobiografii* (Moscow: Paleia, 1993), p. 63.

21. "Ob opasnosti politicheskogo ekstremizma" (copy of original unpublished document available in the archives of the Gorbachev Foundation in Moscow).

22. See note 19 above for the specific citations. For the authorship of the open letter, see J. B. Urban's interview with Boris F. Slavin in the editorial offices of *Pravda,* June 12, 1996.

23. Text in *Sovetskaia Rossiia,* July 22, 1993, p. 3.

24. See the text of the Presidium's letter in *Pravda,* August 28, 1993, p. 2.

25. Ibid.

26. Ibid.

27. Ziuganov, *Drama vlasti,* p. 178.

28. Gennadii A. Ziuganov, *Derzhava* (Moscow: Informpechat, 1994), p. 33.

29. Gennadii A. Ziuganov, "Vesna illiuzii," *Sovetskaia Rossiia,* June 1, 1993, p. 2.

30. "Za edinstvo Rossii: Pismo Prezidiuma Tsik KPRF," *Sovetskaia Rossiia* (special issue No. 3), August 5, 1993, p. 4; see also the electoral platform, *Sovetskaia Rossiia,* July 22, 1993, p. 3.

31. Ibid.

32. Text in *Pravda,* August 28, 1993, p. 2.

33. Ibid.

34. For information on Toiling Russia, see *Politicheskie partii sovremennoi Rossii: Spravochnik* (Moscow: "Rossiiskaia politicheskaia entsiklopediia," 1993), p. 338; Vladimir Pribylovskii, *Slovar novykh politicheskikh partii i organizatsii Rossii* (Moscow: Informatsionno-ekspertnaia gruppa "Panorama," 1992), pp. 140–141; and *Rossiia: partii, assotsiatsii, soiuzy, kluby—Sbornik dokumentov,* 10 vols. (Moscow: "RAU-Press," 1992–1993), vol. 10, pp. 72–74.

35. This estimate, made by seasoned observers on the scene, was some ten times higher than the officially released figure regarding the number of marchers.

36. Authors' interview with Prigarin's aide, Sergei F. Cherniakhovskii, at Moscow State University in May 1994.

37. "Sozdan shtab," *Sovetskaia Rossiia,* May 8, 1993, p. 2.

38. "Zaiavlenie Tsentralnogo Komiteta Vsesoiuznoi Kommunisticheskoi Partii Bolshevikov," *Bolshevik* (Murmansk), No. 19 (1993), p. 4.

39. Text in Ziuganov, *Drama vlasti,* pp. 67–68.

40. Pribylovskii, *Slovar novykh politicheskikh partii,* p. 67.

41. Ibid.

42. See Ziuganov, *Drama vlasti*, pp. 92 and 94.

43. For more on the Russian Unity bloc, see Pribylovskii, *Slovar novykh politicheskikh partii*, p. 104.

44. For the views of the radical neocommunists toward the National Salvation Front, see *Politicheskie partii sovremennoi Rossii*, pp. 314, 351, and 352; see also Pribylovskii, *Slovar novykh politicheskikh partii*, pp. 67–68, 96, 98, and 142–143.

45. Ziuganov, "Vesna illiuzii," *Sovetskaia Rossiia*, June 1, 1993, p. 2.

46. "Manifest Kongressa narodov," *Pravda*, September 25, 1993, p. 1.

47. Yevgenii Krasnikov, "Ruslan Khasbulatov i oppositsiia prisvali k vozrozhdeniiu SSSR," *Nezavisimaia gazeta*, September 21, 1993, p. 2.

48. Gulbinskii and Shakina, *Afganistan . . . Kreml*, p. 299.

49. See *93. Oktiabr. Moskva: Khronika tekushchikh sobytii* (Moscow: Vek XX i Mir, 1994), p. 13; see also *Pravda*, September 24, 1993, p. 2.

50. See *Politicheskie partii sovremennoi Rossii*, pp. 283, 321, and 327; also, "Vsiu vlast Sovetam," *Pravda*, September 25, 1993, p. 2.

51. See *93. Oktiabr. Moskva*, p. 16.

52. Ibid., p. 23.

53. Ibid., p. 50.

54. Galina Orekhanova, "Tragediia," *Sovetskaia Rossiia*, September 25, 1993, p. 2.

55. See Yevgenii Krasnikov, "Partii podeleny po stepeni neblagonadezhnosti: Chto za etim posleduet?" *Nezavisimaia gazeta*, October 8, 1993, p. 2.

56. Authors' interview with Sergei F. Cherniakhovskii, a close associate of Shenin and Prigarin, in the editorial offices of *Golos kommunista*, December 7, 1995.

57. "Ot Rossii eltsinskoi — k Rossii sotsialisticheskoi (Vystuplenie secretaria TsK VKPB Belitskogo A. I. na Leningradskom Veche 3 oktiabria 1993 g.)," *Bolshevik*, No. 21 (1993), p. 1.

58. Ibid.

59. See Krasnikov, "Partii podeleny po stepeni neblagonadezhnosti," *Nezavisimaia gazeta*, October 8, 1993, p. 2.

60. *93. Oktiabr. Moskva*, p. 10.

61. Text in *Sovetskaia Rossiia*, September 23, 1993, p. 2.

62. Text in *Pravda*, September 23, 1993, p. 2.

63. See *93. Oktiabr. Moskva*, p. 74.

64. Authors' interview with Sergei F. Cherniakhovskii, December 7, 1995. Cherniakhovskii was frequently in the White House during the crisis.

65. "Agrarii protiv diktatury," *Pravda*, September 25, 1993, p. 2.

66. "Zaiavlenie Pravleniia Federalnogo Soveta Sotsialisticheskoi partii trudiashchikhsia" (unpublished party document in authors' possession), September 21, 1993.

67. Ibid.

68. *93. Oktiabr. Moskva*, p. 98.

69. See Nadezhda Garifullina, "Krov padet na putchistov," *Sovetskaia Rossiia*, September 30, 1993, p. 2.

70. See "Ob otvetstvennosti: Gubitelno dlia Rossii," *Sovetskaia Rossiia*, October 2, 1993, p. 1.

71. The latter point of view is presented in Sergei Kurginian, "Eto vse sdelala koliuchaia provoloka," *Argumenty i fakty*, No. 40 (1993), p. 3; and Nataliia Gevorkian and

Aleksandr Zhilin, "Lovushka prezidenta. Lovushka dlia prezidenta: Versiia tragicheskikh sobytii v Moskve," *Moskovskie novosti*, No. 42 (October 17, 1993), pp. 4–5.

72. *93. Oktiabr. Moskva*, pp. 123–124.

73. E. A. Kozlov, "Na mitingakh v Moskve," *Kommunist Leningrada* (St. Petersburg), No. 5 (1993), pp. 2–3.

74. *93. Oktiabr. Moskva*, pp. 211–212.

75. "Moscow Russian Television Network in Russian, 2000 GMT, October 1, 1993," in *Federal Broadcast Information Service: Central Eurasia*, No. 190-S, October 4, 1993, p. 66; also Yevgenii Krasnikov, "Ot kommunistov do natsionalistov: Kto oni, zapreshchennye partii i gazety?" *Nezavisimaia gazeta*, October 7, 1993, p. 2. According to CPRF deputy chairman Aleksandr A. Shabanov, his party gave food and water to the White House defenders but cautioned them to avoid confrontation: "Ziuganov said as much to large crowds on October 1 and 2"; authors' interview with Shabanov in the CPRF's Duma fraction offices, May 27, 1994.

76. See "Fenomen Ziuganova," *Sovetskaia Rossiia*, October 24, 1995, p. 2.

77. Ruslan I. Khasbulatov, *Velikaia Rossiiskaia tragediia* (Moscow: 1994), Vol. 1, pp. 316 and 319.

78. Authors' interview with Prigarin's close associate, Sergei F. Cherniakhovskii, December 7, 1995.

79. Lev Sigal, "Sostav prestupleniia: oshibki," *93. Oktiabr. Moskva*, p. 150.

80. Krasnikov, "Partii podeleny," *Nezavisimaia gazeta*, October 8, 1993, p. 2.

81. See "Kommunistov i patriotov ostavili bez deneg," *Nezavisimaia gazeta*, October 6, 1993, p. 2; also Krasnikov, "Ot kommunistov do natsionalistov," *Nezavisimaia gazeta*, October 7, 1993, p. 2.

5
Ziuganovism in Theory and Practice

In the aftermath of the October 1993 crisis, the Russian political scene changed dramatically. Whereas in the April 1993 referendum a majority of Russian voters still endorsed Yeltsin's person and policies, the results of the December 1993 elections to the new Russian legislature came as a shock because of the low voter turnout as well as the protest vote registered by many who did cast ballots. The unexpected and frightening success of the ultra-nationalist Vladimir V. Zhirinovskii, whose misnamed Liberal Democratic Party of Russia won a plurality (about 23 percent) of the party list vote, symbolized the change in the political atmosphere of the country as a whole. And many analysts later contended that the fifty percent voter turnout needed to legitimize the constitutional referendum, which was held simultaneously with the parliamentary elections, was in fact fraudulently attained.

The CPRF's fortunes also underwent a profound if more positive type of transformation. From a party still struggling to recapture a public image of legitimacy, it suddenly became a respected parliamentary fraction in the new Russian State Duma. This was in large part due to the policy choices made by CPRF chairman Gennadii Ziuganov. In a word, the party that had been banned by the Yeltsin regime only a little more than two years earlier decided to play by the rules of the game, as set forth in the president's new constitution. That decision, in turn, enraged the radical neocommunist formations. This was all the more the case in that the CPRF was now able to use its parliamentary perquisites to strengthen its regional network.

Meanwhile, in a series of essays and booklets, Ziuganov was articulating a worldview and set of political ideas which diverged markedly from traditional Soviet Marxism-Leninism. The extra-parliamentary communist radicals thus launched a polemical and organizational campaign against their ever more powerful rival, the CPRF, in which they denounced both Ziuganov's ideological deviationism and his party's "collaboration" with the Yeltsin regime.

Russia and the World, According to Gennadii Ziuganov

Ziuganov set forth his interpretation of the history of Russia and her place in the contemporary world in three books: *Drama vlasti* (*The Drama of Power*), a collection of his articles and documents, with commentary, published in 1993; *Derzhava* (*Great Power*), dated 1994; and *Za Gorizontom* (*Beyond the Horizon*), which came out on the eve of the Third CPRF Congress.[1] Together they formed the basis of Ziuganov's doctoral dissertation, "The Basic Tendencies and Mechanisms of the Social-Political Changes in Contemporary Russia," which he defended in the faculty of philosophy at Moscow State University in the spring of 1995.

Intertwined in Ziuganov's worldview were three facets, pertaining respectively to geopolitics, political culture, and the multiplicity of world civilizations. With regard to the last, Ziuganov maintained that "Russia embodies her own special type of civilization, inheriting and continuing the thousand-year-old tradition of Kievan Rus, Moscovite tsarism, the Russian Empire, and the Soviet Union."[2] In support of this he cited both Western and Russian political thinkers and philosophers whose basic assumption was that there are multiple world civilizations. The Russians he mentioned included Nikolai Danilevskii, Konstantin Leontiev, and the so-called "Eurasians." Among the Westerners he referred to were Oswald Spengler, Arnold Toynbee, and Samuel Huntington. Here it might be noted that Huntington's renowned article, "The Clash of Civilizations," had become a powerful weapon in the hands of Russian nationalists of all political stripes, for it enabled them to claim that even a world-class Harvard professor held that Russia represented a special civilization and that conflicts among civilizations were all but inevitable.

But who was to be the transmitter of values in one or another civilization? "The representatives of civilizations, their bearers and protectors, the chief actors on the stage of world history," declared Ziuganov, "are always *ethnic* groups: nations and peoples as well as their wider collectivities. . . ."[3] Pursuing this thought to its logical conclusion, one can only assume that precisely the *ethnic group* represented the highest value. Here it should be mentioned that a significant part of the Russian opposition categorically rejected the modern Western equation of "nation as citizenship," in which the nation was understood as a supra-ethnic community. Characteristic of the nationalists, and many other Russians as well, was the traditional Soviet notion of the "nation as ethnicity," with roots stretching back to the formation of nation states in Europe.

As for geopolitics, the crux of Ziuganov's view was that Russia was "the pivot and chief bulwark of the Eurasian continental bloc, the interests of which conflict with the hegemonic tendencies of the United States 'ocean power' and the greater Atlantic seaboard."[4] On this point he relied above all on the work of the early twentieth century English geopolitician, Sir Halford Mackinder, for whom the central theme of human history was the ceaseless confrontation between land and sea powers. For Mackinder, the stronghold of land power lay in the center of Asia, which he initially called "the pivot of world history" and later the "heartland." According to him, the country which controlled the heartland was potentially capable of dominating the whole world.

Since the greater part of the Mackinder heartland was located in the territory of the Russian Empire/Soviet Union, Ziuganov readily concluded that precisely Russia was fated to be the global hegemon. These visions of grandeur had not been fulfilled, however, because of the competition of the "sea powers," which were inevitably hostile toward Russia, the bulwark of continentalism. The first seapower hegemon was of course Great Britain, but in the twentieth century the U.S.A. inherited her role. For the CPRF chairman this proved with "mathematical precision" that the U.S.A. was, is, and would remain the chief opponent of Russia, committed to weakening and dominating her.

It is most likely that Ziuganov became acquainted with these geopolitical notions only indirectly, through several works of the small group of contemporary West European intellectuals known as the "new right." From the end of 1991 their works began to be published in Russia, and representatives of this group visited Moscow several times, holding seminars and press conferences in which Ziuganov participated.[5] It evidently did not bother him that the "new right" was a marginal intellectual current or that the geopolitical "discoveries" set forth by its proponents as the latest truth had long since been deemed "old thinking" in the West. Indeed, in his geopolitical ruminations Ziuganov relied upon theoretical constructs the latest of which dated back to the 1930s. He gave a modern cast to his geopolitical conceptions only to the extent that he included the widespread present-day notion concerning the global hemispheric contradiction between the rich post-industrial "North" and the impoverished underdeveloped "South."

According to Ziuganov, Russia was the direct antithesis of the West in terms not only of geopolitics and holistically conceived civilizations but of political culture as well. In *Za Gorizontom* he described her political culture as "the expression of a cultural-historical and moral tradition whose fundamental values are collectivism, *sobornost* [organic spiritual unity], statehood, and the striving for the embodiment of the highest ideals of goodness and justice."[6] The fundamental values of Western civilization were not only different from the spiritual bases on which Russian political culture and civilization were founded, but—and this must again be emphasized—also diametrically opposed to it. "Contemporary Western civilization," wrote Ziuganov,

> is based in the final analysis on an atomized, mechanical picture of the world. . . . Market individualism has become the basic human disposition. . . . Hence the absolutization of the rights of the individual, which in the nationality sphere has justified the melding of tiny peoples into nations; hence the "war of all against all" in the social arena.[7]

In the West the state had been deprived of the sacred meaning with which it was endowed in Russia; it had become only the "night watchman" for the market.[8]

Ziuganov depicted a simplistic, abstract image of the West which did not correspond to the much more complicated and many-sided reality. Yet it is hard to believe that he knew nothing about the active role of Western governments in their economies (Keynesianism), the successful functioning of social welfare oriented market economies in a number of West European countries, or Western policies of broad ethno-cultural pluralism. We can therefore surmise that the CPRF chairman was leading the reader on. Ziuganov invoked a Manichean picture of the world in which the center of goodness, light, of all conceivable and inconceivable virtues—Russia!—was counterposed to the pole of evil—the West. This was reminiscent of former president Ronald Reagan's idea regarding the Soviet Union as the "evil empire"; only Ziuganov had reversed the roles.

To support his views on political culture, Ziuganov drew upon the Russian philosophic and political tradition, turning to authorities whose arguments were often directly contradictory. Among others, he referred to the already mentioned Eurasians—a small group of Russian intellectual emigrés of the 1920s who sought to show that Russia was neither East nor West but a special cultural-historical world, a unique synthesis uniting within itself both Europe and Asia.[9] It goes without saying that he also turned to the Slavophiles and their conception of *sobornost*, that is, the organic spiritual unity of the ethnic Russians.[10] Moreover, from the Russian *narodniki*, the peasant socialists of the 1860s–1880s, Ziuganov borrowed his postulates regarding the spontaneous democracy of the Russian people and their inherent predisposition to socialism. In addition, Ziuganov invoked the Middle Age's messianic ideal of Moscow as the "Third Rome," according to which Russia was seen as the chief protector of the purity of Christianity and the herald of its truth to the world.[11] To be sure, he gave this notion an abstract cultural rather than a concrete religious meaning: Russia was predestined to "show to the world the treasures of the human spirit, as embodied in her personal and family way of life, her social structure, and her great power statehood."[12] At the same time, for Ziuganov communist ideology was fully compatible with the biblical ethic and even to a certain degree flowed from it. As he put it, "The basic moral precepts which were written in the Moral Code [that is, the 'Moral Code of the Builders of Communism' from the 1961 CPSU Program] fully coincided with the Orthodox ethic, the Biblical ethic."[13]

Ziuganov's most controversial source of "inspiration" was the so-called doctrine of "official national character," imperial Russia's establishment ideology during the reign of Tsar Nicholas I at the end of the first third of the nineteenth century. The formula "Orthodoxy, autocracy, nationality" expounded by his minister of culture, Count Uvarov, has always been sharply criticized by educated strata of Russian society. Both democratic Russian and Soviet historiography judged it downright "reactionary." But these considerations did not deter Ziuganov. He disengaged himself from the concrete social meaning of Uvarov's "triad" and contended that it possessed a "wider cultural-historical meaning": it was neither more nor less than the constant, invariable characteristic of Russian history.[14] Here is how this invariability looked to Ziuganov with regard to the Soviet era: "Instead of God . . . , the secular form of Christianity was the socialist ideal. . . ." "They tried," furthermore, "to get along without a tsar but nothing came of it. There appeared the Gensec."[15] The idea of nationality, finally, found its embodiment in the classic Soviet propaganda formula regarding "the Soviet people as a new historical community."[16]

Such a popular, even primitive, style of exposition was plainly aimed at the rank-and-file party members, those who yearned for familiar terms and customary identification marks. At the same time, the traditionalist communists could only be flattered by the argument that the CPSU to whose legacy they clung was, it turned out, the embodiment of the Russian historical spirit and the continuer of Russian tradition—not the usurper of power and hangman of Russia which democratic thinking made it out to be. In short, Ziuganov turned to the past to deliver his comrades from their inferiority complex.

Ziuganov argued, moreover, that Russia could not exist except in imperial form. Everyone curses the empire, he wrote, yet the empire was "historically and geopolitically the generalized form of development of the Russian state."[17] For what is "Great Russia"? Wrote Ziuganov,

> I understand these words to mean the Russian state including unconditionally all the territories in which a compact Russian or Russian speaking population lives, a state based on the indissoluble fraternal union of the great Russians, the little Russians and the white Russians, and also all the tribes and nationalities that voluntarily wish to unite with that union. I do not think that its boundaries will differ essentially from the boundaries of the U.S.S.R.[18]

With one paragraph the CPRF leader killed two birds: he soothed the souls of the Russian nationalists who sought the recreation of the empire but with Russian domination; and he reassured orthodox communists that this Russian empire would be the reborn Soviet Union they so much desired.

The validity of the ideas Ziuganov used to construct his worldview were extremely doubtful. The elements themselves were sometimes even mutually exclusive. Thus Slavophilism stood in sharp contrast to the tsarist regime's doctrine of "official national character." The Slavophiles were among the most notable critics of that concept, while the officialdom of Nicholas I viewed them, in turn, with suspicion. Moreover, Count Uvarov's reactionary formula could in no way be linked with the leftist views of the Russian populists, or *narodniki*. The patriarchal and archaic doctrine of the latter had still less in common with the totalitarian cruelty of the Stalinist regime. Finally, on a series of essential points Eurasianism was deeply alien to all these views.

Ziuganov was probably aware of the eclectic nature and internal inconsistency of his theoretical propositions, all the more so since leftist critics on more than one occasion pointed out these defects.[19] However, the entire construction was important to him not so much in and of itself but as a propaganda weapon and quasi-scholarly foundation for his overall political message.

The message, in a nutshell, was the following. If the West and Russia were so deeply alien to one another on all accounts, then what was there to expect from the West except enmity and constancy in the striving to destroy Russia? And indeed Ziuganov expected nothing from the West except evil. From the beginning of the twentieth century, he argued, "the struggle with Russia has been . . . the top priority of Western policy."[20] According to Ziuganov, this was because "an independent and self-sufficient Russia is in the contemporary world the chief obstacle in the way of the creation of a 'new world order.'"[21] The West had offered its help for the organization of the Russian revolution in 1917, it had manipulated from behind the scenes the antinational and anti-state policy of *perestroika*, and now it was continuing the policy of weakening Russia in order to transform her into a source of raw materials. And the epicenter of all these influences hostile to Russia was the U.S.A.

Essentially, Ziuganov concocted a variation on the classical theories of "global conspiracy" so popular among many Russians, and not only oppositionists. The difference was that the version proposed by Ziuganov had a modernized character: here one could find geopolitics and the political culture approach along with the most current political terminology. One might say that Ziuganov explained the political history of Russia in recent years as though it had been "programmed" from the outside, and at the root of this "program" lay the method of "controlled catastrophe."[22]

We shall have occasion in the next chapter to elaborate upon Ziuganov's conviction that the collapse of the Soviet Union was the direct result of a Western plot. But for now we must give Ziuganov his due: in contrast to past and present "combatants" against "global conspiracies," he was far from calling for putting an end to the "conspirators" once and for all. To be sure, Russia should insofar as she was able oppose the establishment of a "new world order" headed by the U.S. hegemon, argued Ziuganov; but it did not follow from this that she should become involved in geopolitical adventures such as a "push to the South." As far as one can judge, the CPRF leader was advocating isolationism in the realm of foreign policy. The most important task for contemporary Russia was to concentrate on her internal affairs and concerns.

At this point, a few words are in order regarding Ziuganov's views on two other sensitive issues: the role of Jews in modern society and the place of Stalin in Russian history. For many Western commentators, these were some of the most controversial elements in his thinking.[23]

With regard to the Jewish question, Ziuganov's statements in *Za Gorizontom* raised many eyebrows. As he put it in this essay, originally destined for a limited audience but which he later recommended that all CPRF members read, "The Jewish diaspora, which has traditionally controlled the financial life of the continent," was becoming the "controlling shareholder" in the entire Western economy. Moreover, he continued, the characteristics "of this chosen people, 'predestined' according to the Jews' own religious beliefs for leadership of the world and exclusiveness," were beginning to have a decisive "influence on Western consciousness."[24] Given that these utterances appeared in what was basically a geopolitical tract, one could argue that Ziuganov viewed "Jewishness" not so much as an ethnic or racial category but rather as the fullest incarnation of the essence of Western capitalist Judeo-Christian civilization, so alien and inimical to Russian civilization. At the same time, however, he was doubtless perfectly aware of the sympathetic response such ideas would receive among his anti-semitic, right-wing nationalist friends and would-be allies.

But what about Ziuganov's positive evaluation of Stalin's ideological policies after World War II? In the above-mentioned tract he also noted with unabashed regret that "Stalin missed out on the five to seven years of life he needed in order to make his own 'ideological *perestroika*' irreversible. . . ." Here the CPRF chairman was alluding to Stalin's attempt to synthesize Marxist ideology and Russian nationalism in policies at home, and in Eastern Europe, which the rest of the world viewed as thinly veiled Great Russian chauvinism. Stalin, he declared,

> understood as no one else the necessity for an updated worldview within the framework of the new geopolitical form, the U.S.S.R. He understood the urgent need for a congruence of the new realities with age-old Russian traditions. The result . . . was a sharp change in the state ideology of the Soviet Union during the years 1944–1953.[25]

On the whole, Ziuganov's personal attitude toward Stalin was thus decidedly positive. This was hardly surprising, given that the CPRF chairman himself was trying to implement the Stalinist model of ideological rearmament in the form of Great Russian nationalism. Nevertheless, in his public statements regarding the person and activity of Stalin, Ziuganov had to tread carefully in order to maintain an internal party balance among the more traditionalist, pro-Stalinist sectors of the party membership, especially the elderly, and the Marxist reformers who remained adamant in their denunciation of Stalin's "crimes."

The following conclusions can be drawn with regard to Ziuganov's overall thinking. Its intellectual originality, historical validity, and internal consistency were more than doubtful. To a large extent, it was a compilation of fragments from different theories and authors frequently holding opposing views. In language and style it was a rather whimsical mixture of Slavic terms derived from nineteenth-century Russian thinkers and Western notions from contemporary social and political science. However, this criticism makes sense only if one looks at Ziuganov's works as a set of genuine scholarly treatises. The problem is that we have before us not an academic analysis, however weak, but an *ideological, political, and propagandistic myth* couched in a quasi-scholarly form. Since Ziuganov's goal was to achieve political mobilization, his didactic simplicity and eclecticism acquired the character of virtues rather than defects.

A very astute characterization of the reasons for Ziuganov's construction of this myth was offered by one Russian journalist. It is worthwhile quoting his views at some length.

> It is more than likely that Ziuganov is the overall personification of a broad conservative and "uniquely original" protest against the pro-Western changes in Russian society, a protest by people of various political and ideological orientations who agree with one another on the most important point: "What is happening today is a national catastrophe and in order to save Russia it is necessary to return to the past." And in this past there are soviets and raikoms and state orders and zemstvos and *sobornost* and "Orthodoxy, autocracy, nationality," and so forth and so on. . . .[26]

This conservative protest against Russia's integration into post-industrial global society was, to be sure, often cloaked in the rhetoric of the Westernizer-Slavophile schism among the nineteenth-century Russian intelligentsia. But it also reflected a more contemporary and pervasive sociological reality: namely, the gap between the well educated, outward-looking inhabitants of Russia's many large and medium-size cities and the more traditionalist rural villagers and recent migrants to the cities.

It was one of the ironies of post-Soviet Russia that the countryside, emptied of its most able and ambitious human resources by Stalin's brutal collectivization of agriculture in the early 1930s, was now the wellspring of a particularly intense conservative rejection of modernization. One might even argue that by and large only the dregs of Russian society had remained "on the farm" after World War II. Gennadii Ziuganov was himself a newcomer to urban life. More to the point, a not insignificant portion of the CPRF's supporters and electorate could be similarly characterized. We shall return to these themes in Chapter 8. For now let us simply label this paradox "Stalin's revenge."

Ziuganov's thinking on Russia and the world led to several political corollaries, as discussed in the preceding chapter. First of all, he held that the Marxist-Leninist idea of class struggle was directly counter to the interests of the Russian people, united as they were by shared cultural-historical bonds. Indeed, Ziuganov saw both the internecine bloodshed of the Bolshevik Revolution and subsequent Civil War as national tragedies. Secondly, he maintained that the banner around which all Russians should rally was "state patriotism," that is, the defense of Great Russia against her foreign and domestic enemies, above all the West and its traitorous agents. Thirdly, because of the danger of a bloody crackdown by the Yeltsin regime against its domestic opposition, the CPRF should seek socio-political change only through peaceful, legal methods.

This last point led to a second paradox. The Yeltsin Constitution of 1993 entailed the virtual Europeanization of the Russian Federation's political institutions. Nevertheless, it was none other than the profoundly anti-Western CPRF chairman who summoned his party to adhere to the new rules of political competition. Ziuganov's party, alone among the post-Soviet communist groups, would thus take part in the December 1993 elections to the State Duma.

The CPRF, the Elections of December 1993, and the New State Duma

The Russian Federation's 1993 constitution and related laws incorporated many practices common to the major states of Western Europe after World War II. For one thing, the powers of the president were comparable to those accorded the chief executive under the Fifth French Republic's constitution, inspired by General Charles de Gaulle. In the new Russian constitution, the popularly elected president had the prerogative to determine the basic guidelines for domestic and foreign policy and also to appoint a prime minister to oversee the everyday administration of government. Parliamentary approval of the president's choice of prime minister was required, but in the case of a deadlock the president could dissolve the legislature and call for new elections. He had, moreover, extensive decree powers as well as the right to veto legislation.

With regard to the State Duma, the lower and preeminent house of the new bicameral Federal Assembly (the upper house being the Federation

Council), the electoral laws devised by the Yeltsin team in the fall of 1993 provided for an electoral system roughly approximating that of the Federal Republic of Germany. Half of the deputies (450 altogether) were to be elected in single-member districts and the other half were to be distributed according to the percentage of votes cast for candidate lists fielded by the various political parties or blocs. The latter process also included a five percent barrier, that is, those parties that won less than five percent of the party list vote would receive *none* of the 225 seats distributed according to proportional representation. As had been the case in postwar Germany, the intent of this stipulation was to encourage the aggregation of voter preferences into a small number of competing parties.

The State Duma elected in 1993 was to serve only two years, but thereafter it would be elected for four-year terms. The Duma had the powers to approve the president's nominee for prime minister, to issue votes of no-confidence in the government (the prime minister), to initiate legislation and approve the state budget, to declare amnesties, and to override by a two-thirds vote decisions of the Federation Council as well as presidential vetos.[27]

On September 21, 1993, as discussed in Chapter 4, President Yeltsin issued Edict Number 1400 suspending the existing parliamentary bodies and calling for elections to a bicameral Federal Assembly the following December, by which time the draft of a new Russian Federation constitution was also to be prepared.[28] The opposition's takeover of the Russian parliament building (the White House) and the ensuing bloody clashes less than two weeks later, on October 3–4, 1993, did not deter the holding of the parliamentary elections and referendum on the Yeltsin constitution on December 12, 1993. The crisis did, however, contribute to haste and organizational disarray in preparing for those elections as well as to existential uncertainty on the part of the CPRF.

The latter was not only temporarily banned during the state of emergency declared between October 3 and 18; it was also largely deprived of access to the mass media. *Pravda* was shut down from the October confrontation until November 2. On November 19 it was forced to close again for lack of funds, finally resuming publication just two days before the election, on December 10.[29] Meanwhile, *Sovetskaia Rossiia* was published even more sporadically. And the editors of *Glasnost* withdrew into a state of semi-clandestinity until March 1994, putting out in the interim only a few single-page "flimseys" under the title *Rech (Speech)*. During the three weeks preceding the elections, one free hour of air time was allotted to each of the thirteen competing blocs on the state-owned Ostankino and Russian TV channels as well as on Russian Radio. The CPRF, however, was the one major contender that bought almost no additional paid advertising time.[30] As Ziuganov stated at a press conference shortly before the December 12 balloting, "The mass media are inaccessible for us, the opposition press does not appear—therefore we ourselves went to the regions."[31]

On October 26, 1993, the CPRF leadership convened the first All-Russian Conference of the party to take stock of its situation in the wake of the crisis and to prepare for the coming elections. Little information was available on what transpired on that occasion, partly because of the lack of newspaper outlets but also because the party's sense of vulnerability to official harassment, which was palpable even during the spring and summer of 1993, intensified after the "Black October" crackdown. As Ziuganov put it to the October 26 conference, government repression had "in fact already driven the opposition underground."[32] Indeed, it was only after the election results were in, as a result of which the CPRF won over twelve percent of the party list vote and about ten percent of the seats in the Duma, that the party leaders began to feel less threatened. As would soon become clear, the CPRF's new parliamentary status and related perquisites provided an enormous boost to its organizational development, both in the nation's "center" (Moscow) and in the regions.

At the October 26 party conference, the crux of both Ziuganov's report and an "Appeal to the communists, toilers, and all patriots of Russia" distributed on that occasion[33] was that the CPRF should take part in the elections in order to prevent the new Federal Assembly from becoming a total sham and docile instrument of the Yeltsin "dictatorship." A secondary theme was their condemnation of the "haste" and underhandedness of the regime's preparations for the parliamentary contest, which were said to preclude the authentic expression of the people's will. A few nuances distinguished Ziuganov's report from the formal appeal, which became the party's electoral platform. The CPRF chairman spoke of the regime's betrayal of the nation to "overseas bosses," while the appeal referred to the country as a colonial victim of imperialist exploitation. But their basic thrust was the same: the comrades should suppress their understandable urge to boycott the elections because that would merely play into the hands of government extremism. As pointedly stated in the appeal, "Any vacillation at this moment will only lead to a repetition of our failure in the April [1993] referendum."[34]

Eighty-five of the CPRF's eighty-nine regional organizations reportedly backed the leadership's decision to participate in the elections.[35] The conference thus concluded with the endorsement of a party list of 151 CPRF candidates.[36] As in the case of most blocs competing in the 1993 elections, it took the form of a single undifferentiated list, from the top of which would be taken the names of those who were to receive the mandates distributed according to the party preference vote. Here it might be noted that this single-list approach contrasted with the system of several regional party sublists of candidates which would be required for the 1995 Duma elections in order to ensure more adequate parliamentary representation for all parts of the country (see Chapter 7).

Overall, the results of the 1993 elections signaled a victory for the voice of protest against the Yeltsin regime. If in the April 1993 referendum almost 63 percent of eligible voters turned out to give the president a substantial measure of support (58.7 percent),[37] it remained uncertain whether or not the fifty percent turnout required for validation of the constitutional referendum was achieved on December 12.[38] The government's Central Election Commission claimed that some 54 percent showed up at the polls. But even if one accepts this figure, the pro-reform forces suffered a setback, with the top three party list winners being the Liberal Democratic Party of Russia (LDPR) of Vladimir V. Zhirinovskii (23 percent), the Russia's Choice bloc of Yegor T. Gaidar (15 percent), and the CPRF (12 percent). One-third of the votes thus went to the ultra-nationalists and the recently banned communists. Democratic centrists, as opposed to "shock therapy" advocates, also attracted solid support, along with the oppositionist Agrarian Party of Russia and the recently formed Women of Russia bloc. The communists were particularly gratified by the fact that they won, in addition to 30 mandates in the party list vote, 16 seats in single-member districts—even without the funding enjoyed by many rivals. By way of contrast, Zhirinovskii's LDPR won only five seats and Grigorii A. Yavlinskii's Yabloko bloc only three in single-member constituencies.[39]

The first session of the newly elected Duma opened on January 11, 1994, and continued through July 21 of that year. The initial order of business was to work out its own internal structure and procedures. As of January 14, 1994, those electoral associations that had won at least five percent of the party list vote had formed eight fractions. These included the reform-oriented parties, Gaidar's Russia's Choice, Yavlinskii's Yabloko, and a third less enduring bloc led by Sergei M. Shakhrai, which together claimed 131 seats. The two centrist parties, Women of Russia and Nikolai I. Travkin's Democratic Party of Russia, accounted for 38 seats. The opposition was split between Zhirinovskii's LDPR on the far right, with 63 seats, and the Agrarians and CPRF on the left, with 55 and 45 deputies respectively. In addition, deputies elected from single-member districts who were either independent or affiliated with electoral blocs that received less than five percent of the vote eventually coalesced into three so-called parliamentary groups: Sergei N. Baburin's nationalist Russia's Way, the centrist New Regional Policy group, and Boris G. Fedorov's pro-reform Liberal-Democratic Union of December 12. Altogether they had 105 mandates. The remaining handful of deputies were wholly unaffiliated.[40]

Here it should be noted that the size of the CPRF's fraction remained constant at forty-five members[41] although one deputy, the eminent legal scholar Valentin S. Martemianov, was the victim of what the communists claimed was a political assassination and thereafter replaced in a by-election. Also, Anatolii I. Lukianov, who ran on both the CPRF party list (number eight) and in a single-member district, chose to join Baburin's parliamentary group. Overall, the CPRF fraction was the only one that retained its internal cohesion and discipline throughout the tenure of the Duma elected in 1993.[42]

The political spectrum represented in the Duma was thus more balanced (even if still very broad) than that evident by late 1992 in the former Supreme Soviet/Russian Congress. In addition, the internal procedures, or standing rules, of the new parliament's lower house were entirely different from those of the old one. The chairmen and deputy chairmen of its legislative committees were designated according to the numerical strength of the respective fractions and the political importance of the committee assignments, unlike committee staffs in the Supreme Soviet which had been appointed by that body's chairman (Ruslan Khasbulatov). This general procedure was, once again, similar to the organizing principles common to parliaments in continental Western Europe and the United Kingdom, as opposed to the United States' winner-take-all system. The political affiliations of the Duma speaker and his several deputies were also expected to differ from one another. Furthermore, such personnel appointments as well as the concrete legislative agenda were to be worked out collectively by the Council of the Duma, on which each fraction or group had an equal voice along with the speaker.[43]

Ivan P. Rybkin, who had co-chaired the Communists of Russia fraction in the previous parliament and also played a key role in the CPRF's formation, ran for the Duma on the Agrarians' party list. Elected speaker of the Duma in a very close race,[44] he gradually moved toward the political center, in keeping with his function as mediator among the Duma's various internal groupings and spokesman for the body as a whole vis-à-vis the executive branch. Meanwhile, the CPRF fraction was given the chairmanships of the Committee on Security (Viktor P. Iliukhin) and the Committee on Public Associations and Religious Organizations (Viktor I. Zorkaltsev) as well as some half dozen deputy chairmanships. The communists also received one of the four deputy speakerships. That post was held first by Valentin A. Kovalev and later (after Kovalev joined the Yeltsin government as minister of justice, thereby provoking his expulsion from the CPRF fraction) by Gennadii N. Seleznev.[45]

During the State Duma's first session, from January through July 1994, the CPRF deputies voted on most issues with the Agrarians and the Zhirinovskii fraction. They joined together to ensure the election of Rybkin as Duma speaker (regretfully, Ziuganov would later conclude). They fervently supported a blanket amnesty, which the Duma passed on February 23, 1994, for all those arrested on political grounds after the August 1991 abortive coup and the October 1993 bloodshed. And they were just as firmly opposed to the U.S.-backed U.N. economic sanctions against the rump Yugoslavia as well as to Russia's projected participation in NATO's Partnership for Peace plan. On the other hand, after months of criticism of the government's draft budget bills, all three groups also finally backed the state budget for 1994. By way of justification, Ziuganov explained, "This is the logic of common sense. Any government, regardless of its ideology, if it is going to operate, will be obligated to tackle these questions. . . ."[46] This comment was most likely aimed at the extra-parliamentary neocommunists, whose outrage over the CPRF's parliamentary role had been intensifying since the end of 1993.

The Extra-Parliamentary Communist Parties Versus the CPRF

Shortly after the December 1993 elections, Ziuganov threw down the gauntlet to the radical left-wing CPs which had boycotted the elections to the State Duma and the referendum on the new constitution. As he remarked at a CPRF plenum on Christmas Day, "[O]ne of the political conclusions of the elections, however painful to admit, was the exposure of the essential contradiction between the leadership of our party and the leadership of the other communist parties. . . ."[47] The essential contradiction to which he referred, of course, was the extra-parliamentary communists' adamant opposition to any kind of accommodation with the Yeltsin regime's new constitutional order. The very next day the four parties in question— the All-Union Communist Party of Bolsheviks (ACPB) of Nina A. Andreeva, the Union of Communists (UC) of Aleksei A. Prigarin, the Russian Party of Communists (RPC) of Anatolii V. Kriuchkov, and the Russian Communist Workers' Party (RCWP) led by Viktor A. Tiulkin and Viktor I. Anpilov,[48] along with Richard I. Kosolapov's "Leninist Position" group within the CPRF, held the formative meeting of what was to become known as the *Roskomsoiuz*, or Union of Russian Communists. Ziuganov was invited, but he declined to attend. And in early March 1994 the *Roskomsoiuz* leadership council issued a statement declaring that "the tomorrow of the Russian communist movement is not tied to the Ziuganov line."[49]

What was at stake in this growing conflict, in addition to strategic and ideological differences, was competition for the allegiance of the 450,000 rank-and-file communists said to have been represented at the CPRF's February 1993 congress. At that time, the CPRF's grassroots network was only in the process of revival and its putative membership "pool" was not necessarily locked into any one specific post-Soviet communist orientation. Nonetheless, with only the RCWP commanding a membership in the tens of thousands and the other radical CPs counting their followers in the thousands, the extra-parliamentary groups plainly felt threatened. Indeed, by 1994 the CPRF's electoral success was beginning to have a bandwagoning effect, with its bona fide dues-paying members increasing and the ranks of the *Roskom-soiuz* parties thinning out.[50]

The extra-parliamentary communists thus launched a polemical and organizational attack against the CPRF in the spring of 1994, bitterly denouncing its participation in the State Duma as well as Ziuganov's ever more outspoken ethno-centric Great Russian nationalism. Before examining this confrontation, however, we must turn our attention to yet another neocommunist formation, the Union of Communist Parties–CPSU (UCP-CPSU). As mentioned at the end of Chapter 2, tension had already begun to develop in late 1992 between the communist activists who sought to reconstitute the Russian Communist Party as the CPRF and those who wished to reestablish the former CPSU as the dominant post-Soviet communist party in Russia.

On March 26–27, 1993, supporters of the latter option met at the Moscow movie theater "Orion." Proclaiming their gathering the 29th CPSU Congress, they announced the establishment of the Union of Communist Parties–CPSU and declared it to be "the single successor to the CPSU with all legal rights to general party property."[51] Attended by 416 delegates from all the former Soviet republics except Georgia, Armenia, and Kirghistan, this event could best be described as a mixture of paradox and farce. With only twenty-one representatives on hand from the 400-odd members elected to the last CPSU Central Committee in July 1990, Oleg S. Shenin was chosen as the chairman of the new party. Shenin, who had been appointed secretary for organizational matters at the 28th CPSU Congress, had just completed one and a half years in prison for his role in the failed August 1991 putsch. The individual selected as Shenin's first deputy was a bulldozer operator by the name of Konstantin A. Nikolaev. UC leader Prigarin, whose paramount goal since autumn 1991 had been to recreate the CPSU, was named a deputy chairman.[52]

If in 1990 the proponents of a separate Russian Communist Party had had to surmount the obstacles placed in their path by the much more powerful CPSU *apparat*, the reverse was now the case. The new UCP-CPSU, a party without a country or even a local organizational base, was subject to the maneuvers of the CPRF leadership to reduce it to the role of a mere "information and coordinating organ uniting the leaders of the republic parties" throughout the former Soviet Union.[53] Mention was made in Chapter 2 of the intentional holding of the Second CPRF Congress ahead of the already scheduled 29th CPSU Congress. The CPRF leadership also attempted to persuade the CPSU's organizers to postpone their conclave, ostensibly so as not to jeopardize the CPRF's legal registration with the Russian authorities.[54] When this argument fell on deaf ears, the CPRF sent only a second-echelon delegation consisting of Central Executive Committee members Boris F. Slavin and Grigorii K. Rebrov to the UCP-CPSU founding congress. And once there, they continued to urge the assembly to limit itself to laying the groundwork for a subsequent constituent congress of communist parties rather than reconstituting the CPSU forthwith.[55]

During the proceedings Sergei F. Cherniakhovskii, the young associate of Prigarin to whom we have referred several times in previous chapters, protested that behind the scenes "open sabotage hindered the convening of our congress; there were rumors that 'Russia will not come,' or 'Ukraine will not come,' or there will be a postponement."[56] According to disclosures Cherniakhovskii later made, moreover, Ziuganov had actually ordered the CPRF's local organizations not to send delegates to the 29th CPSU Congress, a directive with which a number of them willingly complied given the cost and inconvenience of attending two congresses in quick succession.[57] Plainly, the CPRF leadership had no intention of letting this self-proclaimed successor to the CPSU upstage it in the post-Soviet communist movement.

Prigarin was the main author of the program provisionally adopted at the UCP-CPSU's founding congress. According to Boris P. Kurashvili, it was "oriented to the recreation of the previous form of socialism more than to the creation of a new form."[58] But in Prigarin's own report to the gathering, he rebutted his critics "on the left" who wanted only to return to conditions as they had existed "until 1953, or until 1965, or until 1983."[59] While calling for the reestablishment of the Soviet Union, the renationalization of the economy, and a reassessment of all economic agreements made with the West in recent years, he also stressed the need for broad workers' self-management under socialism in the future. He made no mention of Stalin, and he explicitly criticized the exclusive use of "coercive methods of struggle" advocated by the Andreeva and Tiulkin-Anpilov parties. He echoed, in other words, the moderate Marxist-Leninist orthodoxy of his own Union of Communists.

Such relative moderation did not, however, feature prominently in the congress debates. Among the ultra-leftists present, Anpilov hailed Stalin's communist credentials, while Tiulkin denounced the CPRF's "social-democratic deviationism."[60] A number of Russian and non-Russian delegates deplored the absence from the congress of the top CPRF leaders, openly voicing suspicions regarding their political probity. Representatives of the non-Russian communist parties pleaded for the speedy restoration of the Soviet Union, plainly smarting from the surveillance or persecution to which many of them were subjected in their new independent homelands. Shenin flatly blamed the dissolution of the U.S.S.R. on a Western plot and bitterly condemned Gorbachev and Yeltsin for their race to prove which could be more useful to the West.[61] And Yurii P. Iziumov proudly confirmed that *Glasnost* (of which he was editor-in-chief) "was, is, and will be the newspaper of the CPSU."[62]

Before adjourning, the congress elected a 28-member Political Executive Committee (of the so-called UCP-CPSU Council) that included such disparate figures as Yegor K. Ligachev and the radical Stalinist, feminist, and U.S.S.R. restorationist, Sazhi Z. Umalatova. The list also included eight members of the CPRF's Central Executive Committee (to which Shenin himself belonged) as well as a number of representatives from communist parties in the "near abroad." As already indicated, Shenin was elected chairman and Nikolaev his first deputy, while Prigarin was one of five deputy chairmen.[63] At an August 12, 1993, meeting of the Political Executive Committee, its membership had increased to thirty-two, and Ligachev was identified as a member of the UCP-CPSU's committee on socio-economic problems.[64]

The controversy that erupted in early 1994 among the post-Soviet communist groups thus took on a triangular configuration, with the UCP-CPSU seeking preeminence among the whole lot. Before returning to our discussion of this intra-mural squabbling, however, we must reiterate that on certain basic points the CPRF and its more leftist communist challengers had always been in agreement. All the post-Soviet Russian CPs saw the neocapitalist development of Russia, with its vast income disparities between rich and poor and its destruction of the social safety net, as a vindication of Marx's writings on the evils of capitalism and the need for socialism. There was likewise agreement that the imperialist West, above all the United States, was turning Russia into a neo-colonial outpost, a source of raw materials and an export market for Western manufactured goods. Furthermore, the CPRF's Marxist-Leninist modernizers and Ziuganov nationalists as well as the extra-parliamentary CPs attributed the collapse of the old communist order and the Soviet state itself to the bourgeoisification and betrayal of the CPSU elite, with Gorbachev and Yeltsin the arch traitors. Where they differed was in their strategies for overcoming these multiple ills and their visions of a future socialist society.

Prigarin's Union of Communists took the lead in the organizational campaign against the CPRF. At its Second Extraordinary Congress on December 4, 1993, the UC declared that the CPRF's key documents and many of its actions demonstrated the far-reaching departure of the party's *Presidium* from Marxism-Leninism. It thus announced its own "organizational demarcation from all the right-opportunist and nationalist forces in the CPRF" and called upon the UC's members to withdraw from the CPRF except in the case of local organizations that had decided to also join Shenin's UCP-CPSU.[65]

A few months later the March 1994 issue of the UC's monthly newspaper, *Golos kommunista* (with a print-run ten times larger than its normal circulation) announced the imminent convening of the "30th Conference" of the CPSU's former Moscow city organization.[66] This would turn out to be a blatant move to split the CPRF's local Moscow network by creating a rival to it. After denouncing by name Ziuganov, Yurii P. Belov, and Valentin A. Kuptsov, not to mention Rybkin, the UC organ appealed for the support of all communists who agreed with the decisions of the 29th CPSU Congress in March 1993.[67] Soon thereafter, on April 2, 1994, the Prigarin group reconstituted the "Moscow City Organization of the CPSU," describing it as "committed to Marxist-Leninist positions and free from opportunism and nationalism." Prigarin was elected first secretary and Cherniakhovskii, who had been editor of *Golos kommunista* since the previous December, became secretary for ideological-political work.[68] This organizational challenge, while numerically insignificant (the new city unit siphoned off fewer than five percent of the CPRF's Moscow members),[69] underscored the depth of the escalating rivalry between the CPRF and its more leftist opponents.

Organizational moves against the CPRF were accompanied by polemical attacks. One particularly notable example of the latter was Boris Slavin's "Open Letter to G. A. Ziuganov," a partial version of which appeared in *Golos kommunista* in May 1994 and the full text of which was published in *Mysl*, the journal of Kriuchkov's Russian Party of Communists. Slavin criticized Ziuganov's rejection of the core Marxist tenets of proletarian internationalism and class struggle and his support instead for state patriotism and such nineteenth-century Slavophile notions as *sobornost*. While his arguments were couched in reasoned theoretical discourse, his basic point was unequivocal: Ziuganov's views amounted to right-wing opportunism.[70] As a member of the CPRF's Central Executive Committee, Slavin's decision to oppose Ziuganov publicly on these issues was indicative of considerable disagreement within the party's upper ranks, about which we will have more to say in the next chapter.

Meanwhile, the CPRF leadership took a two-pronged approach to the radical CPs' challenge. It began to mend its fences with Shenin's UCP-CPSU, on the one hand, and to dismiss its leftist challengers as inconsequential sectarians on the other. In February 1994 Ligachev had publicly regretted the CPRF leadership's decision to join the Shenin organization as only an "associate" member.[71] But in Ziuganov's opening report to his party's Second All-Russian Conference in late April 1994, he expressed readiness to cooperate with the successor CPSU "on the basis of solidarity, independence, and mutual assistance."[72] The conference thereupon passed a resolution, "On the Union of Communist Parties," in which it declared the CPRF to be a "constituent" member of the UCP-CPSU (all the while retaining its organizational and programmatic independence); it also endorsed the convening of a coordinating meeting of all communist parties, from both Russia and the "near-abroad," at which the CPRF would be represented by a plenipotentiary delegation.[73]

Such a meeting was subsequently held outside Moscow on May 21–22, 1994, with Ziuganov's participation.[74] During its deliberations the participants called upon the UCP-CPSU leadership to update its program and statutes in order to bring them more in line with the contemporary conditions under which its member parties operated.[75] Two months later, on July 9–10, a UCP-CPSU plenum denounced Prigarin for "schismatic activities," and Shenin invited his deputy to withdraw from the group's Political Executive Committee.[76] Ziuganov and Shenin had evidently reached an agreement whereby their two organizations would cooperate more closely in exchange for the UCP-CPSU Central Executive Committee's promise, first, to revise its original 1993 position on the unitary character of its multi-party formation and, second, to disavow its own radical members' organizational challenge to the CPRF.

All the while, Ziuganov denounced the activities of the *Roskomsoiuz* in general.[77] And in his concluding speech to the Third CPRF Congress in January 1995, he derided the extra-parliamentary CPs, except for the Russian Communist Workers' Party, as "simply *kruzhki,*" that is, small isolated circles of like-minded radicals.[78]

Meanwhile, the radical left CPs persevered in their efforts to unite their forces against both the Yeltsin regime and the CPRF. On July 16–17, 1994, an All-Russian (Inter-party) Conference of Communists met in Moscow. Attended by 196 delegates, including the leaders of the ACPB, RCWP, RPC, UC, Kosolapov's "Leninist position" wing of the CPRF, and the new Moscow organization of the CPSU (the Prigarin-Cherniakhovskii group), the conference formally recognized the existence of the *Roskomsoiuz* since December 26, 1993. It also denounced Ziuganov for conciliationism and submissiveness to Yeltsin as well as for undermining the communist movement from within. And Anpilov insisted on a struggle for the hearts and minds of the rank-and-file CPRF members in order to free them from Ziuganov's baleful influence.[79]

When it came to organizational matters, however, the participants were every bit as divided as they had been during the fall and winter of 1992–1993, on the eve of the reconstitution of the CPRF. The ACPB representative favored only unity of action and opposed any kind of organizational cooperation. Tiulkin called instead for an organic union. Kriuchkov insisted on a gradual, step-by-step approach to unification. And Prigarin spoke of the transformation of the *Roskomsoiuz* into an All-Russian Communist Party that would eventually join the UCP-CPSU.[80]

In the end, only Prigarin and Cherniakhovskii would move on to form their own Russian Communist Party–CPSU in April 1995. For their efforts, they were denounced by the UCP-CPSU Central Executive Committee by a vote of six to three and expelled from the organization's membership Council. They were also excluded from participation in the forthcoming Thirtieth

Congress of the UCP-CPSU.[81] This did not, however, signify that relations between the Shenin group and the CPRF were developing smoothly. On the contrary, Shenin himself refused to be a candidate on the CPRF's party list for the December 1995 parliamentary elections.[82]

The CPRF would thus be hounded constantly by opposition from its left flank as it undertook to formulate an official party program during the second half of 1994 and, more importantly, as it geared up for parliamentary and presidential elections in December 1995 and June 1996. Not only that, but the virulent Great Russian chauvinism espoused by Ziuganov in his political tracts would offer a ready target to his enemies on both sides of the left-right ideological barricade. It would, in short, obscure the more moderate tenets of both Ziuganov's thinking and the CPRF's program and practice.

Notes

1. They were all published in Moscow, the 1993 volume by Paleia and the later two by Informpechat.

2. Ziuganov, *Za Gorizontom*, p. 71.

3. Ibid., p. 10; emphasis added.

4. Ibid., p. 71.

5. On this group and its influence on the contemporary Russian opposition, see Walter Laqueur, *Black Hundred: The Rise of the Extreme Right in Russia* (New York: HarperCollins, 1993), pp. 138–142. For Ziuganov's meeting with representatives of the European new right, see *Den*, May 31–June 6, 1992; the authors are grateful to Veljko Vujacic for this reference (see note 23 below).

6. Ziuganov, *Za Gorizontom*, p. 71.

7. Ziuganov, *Drama vlasti*, p. 175.

8. Ibid., p. 176.

9. For more about the Eurasians, see Nicholas Riasanovsky, *The Emergence of Eurasianism* (Berkeley: California Slavic Studies, 1967); also Laqueur, *Black Hundred*, pp. 174–176.

10. Outstanding among the many Western and Russian works on the Slavophiles is A. Walicki, *The Slavophile Controversy* (Oxford: Oxford University Press, 1975). For an analysis of Ziuganov's Slavophile tendencies, see James P. Scanlon, "The Russian Idea from Dostoevskii to Ziuganov," *Problems of Post-Communism*, Vol. 43, No. 4 (July-August 1996): 35–42.

11. For more on this idea see Leon Poliakov, *Moscow—The Third Rome* (Paris: 1989).

12. Ziuganov, *Drama vlasti*, p. 184.

13. Ziuganov, *Derzhava*, p. 8.

14. Ibid., p. 16.

15. Ziuganov, *Drama vlasti*, p. 50.

16. Ziuganov, *Derzhava*, p. 16.

17. Ibid., p. 14.

18. Ibid., p. 43.

19. See, for example, the interesting article by an author who most likely was using a pseudonym: P. Aleev, "There he is, Ziuganov. . . ." *Alternativy*, No. 1, 1994, p. 4.

20. Ziuganov, *Za Gorizontom*, p. 18.

21. Ziuganov, *Drama vlasti*, p. 182.

22. Ziuganov, *Derzhava*, p. 52

23. See, for example, David Remnick, "Hammer, Sickle and Book," *The New York Review of Books*, May 23, 1996, p. 50; cf. Veljko Vujacic, "Between the Soviet Left and the Russian Right: Russian Nationalism, Gennadii Ziuganov and the Third Road," forthcoming in *Post-Soviet Affairs*, passim.

24. Ziuganov, *Za Gorizontom*, pp. 17–18. As Ziuganov informed a special meeting of the delegates to the Third CPRF Congress in January 1995, this work was initially published "in the restricted journal *Obozrevatel*, which has a circulation of altogether 1000 copies and is intended for leading politicians"; see "Zakliuchitelnoe slovo G. A. Ziuganova na III Sezde KPRF (utrennee zasedanie 23 ianvaria)," *Informatsionnyi biulleten*, No. 2 (14), February 1, 1995, p. 30. *Obozrevatel* was published by the RAU-Corporation, the president of which was Ziuganov's close associate, Aleksei I. Podberezkin.

25. Ziuganov, *Za Gorizontom*, pp. 47–48.

26. "Konservator c kommunisticheskim litsom: Beseda c Ziuganovym," *Obshchaia gazeta*, No. 3 (1995), p. 6.

27. For the structure of the Russian Federation government, see Jeffrey W. Hahn, ed., *Democratization in Russia: The Development of Legislative Institutions* (Armonk: M.E. Sharpe, 1996), pp. 283–289.

28. See text of Edict Number 1400 in *Trud*, September 22, 1993, pp. 1–2, trans. in *Federal Broadcast Information Service: Central Eurorasia* (henceforth *FBIS-SOV*), No. 182-S, September 22, 1993, pp. 3–5. For Yeltsin's decree that a constitutional referendum be held on December 12, 1993, see Moscow ITAR-TASS in English in *FBIS-SOV*, No. 199, October 18, 1993, p. 16.

29. "*Pravda* Returns to Newsstands 10 December" (Editorial Report), *FBIS-SOV*, No. 236, December 10, 1993, p. 41. The December 10 issue carried a long piece by Ziuganov on Russian foreign policy, which was a distilled and somewhat more moderate version of his geopolitical views described at the beginning of this chapter.

30. This did necessarily work against the interests of the CPRF; there were several blocs, including the Civic Union, which spent large sums on paid advertising but did very poorly in the elections. See the brilliant piece by Daphne Skillen, "Media Coverage in the Elections," in *Elections and Political Order In Russia*, ed. by Peter Lentini (Budapest: Central European University Press, 1995), pp. 97–123.

31. Quoted by Dmitrii Kuznets in "Oppositsiia," *Segodnia*, December 11, 1993, p. 2.

32. Ziuganov's report to the October 26, 1993, CPRF Conference was circulated among political activists. A copy is in the archives of the Gorbachev Foundation in Moscow, and was made available to the authors.

33. See ibid. and "Obrashchenie k kommunistam, trudiashchimsia, vsem patriotam Rossii," typescript manifesto on CPRF letterhead paper, a copy of which was made available to the authors from the Gorbachev Foundation archives.

34. Ibid., p. 3.

35. Ziuganov said as much in an interview in *Pravda*, November 4, 1993, p. 1.

36. See *Rossiiskaia gazeta*, November 12, 1993, p. 7.

37. Thomas F. Remington, "Representative Power and the Russian State," in Stephen White, Alex Pravda, and Avi Gitelman, eds., *Developments in Russian & Post-Soviet Politics*, 3rd ed. (Durham, NC: Duke University Press, 1994), p. 78.

38. Peter Lentini, "Overview of the Campaign," in his edited volume, *Elections and Political Order in Russia: The implications of the 1993 elections to the Federal Assembly* (Budapest: Central European Press, 1995), p. 85.

39. Ibid., p. 84. Lentini overstates the CPRF party list seats, putting them at 32, a number that was subsequently reduced to 30, as will be elaborated below.

40. See Jeffrey W. Hahn, "Studying the Russian Experience," in his edited volume, *Democratization in Russia*, p. 254. We do not entirely agree with Hahn's political classification of the above groups, however.

41. Ibid.

42. Natalia Konstantinova, "Dva goda Rossiiskogo parlamentarizma," *Nezavisimaia gazeta*, December 2, 1995, pp. 1–2.

43. For the initial distribution of Duma positions to the various party fractions and groups, see *Argumenti i fakty*, No. 4, January 1994, p. 2.

44. He was elected by a single vote; see Remington, "Representative Power and the Russian State," in White et al., *Developments*, p. 84.

45. Ibid.

46. Quoted in the unpublished paper by Richard Harris, "The Opposition in the State Duma" (Washington, DC: The Catholic University of America, 1994).

47. Gennadii Ziuganov, "Iz doklada na plenume Tsik KPRF," *Sovetskaia Rossiia*, December 28, 1993, p. 3.

48. Only the RCWP was actually barred from registering for the elections by President Yeltsin's October 19, 1993, decree, "On some measures to maintain national security during the 1993 election campaign"; see *FBIS-SOV*, No. 202, October 21, 1993, p. 35. The other three extra-parliamentary CPs decided on their own to boycott the elections.

49. *Golos kommunista*, No. 3 (March 1994); quoted in *Raznogolositsa*, No. 11, March 21–27, 1994, p. 3.

50. By January 1995 the CPRF claimed 530,000 members representing all 89 regions of Russia, while by late 1994 the RCWP's membership had fallen from 80,000 to 40,000 representing 51 regions (*Pravda*, December 21, 1994), that of the UC from 10,000 to some 5,000 to 7,000 (authors' interview with UC leader Aleksei Prigarin in his home, November 3, 1994), and the other CPs had even fewer members than Prigarin's group. See also the figures cited in *Raznogolositsa*, No. 28, July 28–24, 1994, p. 22.

51. See the communiqués in *Glasnost*, No. 13, April 1–7, 1993, p. 1.

52. See the section on the UCP-CPSU in *Kto est Chto: Politicheskaia Moskva 1994*, Vol. 1 (Moscow: Pushchinskii nauchnyi tsentr RAN, 1994), pp. 487–489.

53. Kurashvili, *Kuda idet Rossiia?* (Moscow, "Prometei," 1994), pp. 52–53.

54. This was disclosed during the debates at the congress; see the account in *Materialy XXIX sezda KPSS* (Moscow: Redaktsia "Glasnost," 1993), pp. 42 and 49.

55. Ibid., pp. 42 and 48.

56. Quoted in ibid., p. 46.

57. J. B. Urban's interview with Cherniakhovskii in the editorial offices of *Golos kommunista*, May 12, 1995.

58. Kurashvili, *Kuda idet Rossiia?*, p. 52.

59. Text in *Glasnost*, No. 14, April 8–14, 1993, p. 3.

60. *Materialy XXIX sezda KPSS*, pp. 41 and 43.

61. Ibid., p. 54.

62. Ibid., p. 55.

63. Ibid., p. 103.

64. "Raspredelenie obiazannostei v Politispolkome Soveta SKP-KPSS," *Glasnost*, No. 30, August 19–25, 1993, p. 4.

65. "Postanovlenie 2-go Chrezvychainogo sezda partii Soiuz kommunistov: Za obedinenie kommunistov Rossiiskoi Federatsii-Chlenov KPSS," *Golos kommunista*, No. 5, January 1994, p. 3.

66. "2 Aprelia—XXX Moskovskaia Konferentiia KPSS," *Golos kommunista*, No. 4 (8), March 1994, p. 1.

67. Ibid., p. 3.

68. *Golos kommunista*, No. 5 (9), April-May 1994, passim. It should be noted that during this period Boris P. Kurashvili was on the board of directors of the UC organ.

69. In autumn 1994 the CPRF's Moscow organization had about 19,000 members, the new city unit of the Prigarin-Cherniakhovskii group some 1,500. About half the latter were former CPRF members or those with dual membership in Kosolapov's "Leninist position" group; the rest were individuals entirely new to the communist movement (generally intellectuals aged thirty to fifty) or former CPSU members for whom the only acceptable option was Shenin's reconstituted CPSU. These data come from the authors' interview with Sergei Cherniakhovskii at Moscow State University on November 3, 1994.

70. See *Golos kommunista*, No. 6 (10), May 1994, and *Mysl*, No. 10, 1994. The full text, "Otkaz ot marksizma pogubit kompartiiu (otkrytoe pismo Ziuganovu G. A.)," was republished in the joint Russian-British journal *Alternativy/Alternatives*, No. 3 (Moscow, 1995), pp. 168–174.

71. Yegor Ligachev, "Kommunisty obediniaiutsia," *Sovetskaia Rossiia*, February 15, 1994, p. 2.

72. See Ziuganov's report in *Materialy Vserossiiskoi konferentsii Kommunisticheskoi partii Rossiiskoi Federatsii* (Moscow: 1994), p. 17.

73. Text in ibid., p. 79.

74. "Shag vpered i ni shagu nazad!," *Glasnost*, No. 8, May 27–June 2, 1994, p. 3.

75. "Rezoliutsiia koordinatsionnoi vstrechi kommunisticheskikh partii," ibid., p. 2.

76. See the plenum documents in *Glasnost*, Nos. 12–13, July 29–August 11, 1994, pp. 3–5; cf. authors' interview with Aleksei Prigarin in his home November 3, 1994.

77. Cf. his report in *Materialy Vserossiiskoi konferentsii*, p. 17.

78. Text in CPRF's Informatsionnyi biulleten, No. 2 (14), February 1, 1995, pp. 23–30 at p. 25.

79. *Raznogolositsa*, No. 28, July 18–24, 1994, p. 22.

80. Marina Romanova, "Levoe plecho—vpered!," *Golos kommunista*, No. 8 (12), 1994, p. 2.

81. See the documentation in *Golos kommunista*, No. 10 (28), 1995, p. 3.

82. O. Shenin, "Vserossiiskoi Konferentsii KPRF: Zaiavlenie," *Glasnost*, No. 17, September 1–15, 1995, p. 3.

6

The Political Evolution
of the CPRF, 1994–1995

From its Second Congress in February 1993 to its Third Congress in January 1995, the CPRF underwent substantial political and programmatic development. The "correlation of forces" among the various tendencies inside the CPRF altered in tandem with the worsening socio-economic and political environment: unremitting stagflation on top of ever growing crime and corruption; the sudden drop in the ruble's value on October 11, 1994 (black Tuesday); and the looming civil war in Chechnia. If the center of political gravity lay with the Marxist reformers in February 1993, it shifted to the ethno-centric Russian nationalists led by Gennadii Ziuganov during the first half of 1994 and thereafter turned in the direction of the Marxist-Leninist modernizers during the final preparations for the Third CPRF Congress.

This chapter begins with the CPRF's preliminary discussion of an official program during the first half of 1994, starting with the program theses considered by the Central Executive Committee in March 1994 and continuing with the deliberations at the party's Second All-Russian Conference the following month. In October 1994 a fully elaborated draft program embracing many of Ziuganov's views was accepted by a Central Executive Committee plenum as a basis for discussion at all levels of the party. The second section of this chapter focuses on the contrast between that October 1994 "Ziuganov draft" and the document ultimately endorsed at the Third CPRF Congress on January 21–22, 1995. On that occasion 345 delegates, representing some 530,000 party members, formally approved a CPRF Program that differed substantially from the October 1994 version in its heightened emphasis upon Marxist-Leninist principles and downplaying of Russian nationalist thinking. The chapter concludes, in its third section, with an analysis of the reasons for this seemingly paradoxical turn to the left at a time when the CPRF was gearing up for the coming round of parliamentary and presidential elections scheduled for late 1995 and mid-1996.

The CPRF's Spring 1994 Programmatic Evolution: Ziuganov's Ascendancy

As the CPRF settled into its new role as one of the larger parliamentary fractions in the State Duma, its leaders began to grapple with the task of clarifying their party's political profile. Work thus began in early 1994 on the formulation of an official CPRF program. The drafting process embraced such topics as the party's interpretation of the Soviet past, its electoral strategy and policy agenda for the near term, and its vision of the future. Such a programmatic articulation of its views was needed both to forge unity among the various tendencies within the party's activist core and to mobilize its half million or so rank-and-file members for agitation, electioneering, and membership recruitment at the grassroots.

During the spring of 1994 the drafting process went through two stages. The first major benchmark was a plenum of the Central Executive Committee in mid-March. At that time, the party leadership underscored the need for an official program, discussed the general parameters of such a document, and appointed a commission to edit a preliminary draft. The result was a set of programmatic theses which was disseminated for discussion at all levels of the party. This initial draft still bore many of the hallmarks of the Marxist reformers although several ideas that reflected Ziuganov's specific views were also included. A month later, in late April, a Second All-Russian Conference of the CPRF was convened to deliberate upon the many amendments and additions to the March theses which had been made in the interim. On this occasion Ziuganov took the center stage. In his opening report he rebutted some of the criticisms which had already been raised and elaborated upon his own views in far greater detail than he had hitherto done at formal party meetings. More importantly, the documents the conference approved and the resolutions it passed bore the unmistakable imprint of Ziuganov's thinking regarding Russia and the world, as described in Chapter 5. During this same period, moreover, Ziuganov and several like-minded CPRF associates launched an attempt to create an opposition national front-style coalition with non-communist nationalists called "Accord in the Name of Russia."

The March 1994 Plenum of the CPRF's Central Executive Committee

Ziuganov opened his report to the March 15, 1994, plenum—the sixth to be held since the CPRF's February 1993 congress—by setting forth an agenda that included discussion of both the projected party program and the CPRF's attitude toward religion and "state patriotism."[1] Above all, he stressed the need for a comprehensive theoretical program, noting the contribution in this regard of both the 1993 congress's "Programmatic Declaration" and the party Presidium's late summer 1993 "open letter" to the communists of Russia. As discussed in chapters 3 and 4, the former emphasized the policy preferences of the Marxist reformers while the latter, written by Ziuganov's close ideological ally, Yurii P. Belov, expounded upon the uniqueness of Russia's historical political culture and the centrality of Russian "state patriotism" to the creation of a broad coalition of forces opposing the Yeltsin regime.

At the same time, Ziuganov was notably restrained when it came to advancing concrete programmatic suggestions, at least in his public address to the March plenum. He cautioned against the "simple repetition of tested positions of Marxist-Leninist teaching" in dealing with the problems of contemporary Russian society, and he alluded to the need to "carefully analyze" the reasons for the crisis and collapse of Soviet socialism. He also underscored the importance of innovative thinking, declaring that "Our slogan is not 'back to socialism' but 'forward to socialism.'" Still, he refrained from spelling out his interpretation of what had gone wrong in the Soviet past or his preferences regarding a socialist future. With respect to details, he confined himself to stating that an opposition coalition should range "from communists and socialists through national-patriots and centrists to democrats without quotation marks." In other words, it should be patterned after Moscow's wartime national front directives to communists in fascist-occupied Europe. Such a coalition should strive, moreover, for the creation of a "government of national trust."

If Ziuganov was less than concrete in his plenum report, the same cannot be said of Yurii Belov, the head of the CPRF organization in the Leningrad region. Belov was a self-proclaimed "first generation intellectual [*intelligent*]" who, like Ziuganov, had done his military service in the German Democratic Republic. Significantly, Belov described the G.D.R. as a place where "Union" and "Russia" were inextricably linked in the minds of the Red Army troops.[2] It is worth reflecting on this remark. In the case of both Ziuganov and Belov it may well be that their Great Russian nationalism (so distinct from Soviet superpower patriotism and "proletarian internationalism") can be ascribed in part to their service in the Soviet Forces in Germany during the 1960s. In that pre-*detente* era memories of World War II were still vivid, and the attitude of Russians toward Germans was more likely that of wartime victors than Cold War allies. One may surmise that under these circumstances feelings of Russian ethnic identity and national pride became stronger while ideologically prescribed internationalist solidarity went by the board.

In a *Pravda* article published the same day the March plenum met, Belov set forth a series of policy prescriptions with which Ziuganov doubtless concurred. On the one hand, Belov baldly asserted that a "mixed economy is the path to socialism," praising in this context both Lenin's New Economic Policy and present-day "native [*otechestvennye*] entrepreneurs." On the other hand, he argued that a strong coalition of "state-patriotic forces" was essential in order to combat the "anti-state, destructive, *cosmopolitan* forces" threatening Russia today.[3] Here it should be pointed out that in Russian usage "cosmopolitan" is a loaded term, denoting Zionist influences and an outright anti-Russian orientation. On this score Belov did not mince his words: Russia, he declared, was presently the object of a "plot devised by the strategists of global geopolitics to bring about the political, economic, and spiritual enslavement of our country." The similarity of such ideas to Ziuganov's geopolitical thinking was striking. Furthermore, as if to demarcate his own views from those of the Marxist reformers, Belov went on to praise both the current Chinese model of a mixed economy and the past economic reform initiatives of such Soviet leaders as Aleksei N. Kosygin and Yurii V. Andropov.

Before turning to a discussion of the theses approved at the Sixth Plenum, it should be pointed out that a stenographic account of the proceedings was not published, nor was an initial version of the theses which had already been discussed at regional party conferences in Krasnoiarsk, Saratov, Yaroslav, Orel, Voronezh, and the Leningrad and Moscow regions. However, an "overwhelming majority" of those at the plenum (which was attended by 78 of 120-plus members of the Central Executive Committee as well as by members of the Central Control-Auditing Committee and the party's Duma fraction) reportedly endorsed the revised theses for further discussion in the party's primary organizations after their reworking by an editorial commission.[4] With regard to the editorial commission, moreover, it is well to identify the eleven individuals on it because they represented the three major CPRF tendencies. Thus, the nationalists included, in addition to Ziuganov and Belov, Aleksandr A. Shabanov, Ziuganov's chief aide in the Duma fraction offices; the Marxist reformers were represented by Viktor I. Zorkaltsev, Valentin A. Kuptsov, Ivan I. Melnikov, Kazbek A. Tsiku, and Boris F. Slavin; and the Marxist-Leninist modernizers by Richard I. Kosolapov and Ivan P. Osadchii. The eleventh commission member, Anatolii I. Lukianov, was probably closest to the last-mentioned group.[5]

The final product of their labors, "From Crisis to Balanced Development, People's Power, and Socialism: Theses for the Elaboration of a Program of the Communist Party of the Russian Federation," was published on March 24, 1994.[6] As was to be expected, it constituted a judicious blend of ideas favored by the Marxist reformers and/or the ethnocentric Russian nationalists. Perhaps the most telling victory of the Marxist reformers was the definition of the CPRF as the party of "creative Marxism." Indeed, the customary Soviet-era phrases, "Marxism-Leninism" and "democratic centralism," did not appear anywhere in the text. But equally significant, if less pointed, was the attribution of the CPSU's crisis and downfall to the breach that had developed over the years between the party's base and the *apparat*, the latter of which was referred to in the document as the "party-official bureaucracy" and "careerists." With regard to this fundamental organizational differentiation, however, there was as yet no hint of betrayal on the part of the *apparat* or of subversion from without. Finally, the endorsement in the March theses of the ideas of a mixed economy and limited, indigenous private entrepreneurship, which were acceptable to both the Marxist reformers and the CPRF nationalists, was also accompanied by the call for a coalition of "*progressive* state-patriotic forces" and the eventual creation of a "government of *people's* trust."[7] These seemingly obscure nuances were at odds with Ziuganov's appeal for a broader national front-style opposition bloc and a "government of national trust."

At the same time, Ziuganov and his like-minded colleagues also had their say. Not only did the March draft assert that "the CPRF defines state patriotism as the idea of Great Russia"; it also insisted on according due prestige "to the [Russian historical] traditions of community and collectivism, to the Russian language," and on halting both "historical vandalism" and the inculcation of "Westernization and Americanism [sic]." Moreover, the greater emphasis in the March theses than heretofore on resurrecting the U.S.S.R., albeit peacefully, and on reasserting an independent Russian foreign policy— to the point of abrogating international treaties if necessary—can likewise be interpreted as policies favored more by the Ziuganov nationalists than by the Marxist reformers. Indeed, in May 1994 Ziuganov's aide and ally, deputy CPRF chairman Shabanov, called for the reconstitution of the Soviet Union according to the following sequence: first Russia and Belarus; then Ukraine and Kazakhstan; later the rest of the Central Asian republics along with Azerbaidjan and Armenia; Georgia last; and the Baltic states "never."[8] Such foreign policy aims were doubtless also backed by the Marxist-Leninist modernizers. But the influence of this third CPRF tendency was otherwise not much in evidence unless we assume that they were the ones who insisted upon the inclusion in the March theses of a projected three-stage evolution of Russia from a mixed economy and political pluralism under a "government of people's trust" to the eventual restoration of socialism.[9]

The April 1994 Second All-Russian Conference of the CPRF

On April 23–24, 1994, the CPRF convened its Second All-Russian Conference, which took place in the Moscow suburb of Zvenigorod and was attended by about 270 delegates representing all 89 Russian regions. On this occasion the intra-party alignments underwent a perceptible transformation. On the one hand, a more orthodox brand of Marxist-Leninist argumentation began to be heard. On the other hand, Ziuganov and his allies started an all-out campaign to make "state patriotism" the banner around which a broad anti-Yeltsin national front-type coalition might coalesce. According to Slavin, whose "open letter" to Ziuganov we discussed in the last chapter, about thirty percent of the delegates present voiced opposition, albeit from a variety of vantage points, to the emphasis upon "state patriotism."[10] In a further indication of the controversy surrounding this event, the conference's editorial commission, composed of representatives from forty-one regional party organizations, received over 2,000 additions and amendments to the March theses.[11]

Unfortunately, as was the custom in the case of CPRF meetings, the conference debates were not published. Nevertheless, from the abbreviated reports in *Pravda* and *Sovetskaia Rossiia* one can glean some insight into the nature of the differences voiced at the gathering. As described in *Pravda*, those who spoke during the deliberations (about thirty) "*warned against enthusiasm for the slogan of state patriotism.* They insistently spoke out on the impermissibility of rejecting class struggle, of conciliationism, and of sliding into parliamentarism."[12] By way of contrast, *Sovetskaia Rossiia* reported that "*the conference insistently defended the thesis on state patriotism* as the leading idea in the reconstitution of a great power and the acquisition of reliable allies beyond its frontiers."[13] Not only did these two contradictory versions offer an insight into the opposing tendencies among the CPRF's activists; they also underscored the divergent political profiles of the two major Russian left-wing newspapers. While *Sovetskaia Rossiia* had become a staunch supporter of the Ziuganov position (and, not coincidentally, a recipient of donations from CPRF Duma deputies[14]), *Pravda* served as an outlet for a variety of more traditional Marxist-Leninist viewpoints.

In his opening report to the April conference, Ziuganov accentuated the positive attributes of Russia's political culture through the ages and the strategic importance of "state patriotism," as he had done in his official addresses ever since the party leadership's "open letter" to the Russian communists in mid-1993. He also discoursed upon the innate incompatibility of Western and Russian civilization and bemoaned the absence of morality and the work ethic among present-day Russian youth, familiar themes in his journalistic writing. But most significantly, for the first time at a formal party conclave—and just two weeks after his first trip to the United States[15]—he spelled out his conspiracy theory regarding the Soviet Union's demise. From the start of the Cold War, he argued, the West had launched a secret plan for the destruction of the U.S.S.R. It first provoked the Soviet Union into a race for global "symmetry" (i.e., the arms race) in order to precipitate the

U.S.S.R.'s economic decline. Thereafter, *perestroika* served the plans of Russia's enemies by providing an ideological rationale for her collapse, namely, Russophobia, anti-communism, and "deafening, importunate propaganda regarding the 'charms' of the liberal-democratic worldview." During 1990–1991, the third stage of this "global geopolitical diversion," the "democratic" leadership of Russia became the enemies' "battering ram" for the destruction of the Soviet Union.[16] The CPRF leader, in other words, sketched out a case for bringing charges of treason against both the Gorbachev reformers and Yeltsin's entourage.

Ziuganov's keynote address was followed by Zorkaltsev's report on the work of the CPRF's fraction in the State Duma and Kuptsov's report on the development of the party's organizational network. Neither one broached Ziuganov's theme of "state patriotism" or his conspiracy theory regarding the U.S.S.R.'s collapse. At the same time, both men seemed more circumspect with regard to the reformist orientation with which they had been associated at the Second CPRF Congress in February 1993.

Zorkaltsev was straightforward and pragmatic in his discussion of the need for the party fraction's ongoing consultations, cooperation, and compromises with other Duma groups on legislative matters, pointing to the CPRF's control of only ten percent of the total votes. At the same time, however, he sounded a bit defensive when he explained the party's vote in support of the 1994 government budget and when he repeatedly called for stronger ties between the CPRF's Duma deputies and its regional organizations so that the latter might give timely advice and "correctives."[17] One got the impression that the party's parliamentary activity was receiving critical flak from its own rank-and-file members as well as from its extraparliamentary rivals on the left.

Kuptsov's report focused on the tasks of the CPRF's 89 regional, 2,000 local, and 20,000 primary party organizations. Given the preponderance of elderly people in the party, he explained, top priority had to be given to the recruitment of new members, especially among young people (only 3,000 new CPRF recruits, he noted, had been registered since October 1993[18]). With an eye to the electoral campaigns ahead, moreover, he admonished party organizations at all levels to shed old habits and to enlist supporters and sympathizers from the general population in various party activities but without imposing upon them undue burdens or pressure of any kind. And in order to exchange and/or disseminate information about the party's work, he encouraged horizontal ties among local party organizations (a sharp departure from the strictly vertical structures of the old CPSU).

However, Kuptsov also emphasized the need for strengthening internal party discipline. If Zorkaltsev seemed on the defensive, Kuptsov sounded downright orthodox in his denunciation of "non-payment of membership dues, violation of the principles of democratic centralism, dual membership, factionalism," and so on.[19] In the same vein, he declared that the party's active participation in parliamentary activity in no way signified its rejection of the "revolutionary and democratic traditions of the communist and workers' movement." He also insisted that the process of re-registering CPSU cardholders wishing to become members of the CPRF should be concluded by July 1, 1994. Plainly, Kuptsov sought to tighten up membership admissions as well as discipline in the face of the radical left's organizational challenge discussed in Chapter 5.

Furthermore, both Zorkaltsev and Kuptsov alluded to a problem that had vexed the CPRF leadership from the start: the so-called "information blockade" of their activities by the mainstream Russian media. Zorkaltsev described how the party's Duma deputies had helped to overcome this "information vacuum" by addressing hundreds of local CPRF meetings and writing dozens of articles in newspapers and journals. Still, the conference resolution on Kuptsov's report made it clear that "the creation of our own newspaper or, at a minimum, an information bulletin" was an urgent task.[20] Kuptsov linked the non-payment of membership dues to the failure to set up a party press, but he also conceded that dues alone would not suffice to fund such activities. The CPRF leadership was therefore seeking to find other means of material support by "strengthening its ties with representatives of management who have maintained their socialist convictions, [and] with patriotically oriented entrepreneurs."[21] What was clear from this discussion was that, at least as of April 1994, the party's finances were not in good shape.

The conference passed resolutions on the three reports discussed above as well as on the resolution, "On the Union of Communist Parties," described in Chapter 5. In addition, two documents prepared in advance were submitted to the assembled delegates for deliberation, one entitled "On Patriotism and the Attitude toward the Ruling Regime" and the other "The Communist Party of the Russian Federation on the Path to Accord in the Name of Russia."

The first document, "On Patriotism and the Attitude toward the Ruling Regime,"[22] reiterated the Ziuganov-Belov position that the standard bearers of Russian "state patriotism" had always been the "Russian people," with their historically ingrained "communal-collectivist customs." It therefore appealed for the formation of a "union of state-patriotic forces" composed of the peasantry, indigenous [*otechestvennye*] entrepreneurs, Cossacks, Orthodox believers, military representatives, and the "laboring intelligentsia." And, after the usual denunciations of shock therapy and the Belovezhskie agreements, it concluded with the ominous assertion that those who backed the Yeltsin regime were "aliens in our Fatherland [*Otechestvo*]."

The second document, "The Communist Party of the Russian Federation on the Path to Accord in the Name of Russia," bore all the earmarks of Ziuganov's personal authorship.[23] It plainly constituted his riposte to Yeltsin's

"Treaty on Social Accord" (the president's winter 1994 initiative designed to secure broad inter-party agreement on avoiding the kind of civil conflict that had erupted in autumn 1993).[24] The CPRF chairman now countered with a plan to overturn the Yeltsin government in a peaceful, "civilized" manner by forming a broad coalition of "leftist, centrist, patriotic, and people's-democratic forces," exactly the type of national front opposition that Ziuganov had been urging since the March 1994 plenum. The document warned of the threat of a "spontaneous anarchical rebellion [*bunt*] of déclassé elements" in the face of the mounting "economic, political, and spiritual colonization" of Russia. It thus called for the coming to power, through elections or "some other peaceful, non-coercive path," of a "people's-democratic" coalition. The latter would then carry out the "*general-democratic* tasks" that were the prerequisites for the eventual "peaceful, civilized struggle of the communists for the realization of their further programmatic goals." Here it should be mentioned that those "*general-democratic*" tasks included measures which would later form the core of the CPRF's electoral platform in the fall of 1995.

According to the April 26, 1994, report in *Sovetskaia Rossiia*, the conference approved resolutions on both these documents. In the published conference materials, however, there was no reference to a *resolution* on the second document. The omission could not have been accidental. The absence of a formal resolution may have been related to the fact that Ziuganov had already joined with non-communist political figures weeks earlier to organize a broad national front movement called "Accord in the Name of Russia." This turn of events, about which we will have more to say in the next section, appears to have been a unilateral and hence controversial move on the part of the CPRF's nationalist wing. It was, in other words, one thing to express rhetorical support for the idea of a national front coalition but quite another to initiate its actual formation without prior agreement by the party's leadership bodies.

The political-ideological clashes that occurred at the Second All-Russian Conference, which were attested to both by participants and by the diametrically opposed reports of what had transpired in *Pravda* and *Sovetskaia Rossiia*, resulted in minor albeit contradictory amendments to the March 1994 program theses.[25] The Marxist reformers were probably gratified by the appearance in the revised theses of at least generic support for internationalist solidarity across state and ethnic boundaries. At the same time, the single reference to "revolution" in the March version was changed to read "socialist transformation," a formulation also acceptable to Ziuganov. As for the Marxist-Leninist modernizers, their insistence on a predominant government role in economic matters was reflected in the new draft's ban on private property in land and call for state control over banking, most foreign trade, and capital transfers abroad. The Leninist principle of "democratic centralism" was also once again affirmed, but this should be seen in the context of alarm over the escalating rivalry between the CPRF and its ultra-leftist challengers. All of these modifications were, however, insignificant compared to the altercations over the shape of the final party program which lay in store for the autumn of 1994.

"Accord in the Name of Russia"

As suggested above, the notion of a broad national front coalition of opposition groups was not simply a proposal put forth by Ziuganov at the CPRF's March plenum and April Second All-Russian Conference; it was a concrete action plan that was in the process of implementation even as the party's top deliberative bodies convened during the spring of 1994. On March 18, 1994, the front page of *Pravda* carried the text of a document entitled "Accord in the Name of Russia: Appeal to the Citizens of the RF by the Leaders of the Center-left Opposition." This appeal described "Accord in the Name of Russia" as a political movement aimed at restoring the "strength and might of Russian statehood" and open to all Russian citizens, regardless of political affiliation or occupation.

The sixteen signatories of the appeal included only five individuals directly linked to the CPRF: Aman M. Tuleev, communist leader from the Kemerovo mining region and one of the six candidates in the 1991 Russian presidential election; Valentin V. Chikin, editor-in-chief of *Sovetskaia Rossiia*; Petr V. Romanov, director of the Krasnoiarsk chemical plant, "Yenisei"; Gennadii N. Seleznev, a member of the editorial board of *Pravda* who would be named to the CPRF's five-man secretariat in January 1995 and would later be elected speaker of the State Duma in January 1996; and Ziuganov himself. Among the signatories who were prominent figures in other parties or movements were the recently amnestied Aleksandr V. Rutskoi, the center-left economist Sergei Yu. Glaziev, the Siberian nationalist lawyer Sergei N. Baburin, the social democrat (and co-founder with Rutskoi of People's Party-Free Russia) Vasilii S. Lipitskii, and the renowned film director Stanislav S. Govorukhin. Also included were such notable figures as the editor-in-chief of the ultra-nationalist weekly *Zavtra*, Aleksandr A. Prokhanov; the Oscar-winning director of the film *Burnt by the Sun*, Nikita S. Mikhalkov; and the Gorbachev Foundation political analyst, Aleksandr S. Tsipko.[26]

The "Accord in the Name of Russia" initiative thus constituted a concrete embodiment of the kind of broad-gauged political coalition called for in the document, "The Communist Party of the Russian Federation on the Path to Accord in the Name of Russia," which was presented for deliberation to the Second All-Russian Conference of the CPRF some five weeks later. Plainly Ziuganov and his nationalist associates were trying to stack the deck in their favor by creating a prototype of the kind of coalition they had in mind well before proposing this organizational strategy to the party conference for approval.

But there is another angle from which to view this chain of events. Both the wide political spectrum represented by the signatories of the appeal published in *Pravda* and the document prepared for the April conference bring to mind the Comintern-era national front strategy first adumbrated in the CPRF Presidium's late summer 1993 "open letter to the communists of Russia," as discussed in Chapter 4. Indeed, the open letter stratagem was standard Comintern operating procedure; and the April 1994 document's very phraseology was reminiscent of Moscow's wartime directives to European communist parties to form anti-Nazi national liberation coalitions of "people's-democratic" forces which, after the war, would undertake "general-democratic tasks" to facilitate the eventual transition to socialism.[27] Whether the CPRF proponents of this nuanced, multi-stage approach had in mind the national front strategy implemented in Eastern Europe after World War II, which led to single-party communist domination, or were prepared to pursue the pluralist variant followed during the postwar decades by the West European communist parties would remain one of the proverbial sixty-four dollar questions of contemporary Russian politics.[28]

The "Accord in the Name of Russia" movement was formally launched on May 28, 1994. Amid considerable ceremony and media attention, five hundred or so invited supporters gathered in the Parliamentary Center of the Russian Federation to constitute themselves as the movement's National Council and to listen to the speeches of some half dozen members of the conclave's self-appointed "initiative group": Glaziev, Romanov, Rutskoi, Ziuganov, Tsipko, Govorukhin, and the deputy head of the Agrarian Party of Russia, with Baburin presiding during the afternoon discussion session.[29] However, Ziuganov and Rutskoi, the presumptive leaders of the new movement, immediately diverged from one another regarding the institution of the Russian presidency and the procedures to be followed in selecting the united opposition's candidate for that post. Rutskoi let it be known that he was prepared to run and, if elected, would exercise the "full powers" of the office; whereas Ziuganov not only urged all due deliberation in nominating a candidate but also called for the eventual abolition of the position itself.[30] Both speeches were received with equal but notably restrained applause. In fact, the audience responded most warmly to the anti-regime peroration by the witty and urbane Govorukhin.

The movement soon faded from the scene, with its organizers meeting for the last time in June 1994 and the non-communist participants, Rutskoi, Glaziev, Baburin, Lipitskii, and Govorukhin, running for parliament in December 1995 as candidates in five rival electoral blocs. Nevertheless, the spring 1994 initiative was a trial balloon for Ziuganov's further moves in support of a broad national front strategy, which would become a central

feature of his spring 1996 Russian presidential campaign. He also continued
to cite it as a concrete example to be emulated by those who opposed the
Yeltsin government.[31] Meanwhile, Ziuganov's participation in a so-called
Congress of Patriotic Forces in Kaliningrad on September 16, 1994, which
was backed by a broader and decidedly more right-wing assortment of political figures than that represented in "Accord in the Name of Russia,"[32] was
further evidence of his commitment to the national front approach.

From October 1994 to January 1995: Ziuganov's Line on the Defensive

On October 22, 1994, the Ninth Plenum of the CPRF's Central Executive
Committee endorsed a fully elaborated draft program for discussion by all
lower-level party organizations. It also laid the groundwork for the Third
CPRF Congress, which it scheduled to convene on January 21, 1995. This
October 1994 draft bore the unmistakable imprint of Ziuganov's thinking on
a wide range of topics. However, it underwent substantial changes prior to
being formally approved at the January 1995 congress. Indeed, a comparison
of the draft version and the final document indicates that in the interim a
basic shift occurred among the major tendencies within the party's activist
core: the Marxist reformers, the Marxist-Leninist modernizers, and the Ziuganov nationalists. As will be detailed below, although Ziuganov's views
dominated the October 1994 version, in the final 1995 program a number of
his specific formulations, especially with regard to ethno-centric Great Russian nationalism, were perceptibly modified. In this process of revision, moreover, the ideas of the Marxist-Leninist modernizers gained ground whereas
those of the Marxist reformers were barely detectable. On the whole, Ziuganov remained the paramount leader of the CPRF, as evidenced by the line-
up of forces in the leadership organs designated at the Third Congress. But
he was obviously on the defensive with regard to his nationalist thinking.

Ziuganov himself conceded in his opening report to the Third CPRF
Congress that the final program was "born amid stormy debates."[33] According to him, two concepts set forth in the October draft were particularly
controversial: the idea of balanced global economic development and the
notion of the historical uniqueness and destiny of Russia.[34] Here it should
be noted that "balanced development" was an internationally coined term
denoting the harmonization of ecological concerns with progressive norms.
Its basic thrust was economic development for all within the bounds of environmental protection everywhere. As such, it seemingly embodied a position
to which no one could object. All the same, while championing it in his
keynote report, Ziuganov also remarked that it had led to "the most contradictory judgments."

With regard to the concept of "balanced development," the October 1994 draft argued that "consumer society" in the developed capitalist world threatened the very existence of "human civilization" on Earth through ecological destruction. At the same time, it declared that the individual worker among the "golden billion" living in capitalist societies had been transformed from an "appendage of a machine" into an "appendage of a credit card."[35] These ideas, however, were not readily congruent with orthodox Marxist-Leninist economic reasoning. Accordingly, the official 1995 program spoke not of the threat to "human civilization" but of the growing chasm in living standards between "the golden billion" and the "exploited periphery" of the world. Even more to the point, it argued that consumerism had become the new mechanism of capitalist exploitation, forcing the working class into ever more intensive labor. In place of the term "balanced development," therefore, the 1995 program upheld the goal of "*optimal, socialist development.*"[36]

As for the issue of Ziuganov's Russian nationalist orientation, he had as we have seen already articulated it at the CPRF's Second All-Russian Conference the previous spring. But the various facets of his outlook were set forth with unprecedented specificity in the October 1994 draft program. In a section entitled "The Place of Russia in the History of Civilization," the document described Russia as the embodiment of a "cultural-historical and moral tradition" the basic features of which were *sobornost* (defined here as communitarianism and collectivism), great-powerhood (*derzhavnost*), and spirituality (*dukhovnost*).[37] The draft then made the following assertions: Russia was a "special type of civilization" and the "pivot" of a Eurasian continental bloc counterposed to the U.S.A. and its Atlantic partners; Russia also represented a "unique ethnic community" bound together by a "single Slavic nucleus, the Russian people, including the greatrus, littlerus, and whiterus [*sic*]"; Russia was likewise an "original holistic economic organism" distinct from the Western free market model; last but not least, "Western capitalist civilization and Russian civilization" were essentially incompatible.[38] Not only were the foregoing passages integral to Ziuganov's worldview, as described in Chapter 5; they were also included almost verbatim in his subsequent 1995 treatise, *Russia and the Contemporary World.*[39]

In the final CPRF program of January 1995, however, little remained of the above line of reasoning except for the listing of *sobornost, derzhavnost,* and *dukhovnost* among Russia's historical political-cultural values. In addition, the official 1995 version distilled the following gist from Ziuganov's originally much more lengthy as well as more explicit geopolitical and ethno-centric formulations: "*In its essence the 'Russian idea' is a deeply socialist idea.*"[40]

At the same time, a three-page section in the October draft on the CPRF's goals and tasks was also almost entirely eliminated from the final party program.[41] The deleted passages had a two-fold thrust. First, they equated the reconstitution of the Soviet Union with the "realization of the idea of Great Russia," indeed with the salvation of "Russia as the historical Fatherland of all the nations and peoples inhabiting her." Secondly, they reiterated the depiction of Russia as a "unique ethnic community," one which had been fragmented by "bourgeois counter-revolutionaries acting on the orders of their 'global stage-managers.'" All that remained of this section in the January 1995 party program was a brief call for the creation of a "union of authentically patriotic forces" and the affirmation that the CPRF, as the successor to the CPSU and its precursors, would heed all that was valuable in the "experience of the Russian, Soviet, and world communist movement."[42]

On the other hand, Ziuganov's interpretations on several points were affirmed or even strengthened in the official 1995 program. For instance, the latter denounced the "blackening of *Russian* and Soviet history,"[43] whereas the October 1994 draft deplored only the blackening of "Soviet history."[44] The final program also called for backing "the national-liberation struggle of the Russian people" by seeking allies among "political parties of the socialist, centrist, and consistently democratic spectrum" as well as among "progressive patriotic movements" and numerous other social groups including "religious associations of all the traditional confessions."[45] This oblique reference to a broad national front strategy had the appearance of a mutually acceptable substitute for the October draft's emphasis upon the unique destiny of the ethnic Russians.

A more important case of Ziuganov's views being partially buttressed in the final program had to do with his attribution of the Soviet collapse to a Western conspiracy abetted by traitors in the CPSU, which he had spelled out in his report to the April 1994 Second All-Russian Conference. The October draft merely accused the Soviet bureaucratic elite during *perestroika* of staging a "bourgeois counterrevolution" under the guise of cliches such as "new thinking," "universal values," "the rule of law," and "civil society."[46] The final program went much further. It asserted that the CPSU had been divided throughout its history into two "currents": "the proletarian one and the petty bourgois, the democratic and the bureaucratic"—in the final analysis, the patriots and the traitors. The petty bourgeois bureaucratic traitors were represented at the start by the Trotskyists and at the end by "Gorbachev and Yeltsin, Yakovlev and Shevardnadze."[47] Without taking into account the ceaseless struggle between these two tendencies, the program asserted, one could not make "an objective evaluation of the role of such leaders of the party and state as I. V. Stalin and V. M. Molotov, N. S. Khrushchev and G. M. Malenkov, L. I. Brezhnev and A. N. Kosygin."[48] In short, if the long-vilified Khrushchev was finally given his due, so too was the man he so boldly condemned for "crimes" against the Soviet party-state.

Conspiratorial thinking was as integral to Ziuganov's worldview as it was to Stalin's. Indeed, in this regard the official 1995 program came very close to reiterating the infamous Stalinist formulation from the late 1930s regarding the intensification of class struggle and the need for greater vigilance with the advance of socialism: to wit, "As socialism is created," the CPRF document declared, "the resistance of forces hostile to it not only does not die down, but it frequently acquires the most fierce and misbegotten forms."[49] It seems safe to assume, therefore, that the charges of Western subversion and domestic treason, taken together, constituted a common denominator of agreement between the more orthodox Marxist-Leninist modernizers and the Ziuganov nationalists.

Meanwhile, if the views of the Marxist reformers were still in evidence in October 1994, by the Third CPRF Congress they had lost much ground to the Marxist-Leninist modernizers. The October draft included among its chief goals "freedom of speech, conscience, association in political parties and social organizations."[50] The corresponding list in the January 1995 program omitted the foregoing but insisted on "the liquidation of the exploitation of man by man."[51] As discussed in Chapter 3, this phrase had been left out of the "Programmatic Declaration" of the Second CPRF Congress, much to the consternation of the more orthodox Marxist-Leninist participants on that occasion. But it appeared three times in the 1995 CPRF Program.[52] Lest this be interpreted as a return to dogmatic thinking per se, however, the document also averred that the CPRF was guided by "*developing* Marxist-Leninist teaching."[53]

In general, the 1995 program was suffused with more traditional Marxist-Leninist modes of analysis than the 1994 draft, as already alluded to above. As one further example, the many references in the October version to a "bourgeois counterrevolution" were expunged from the final CPRF Program, doubtless to placate the more orthodox Marxist-Leninists, those for whom subversion and betrayal were more satisfactory explanations of the U.S.S.R.'s fate than the idea of a "bourgeois counterrevolution" under conditions of "developed socialism."

In addition, the January 1995 document included a rather lengthy analysis of the changing nature of productive labor in the twenty-first century, arguing that it would become "*predominantly intellectual*" in character.[54] While couched in Marxist terminology, this assessment was at the same time fully in line with Ziuganov's special emphasis on building bridges to non-party intellectuals. It was also consonant with the presence in the central party leadership of a large number of individuals with post-graduate degrees in what Western educators would call the arts and sciences. It was hardly coincidental that the Third CPRF Congress adopted as the party's new emblem "hammer, sickle, and book." On this theme we will have more to say in the next chapter.

References to pluralist politics and a mixed economy were, finally, watered down in the official CPRF program. The October 1994 draft had called for party pluralism and endorsed a mixed economy even under conditions of communist participation in a coalition "government of people's trust." The January 1995 document omitted the reference to multipartyism, as we have already noted, and it likewise circumscribed the extent and duration of a mixed economy. It did, to be sure, emphasize the use of "legal methods" to establish a "government of people's trust." But the function of such a coalition government was to "change the economic course" and implement "emergency measures of government regulation." And democratic elections and "freedom of speech and political associations" were approved only in the context of an explicit reference to Yuri V. Andropov's purported 1983 initiatives in these directions.[55]

Finally, as in the preliminary March 1994 program theses and the October 1994 draft, the "government of people's trust" was viewed as simply the first stage—signifying the implementation of the "minimum program"—in a three-stage transition to socialism. In the January 1995 program, however, the third stage of socialist transformation was explicitly identified with "Lenin's definition," namely, with an end to the "exploitation of man by man," a "classless society," and "scientific planning and management."[56]

The Third CPRF Congress, January 21–22, 1995: Mixed Signals

The proceedings of the Third CPRF Congress were sufficiently evocative of the Soviet-era CPSU congresses to enhance the impression of a turn to the left in the overall CPRF line. Of the 363 delegates elected by the party's regional organizations (345 were actually present at the congress), 42 were workers, 34 came from the agricultural sector, 68 were economic directors, and 73 were members of elected legislative bodies at the central or regional level; ten percent were under 40, eighty percent were between 40 and 60 years old, and the average age was between 40 and 50; but—in a striking departure from Soviet practice—eighty-six percent of the delegates had higher education, and seventy-one delegates had earned an advanced academic degree.[57] Ziuganov's formal report on behalf of the Central Executive Committee was followed by addresses by Shabanov, Kuptsov, Zorkaltsev, and Sergei A. Potapov dealing, respectively, with the drafting of the CPRF Program, changes in the party statutes, the work of the Duma fraction, and the congress's mandate committee.[58] The delegates voted in favor of the party leadership by a ratio of some ninety-five to five percent on all important documents and key questions.[59]

Furthermore, representatives of communist organizations from eight former Soviet republics as well as forty-five delegations of communist, socialist, and workers' parties from thirty-three countries around the world were the honored guests of the congress. The latter included such stalwart, unreconstructed Marxist-Leninist organizations as the Communist Party of Iraq, the Italian Party of Communist Refoundation, the Korean Workers' Party, the Communist Party of Cuba, the Portuguese Communist Party, the Communist Party of Slovakia, the French Communist Party, the Hungarian Workers' Party, and the Communist Party of the U.S.A.[60] As a final fillip, the new leadership organ elected by the congress delegates was named once again the "Central Committee" of the CPRF.

There were a number of reasons for the leftward shift suggested by the contents of the official CPRF Program adopted by the Third Congress. Among them was growing popular disillusionment with the Yeltsin regime during the second half of 1994 and the left-wing opposition's consequent flexing of its muscles both in the Duma and on the streets. This heightened boldness was evidenced by a motion of no-confidence in the government of Prime Minister Viktor Chernomyrdin brought before the Duma on October 27, 1994. Although the motion received only 194 of the absolute majority of 226 votes required for passage, that was partly because of Yeltsin's surprise appointment earlier the same day of Agrarian Party Duma deputy Aleksandr G. Nazarchuk to the post of minister of agriculture.[61] As a result, nineteen members of the APR fraction declined to vote for the no-confidence resolution.[62] Ten days later, on the November 7 anniversary of the Great October Revolution, the CPRF joined with the main extra-parliamentary communist groups to organize well attended rallies in Moscow and other cities in a show of strength which contrasted sharply with the cowed passivity of the left-wing opposition the year before, in the aftermath of the October 1993 bloodshed.[63] Meanwhile, public discontent was fueled by the ruble's loss of one-quarter of its value in relation to the U.S. dollar on October 11, 1994 (Black Tuesday), by ever more frequent indications of Yeltsin's heavy drinking, and, in December, by the outbreak of war in Chechnia.

Mounting popular opposition to the political establishment also enhanced the appeal of the radical extra-parliamentary CPs, as was to be demonstrated in the December 1995 parliamentary elections when their bloc of candidates would outpoll both the APR and the reformist party of Yegor Gaidar. This, in turn, worked to the advantage of their associates among the CPRF's Marxist-Leninist modernizers. A prominent representative of the latter was Kosolapov, who, it will be recalled, was not only the leader of the "Leninist position" group within the CPRF but also a co-founder of the ultra-radical *Roskomsoiuz*. He himself later maintained that his group did influence the outcome of the deliberations on the final version of the CPRF Program, enabling it to become a "Marxist-Leninist document" even if Ziuganov was a "patriotic social democrat."[64] The self-congratulatory tone of this statement notwithstanding, in May 1995 the newly appointed CPRF secretary in charge of ideology, Nikolai G. Bindiukov, corroborated Kosolapov's claim. Not only had Kosolapov been a member of the Program Commission, Bindiukov confirmed, but some of his views had also been accepted; indeed, the ideology secretary continued, Kosolapov was too serious a scholar to remain in the CPRF if he did not agree with its Program.[65] The influence of the party's left-wing was further suggested by the presence in the final CPRF program of a more conciliatory approach to inter-CP disputes than Ziuganov was wont to display.[66]

Another reason for the more doctrinaire Marxist-Leninist tone of the final CPRF Program had to do with the fundamental shift in the "correlation of forces" that had occurred between the party base and the top leadership, especially when compared to the Soviet era. As related in Chapter 3, the CPRF's precursor, the RCP, had had its origins in a revolt by lower-level party functionaries and local activists against the Gorbachev leadership's reformism "from above." From the time of the February 1993 reconstitution of the party, documents relating to organizational matters had thus constantly affirmed the need to implement *authentic democratic centralism*, with the accent as much upon participatory decision-making as upon unity in the execution of decisions once made. Not coincidentally, such grassroots activism and initiative were also the dictate of necessity under conditions of competitive electoral politics: for the rank-and-file cadres were destined to be the CPRF's shock troops in the coming parliamentary and presidential election campaigns.

As the organizational network was revived, however, it soon became apparent that the local activists were often imbued with more traditionalist, albeit not necessarily dogmatic, Marxist-Leninist thinking than some of their leaders in the CPRF's Duma fraction offices.[67] Precisely because of the reconstituted party's commitment to genuine internal party democracy, these local cadres were evidently able to exert considerable influence on the formulation of the final party program. In the Ivanovo region, for instance, Ziuganov's positions on ethno-centric Russian nationalism were strongly criticized by delegates to the local CPRF conference convened to discuss the October 1994 plenum's draft program later that autumn.[68]

During 1993 and the first half of 1994, to be sure, organizational initiatives and policy directives came from the top down. This was all the more the case when, from early 1994 onward, the CPRF's Central Executive Committee was able to set up its headquarters in the offices of the party's Duma fraction. As Zorkaltsev spelled out in his report to the Second All-Russian Party Conference in April 1994, "The CEC apparatus has been set up at the fraction's expense. The CEC uses the premises, resources, and material supplies of the fraction."[69] A month later Ziuganov elaborated on this theme during a meeting with students and faculty at Moscow State University. While discussing the importance of the party's work in the regions, he pointed out that the CPRF leadership maintained its ties to the localities by means of the "channels of communication the State Duma put at the disposal of the fraction."[70] (He added, however, that operational contacts between the center and periphery were carried out by 100 activists paid from party funds.)

On the other hand, the need to improve the two-way flow of information between the leadership and the base was also emphasized at the April 1994 All-Russian Party Conference. A concrete step in this direction was taken early the following autumn. From September 21 through October 5, 1994, a so-called "All-Russian Party Meeting" took place for the express purpose of launching a campaign to collect signatures in support of a referendum calling for early presidential elections. But an important secondary reason was to take the political pulse of the rank-and-file party membership. During this fifteen-day period some eight thousand party meetings were held in which "just under 500 thousand party members and almost 150 thousand supporters of the party" participated.[71]

At the CPRF's Ninth Plenum on October 22, 1994, Kuptsov reported on what transpired during this massive undertaking. First of all, by then over a million signatures had been collected (just two months later, reported Ziuganov at the Third Congress, that figure had increased to over three million).[72] Plainly this augured well—indeed, it constituted a virtual dry-run—for the party's future collection of the signatures required to nominate candidates for the parliamentary elections in December 1995 and the presidential election in June 1996.

Equally significant, however, were Kuptsov's disclosures regarding party sentiments at the grassroots. He emphasized in particular that communists in the localities had "*insistently advanced proposals for the speedier formulation of a draft Party Program*, for its discussion in the primary party organizations and approval at the Third CPRF Congress."[73] These local activists were, moreover, interested in "theoretical questions" and the "significance of ideology" for the party. "In a word," he concluded, "a theoretical deficit can be observed." Kuptsov also reported that at the local level members of the extra-parliamentary CPs were also participating in the signature collection campaign despite opposition to this venture by their respective party leaderships.[74] It is safe to assume that, in their joint canvassing for signatures, members of the CPRF and the radical left CPs also exchanged "theoretical" views.

As already noted, the draft CPRF Program unveiled at the Ninth Plenum was distributed for critical review to all lower party organizations. Indeed, the plenum directed "party committees at all levels to organize a discussion of the draft CPRF Program and to send their comments to the CPRF CEC by December 20, 1994."[75] According to Ziuganov's opening report to the Third Congress in January 1995, the CEC had received "hundreds" of comments and suggestions on the draft from both party bodies and individuals.[76] Shabanov summed up the crux of those recommendations in his congress report on this party-wide discussion. In a nutshell, he declared that the majority of communists had spoken out in favor of "the development of Marxist-Leninist teaching" and that the fundamental conceptual basis of the new program was "Marxist theory in its contemporary form."[77] The CPRF's Moscow city leader, Aleksandr A. Kuvaev, pointedly summed up the situation in his speech to the Third Congress: "Now, after the approval of the new party Program, our [ultra-leftist] opponents have no basis for accusing us of social democratism."[78]

Shabanov also disclosed that the program commission was aided in its work of revision by an advisory group composed primarily of members of the Central Council of the Society of Russian Scholars of a Socialist Orientation.[79] This organization, known by its acronym RUSO, had held its founding congress on October 1, 1994, at which time 192 delegates elected a Central Council of eighty-seven scholars, some sixteen of whom were members of the CPRF's Central Executive Committee. While that group of sixteen included Slavin, who was an anti-Stalin reformer and Marxist internationalist, the key organizers of RUSO were the Marxist-Leninist modernizers Osadchii and Kosolapov.[80]

In short, we may surmise that the relatively orthodox Marxist-Leninist cast of the official CPRF Program was the result of influences emanating both from the party base and from Marxist-Leninist scholars who were more traditionalist in their thinking than those closely associated with Ziuganov. Shabanov stated in his above-cited report that the final version was adopted "unanimously" at the last session of the program commission. This was most likely the case. For at a CEC meeting prior to the Third Congress, Slavin was the sole participant to speak out against the document approved by the program commission. When he insisted that the party reaffirm the 20th CPSU Congress's criticisms of Stalin, Ziuganov retorted that Slavin should read Belov's articles on Stalin, "The Statesman Genius." Soon thereafter Slavin became the first notable ex-communist in the post-Soviet Russian communist movement.[81]

The implications of this programmatic denouement for the political complexion of the top leadership organs approved at the CPRF's Third Congress will be discussed in Chapter 7. Here suffice it to say that while Ziuganov was overwhelmingly supported for reelection as party chairman, he presided over an organization which remained deeply divided on political-ideological questions and thus, potentially, on key issues of party strategy and public policy.

The new CPRF program, by sending mixed signals regarding the party's ultimate objectives, served to paper over these differences, just as it helped to blunt the ultra-leftist CPs' charges of "right-wing opportunism." But it was ill-suited for the national election campaigns which lay ahead. Indeed, the CPRF's opponents, particularly in the 1996 presidential race, would find it all too easy to use the more doctrinaire elements in the January 1995 program to undermine the credibility of Ziuganov and his party on such matters as respect for the democratic process, the endorsement of a mixed economy, and the normalization of relations with the West.

Notes

1. "Chto delat dalshe?: Doklad Gennadiia Ziuganova na plenume TsIK KPRF 15 marta 1994 goda," *Sovetskaia Rossiia*, March 17, 1994, p. 3.
2. Galina Orekhanova, "Yurii Belov: Dorozhu chuvstvom ravenstva," *Sovetskaia Rossiia*, March 17, 1994, p. 2.
3. Yurii Belov, "KPRF: partiia staraia ili novaia?" *Pravda*, March 15, 1994, p. 2; emphasis added.
4. *Sovetskaia Rossiia*, March 17, 1994, p. 3.
5. *Pravda Rossii*, No. 11; see insert in *Sovetskaia Rossiia*, March 24, 1994, p. 3.
6. Ibid.
7. Ibid.; emphasis added.
8. Authors' interview with Shabanov in the CPRF's Duma fraction offices, May 27, 1994. Shabanov was silent on the future of Moldova.
9. This was implied during the interview cited in the preceding note. To be sure, Shabanov was not speaking of the Marxist-Leninist modernizers per se but of the many "older members" of the CPRF who insisted on seeing the "goal" of stage three incorporated into the party program.
10. J. B. Urban's interview with Boris Slavin in the editorial offices of *Pravda* on December 14, 1995.
11. Galina Orekhanova, "Aprelskaia konferentsiia devianosto chetvertogo," *Sovetskaia Rossiia*, April 26, 1994, p. 1.
12. Ivan Boltovskii, "Aprelskie tezisy yzhe est," *Pravda*, April 26, 1994, p. 1; emphasis added.
13. Orekhanova, "Aprelskaia konferentsiia," *Sovetskaia Rossiia*, April 26, 1994, p. 1; emphasis added.
14. This was reported by Viktor Zorkaltsev in his report to the CPRF's Second All-Russian Conference in April 1994; see note 17 below.
15. For Ziuganov's reflections on that trip, which took place the first week in April, see the second edition of *Derzhava* (Moscow: Informpechat, 1994), pp. 129–162; they also appeared under the title "Imperiia i imperialisty. K 200-letiiu Amerikanskoi mechty," in *Nash sovremennik*, No. 8 (1994).
16. "Za Delo naroda, Vo imia otechestva: Doklad predsedatelia Tsik KPRF G. Ziuganov," *Sovetskaia Rossiia*, April 26, 1994, p. 2; cf. "O politicheskom i eko-

nomicheskom polozhenii v Rossii i zadachakh partii: Doklad Predsedatelia Tsik KPRF tov. G. A. Ziuganova," *Materialy Vserossiiskoi konferentsii Kommunisticheskoi partii Rossiiskoi Federatsii* (Moscow, 1994), pp. 4–18.

17. "Otchet fraktsii 'Kommunisticheskaia partiia Rossiiskoi Federatsii' v Gosudarstvennoi Dume Federalnogo Sobraniia RF: Doklad zamestitelia Predsedatelia Tsik KPRF tov. V. I. Zorkaltseva," ibid., pp. 19–27.

18. "Za organizatsionnoe ukreplenie partii: Doklad pervogo zamestitelia Predsedatelia Tsik KPRF tov. V. A. Kuptsova," ibid., pp. 28–40 at p. 31.

19. Ibid., p. 33.

20. "Rezoliutsiia 'Ob organizatsionnom ukreplenii partii,'" ibid., pp. 47–50 at p. 49.

21. "Za organizatsionnoe ukreplenie partii," ibid., p. 39.

22. "Rezoliutsiia 'O patriotizme i otnoshenii k praviashchemu rezhimu'," ibid, pp. 64–68. The document was also published in *Sovetskaia Rossiia*, April 28, 1994, p. 2.

23. "Kommunisticheskaia partiia Rossiiskoi Federatsii na puti k soglasiiu vo imia Rossii," *Materialy Vserossiiskoi konferentsii*, pp. 70–78. The text was also published in *Glasnost*, No. 8, May 27–June 2, 1994, pp. 4–5.

24. This linkage to Yeltsin's initiative was spelled out in the resolution, "Ob otnoshenii k proektu, 'Dogovora ob obshchestvennom soglasii'," *Materialy Vserossiiskoi konferentsii*, p. 69.

25. For the text of the revised theses, see ibid., pp. 51–63.

26. The remaining three signatories were Valerii D. Zorkin, former chief justice of the Constitutional Court; Mikhail I. Lapshin, head of the Agrarian Party of Russia; and A. Shilov, a well-known artist. The appeal itself was first drafted by Prokhanov and then revised in its final version by Tsipko.

27. Joan Barth Urban, *Moscow and the Italian Communist Party: From Togliatti to Berlinguer* (Ithaca, NY: Cornell University Press, 1986), Chapter 5.

28. In East Europe the national front movements, variously named, became mass organizational facades for communist-party domination in the mid-to-late 1940s. In West Europe the Italian Communist Party participated in the broad-based Committee of National Liberation during the wartime Resistance, while in France the Communist-dominated National Front cooperated but did not unite with other anti-Nazi groups. In both Italy and France, however, the communist parties participated as minority partners in authentically democratic coalition governments during the mid-1940s. See ibid.

29. Each member of the "initiative group" was entitled to invite thirty to forty supporters to this National Council meeting; the authors of this book received invitations from Tsipko. See Yelena Chepkasova and Yevgenii Krasnikov, "Radikaldemokraty reshali, kakoi budet partiia novogo tipa: Oppozitsiia oseniu izberet 'tenevoe pravitelstvo,'" *Nezavisimaia gazeta*, May 31, 1994, p. 1.

30. Ibid.; also Dmitrii Kuznets and Gleb Cherkasov, "Nachalas dvunadesiataia popytka obedineniia oppozitsii," *Segodnia*, May 31, 1994, p. 3. A week earlier, Rutskoi had publicly disclosed his doubts about the "Accord in the Name of Russia" movement and his preference for building a strong "right-wing" opposition before becoming too closely involved with it; see Gleb Cherkasov, "10 shagov ot propasti," *Segodnia*, May 24, 1994, p. 3.

31. See, for example, the lengthy interview with Ziuganov in *Nezavisimaia gazeta*, November 4, 1994, p. 5.

32. See the joint declaration, "Russkii rubezh: Ot Kaliningrada do Kuril," signed by the major political leaders attending the congress in *Interviu: Zdravyi smysl*, No. 11 (14), 1994, p. 1.

33. Text in *III Sezd Kommunisticheskoi Partii Rossiiskoi Federatsii: Materialy i Dokumenty* (Moscow: Informpechat, 1995), p. 26.

34. Ibid., pp. 27–28.

35. Text in *Materialy IX Plenuma Tsentralnogo Ispolnitelnogo Komiteta KPRF* (Moscow: 1994), pp. 46–63 at pp. 49–50.

36. *Programma Kommunisticheskoi partii Rossiiskoi Federatsii* (Moscow: "Informpechat," 1995), pp. 7–9; emphasis in the original.

37. *Materialy IX Plenuma*, pp. 50–51.

38. Ibid., p. 51.

39. Gennadii Ziuganov, "Russia and the Contemporary World," *The Brown Journal of World Affairs*, Vol. II, No. 2 (Summer 1995): 123; this translation is an abridged version of Ziuganov's *Rossiia i sovremennyi mir* (Moscow: Informpechat, 1995).

40. *Programma Kommunisticheskoi partii Rossiiskoi Federatsii*, p. 13; emphasis in the original.

41. *Materialy IX Plenuma*, pp. 59–61.

42. *Programma Kommunisticheskoi partii Rossiiskoi Federatsii*, p. 28.

43. Ibid., p. 23; emphasis added.

44. *Materialy IX Plenuma*, pp. 52 and 57.

45. *Programma Kommunisticheskoi partii Rossiiskoi Federatsii*, p. 20.

46. *Materialy IX Plenuma*, p. 47.

47. Here it is worth quoting the program verbatim: "Gorbachev and Yakovlev, Yeltsin and Shevardnadze bear personal responsibility for betrayal of the party, for neglect of the national interests, for the destruction of our Fatherland." See *Programma Kommunisticheskoi partii Rossiiskoi Federatsii*, p. 18.

48. Ibid., pp. 16–17.

49. Ibid., p. 19.

50. *Materialy IX Plenuma*, pp. 46–47.

51. *Programma Kommunisticheskoi partii Rossiiskoi Federatsii*, p. 5.

52. Ibid.; see also pp. 21–22 and 26.

53. Ibid., p. 6; emphasis added. The October 1994 draft referred simply to "Marxist-Leninist teaching."

54. Ibid., pp. 9–11; emphasis in the original.

55. Ibid., p. 17.

56. Ibid., pp. 21–22.

57. "Doklad mandatnoi komissii," *III Sezd Kommunisticheskoi partii Rossiiskoi Federatsii*, pp. 61–62; cf. "Vpered—k sotsializmu!" *Pravda*, January 24, 1995, pp. 1 and 3. One delegate was elected for every 1,400 party members.

58. A report was also delivered on the work of the Central Control-Auditing Commission.

59. *Sovetskaia Rossiia*, January 26, 1995, p. 3. For a synopsis of the criticisms of the proposed CPRF program which were voiced even at the congress, only to be decisively voted down, see the account in *Glasnost*, No. 5–6 (180), February 1–14, 1995, pp. 4–5.

60. The complete list of foreign communist delegations was published in *III Sezd Kommunisticheskoi partii RF*, pp. 122–128. Ziuganov, it might be noted, had represented the CPRF at the 28th Congress of the French Communist Party in January 1994; see *L'Humanité* (Paris), January 26, 1994, p. 15.

61. Nazarchuk replaced Viktor Khlystun, who had reportedly proferred his resignation several months earlier for reasons of poor health. However, in the spring of 1996, after the APR's poor showing in the December 1995 parliamentary elections, Khlystun returned to the post of minister of agriculture.

62. *Raznogolositsa*, No. 42 (October 24–30, 1994): 24.

63. On November 6, 1994, Ziuganov led a solemn procession of several thousand CPRF activists to the Lenin Mausoleum, while the next day some fifty to seventy-five thousand leftists of all stripes marched in orderly formation from October Square to the center of Moscow to celebrate the seventy-seventh anniversary of the Bolshevik Revolution; personal observations of the authors.

64. J. B. Urban's interview with Richard I. Kosolapov at Moscow State University, May 22, 1995.

65. J. B. Urban's interview with Nikolai G. Bindiukov in the CPRF's Duma fraction offices, May 26, 1995.

66. Compare the October draft, *Materialy IX Plenuma*, p. 61, to *Programma Kommunisticheskoi partii RF*, p. 29.

67. On this point, see the findings from a study of voting behavior before and after the 1993 Duma elections in Mathew Wyman, Bill Miller, Stephen White and Paul Heywood, "Parties and Voters in the Elections," in Peter Lentini, ed., *Elections and Political Order in Russia* (Budapest: Central European University Press, 1995), esp. pp. 136–139.

68. This information was conveyed to the authors by a member of the Ivanovo city party committee, a woman in her sixties who was an anti-Stalin Marxist internationalist. The authors were the guests of the Ivanovo city and regional CPRF committees on June 13, 1996. This whole subject of local CPRF attitudes and structures is in need of systematic field research.

69. Zorkaltsev, "Otchet Fraktsii 'Kommunisticheskoi partii Rossiiskoi Federatsii' v Gosudarstvennoi Dume," *Materialy Vserossiiskoi konferentsii*, p. 26.

70. Viktor Khamraev, "KPRF rasschityvaet mirno vstat k ruliu: Gosduma stala dlia partii bolshim podsporem," *Segodnia*, May 21, 1994.

71. "O sostoiavshemsia IX plenume TsIK KPRF," *Informatsionnyi biulleten*, No. 9, October 25, 1994, p. 3.

72. See Ziuganov's keynote report, *III Sezd Kommunisticheskoi partii RF*, p. 20; cf. Valentin Kuptsov's report on the "All-Russian Party meeting" and the signature campaign in *Materialy IX Plenuma*, pp. 27–33.

73. Ibid., p. 32; emphasis in the original.

74. Ibid., p. 30.

75. "Dokumenty IX Plenuma," *Materialy IX Plenuma*, p. 40.

76. Ziuganov's report, *III Sezd Kommunisticheskoi partii RF*, p. 25.

77. See the report of A. A. Shabanov in *III Sezd Kommunisticheskoi partii RF*, p. 46.

78. Paraphrased in *Glasnost*, No. 5–6 (180), February 1–14, 1996, p. 4.

79. Shabanov, *III Sezd Kommunisticheskoi partii RF*, p. 46.

80. I. Osadchii, "Informatsia o podgotovke i provedenii Uchreditelnogo Sezda Obshchestva 'Rossiiskie uchenye sotsialisticheskoi orientatsii' (RUSO)," *Informatsionnyi biulleten*, No. 8, October 10, 1994, pp. 31–33.

81. J. B. Urban's interviews with Boris F. Slavin in the editorial offices of *Pravda*, December 5 and 14, 1995. In mid-1995 Slavin became an adviser to Sviatoslav Fedorov, whose program he drafted for the 1996 presidential campaign.

7

On the Campaign Trail:
The CPRF's Electoral Strategy

If the January 1995 congress brought to a close the CPRF's process of for-mulating its official party program, it also marked the start of the party's preparations for the Russian Federation's December 1995 parliamentary elections and mid-1996 presidential race. The nineteen-member Presidium and five-man Secretariat named at the time of the Third CPRF Congress would determine the electoral strategy in both contests and steer the party's ranks along their campaign trails. Inasmuch as nine of the top twenty-one ongoing or newly designated CPRF leaders (three of them were simultane-ously members of the Presidium and Secretariat) had been elected Duma deputies in December 1993, the party's Duma fraction offices had already been transformed into its de facto national headquarters. This situation was further facilitated by the Duma's mid-1994 move to the refurbished and en-larged former Gosplan building in downtown Moscow, just off Red Square. Moreover, as a result of the December 1995 parliamentary elections, the number of preeminent CPRF leaders who became Duma deputies rose from nine to nineteen (see Table 7.1), thereby highlighting the party's intent to make the legislative branch of government its organizational locus.

This chapter begins with a discussion of the CPRF's new leadership group as well as an analysis of where its individual members fit according to the classification scheme we have developed with regard to the party's activist core. In the second and third sections we will examine the campaign strate-gies pursued during the successive parliamentary and presidential contests. By way of preliminary overview, it is important to underscore the very differ-ent character of the CPRF's approaches to these respective electoral races.

During the campaign for the new State Duma, the party sought to demar-cate itself sharply from electoral blocs immediately to its left and right and to mobilize its rank-and-file members to get out the vote exclusively for the CPRF's party list candidates and nominees in single-member districts. To this end, the CPRF election platform published in late summer 1995 enumerated

TABLE 7.1   Members of CPRF Presidium and/or Secretariat, 1993–1995

Date of Appointment to Presidium	Elected to Duma, 1993	Elected to Duma, 1995
*February 24, 1993**		
Gennadii A. Ziuganov	✓	✓
Yurii P. Belov		✓
Svetlana P. Goriacheva (resigned late 1993)		(✓)
Valentin A. Kuptsov		✓
(Mikhail I. Lapshin—removed April 1994)	(✓)	
(Ivan P. Rybkin—removed April 1994)	(✓)	
Viktor I. Zorkaltsev	✓	✓
*March 20, 1993**		
Anatolii V. Ionov	✓	✓
Valentin A. Koptiug		
Georgii V. Kostin		✓
Ivan I. Melnikov (also Secretariat as of January 1995)		✓
Aleksandr A. Shabanov		✓
Mikhail S. Surkov		✓
*May 29, 1993**		
Valentin I. Nikitin	✓	✓
Kazbek A. Tsiku	✓	✓
April 24, 1994		
Anatolii I. Lukianov	✓	✓
January 22, 1995		
Alevtina V. Aparina	✓	✓
Nikolai G. Bindiukov (Secretariat only)	✓	✓
Gennadii E. Gamza		✓
Leonid A. Ivanchenko		✓
Viktor P. Peshkov (also Secretariat)		✓
Sergei A. Potapov (also Secretariat)		✓
Gennadii N. Seleznev (Secretariat only)**	✓	✓
Viktor M. Vidmanov (resigned his deputy seat after election)		✓

*Information supplied by personnel in the CPRF Duma fraction offices. Other dates of appointment are part of the public record, as indicated in the following pages.
**Seleznev moved from the Secretariat to the Presidium in May 1996.

a set of proposals which were tantamount to the first stage of the three-stage transition to socialism set forth in the official party program approved in January 1995. The outcome was an indisputable electoral success, especially given the distorting effect of proportional representation combined with the five percent barrier. The CPRF won only 22.3 percent of the party list vote, but that was about double the returns of its nearest competitor and it netted the communists over one third of the deputies elected to the Duma on December 17, 1995. The party's de facto organizational headquarters thus came close to controlling the parliamentary body in which it was housed.

The campaign strategy adopted for the presidential race was, in contrast, targeted to a much broader political spectrum, as required by the constitutional stipulation that the chief executive be elected by an absolute majority of the votes cast. In a nutshell, the CPRF embraced the classic national front stratagem long advocated by Gennadii A. Ziuganov. As the presidential candidate not only of the CPRF but also of the so-called "people's-patriotic forces of Russia," Ziuganov was initially backed by a conglomeration of figurehead or token organizations, characterized by small and often overlapping memberships, which were little more than "communist fronts" according to the conventional usage of that term. By late March–early April 1996, however, Ziuganov's candidacy had won the support of groups ranging from Viktor I. Anpilov's ultra-leftist "Toiling Russia" bloc to Sergei N. Baburin's center-left Russian All-People's Union and Aleksandr V. Rutskoi's *Derzhava* movement.

This decisive broadening of the scope of the "people's-patriotic forces" can be partly attributed to the CPRF-initiated Duma resolution of March 15, 1996, which repudiated, if only symbolically, the legality of the Belovezhskie agreements. For the reestablishment of the U.S.S.R. was a non-negotiable demand of the left-wing radicals represented by Anpilov, whose "Communists–Toiling Russia–for a Soviet Union" bloc won an impressive 4.53 percent of the votes in the December 1995 Duma elections. At the same time, however, in order to appeal to more centrist groups, Ziuganov's personal election platform published toward the end of March 1996 was notable for its sweeping populism and absence of allusions to anything resembling a traditional communist program.

In Chapter 8 we will turn to an analysis of the reasons for the CPRF's relative success in the Duma elections and outright defeat in the presidential contest. That discussion will also include an examination of the demographic and sociological profile of the CPRF's electorate. We will, by way of conclusion, take a look at alternative scenarios of the Russian communist movement's future evolution.

The Political Profile of the CPRF
Leadership After the January 1995 Congress

The most striking aspect of the enlarged CPRF leadership group named at the Third CPRF Congress was the preponderance within it of individuals whom we have designated as Marxist reformers and Russian nationalists. The Marxist-Leninist modernizers, whose influence upon the final version of the CPRF

Program—as recounted in Chapter 6—was so pronounced, did not receive commensurate recognition in the party's new presidium. Apparently, the Ziuganov nationalists and the Marxist reformers agreed to make concessions to the Marxist-Leninist modernizers during the final deliberations on the party program in order to placate the traditionalists at the party's grassroots and to consolidate the party's ranks in general. But neither the Marxist reformers nor the nationalists were prepared to concede to their more orthodox colleagues a substantial role in the CPRF Presidium, the party's top policy-making body.

A second conspicuous feature of the post-congress CPRF leadership was the growing number of its members who were originally academics rather than party or state functionaries. Their presence was reflected in the newly devised CPRF emblem, "hammer, sickle, *and book*,"[1] which was endorsed by the Third Congress. Their influence may have been responsible for Ziuganov's quasi-intellectual aspirations, evidenced by his defense of a doctoral dissertation at Moscow State University in the spring of 1995. More to the point, they were representative of a sizable body of Russian research institute personnel, university faculty, and school teachers who deeply resented the post-Soviet order not only because of the socio-economic degradation they had suffered but also because their research funds had dried up or because they as individuals were unwilling or unable to adapt to the new approaches to history, philosophy, and the social sciences which had been sweeping the Russian academic world since the advent of *glasnost* in the late 1980s. The addition of "book" to the traditional communist symbol of "hammer and sickle" thus not only accorded long overdue recognition to the Soviet-era intelligentsia; it was also designed to appeal to this stratum of psychologically disoriented and politically alienated Russian citizens.

Last but not least with regard to the new CPRF Presidium, Ziuganov continued to exercise paramount leadership in matters of overall policy and electoral campaign strategy. This would become ever more clear as the CPRF geared up for the parliamentary and presidential elections scheduled for December 1995 and June 1996. But from the self-assured tone of Ziuganov's closing speech to the Third Congress the morning of January 23, 1995, it was already apparent that no substantive challenge to his personal authority had been posed during the conclave's proceedings.

Ziuganov's concluding comments were notable both for their candor and for the insight they provided into several internal party organizational issues, not to mention the chairman's own views.[2] Overall, his remarks were delivered in the customary CPSU format of answers to questions raised by delegates to the congress. A number of these queries were rather unexceptional and self-explanatory, for instance, those dealing with the CPRF's call for early elections, for restrictions on presidential power, and for the legalization of primary party organizations in the workplace as well as the party's attitude toward the various neocommunist groups (Ziuganov's reply on this last point has already been discussed in Chapter 5).

Some of the other questions, however, lent themselves to more pointed responses or revelations and thus appeared only in the version published in the party's internal-circulation *Informatsionnyi biulleten*. When asked his opinion of Duma speaker Ivan P. Rybkin, for example, Ziuganov compared him to Gorbachev and Aleksandr N. Yakovlev: to wit, each could just as easily switch from social democracy to fascism since not one of them had "a system of views or a conscience or knowledge or elementary convictions."[3] This pejorative comment was omitted from accounts of the Third Congress aimed at the broader public.

When asked about the role of the CPRF at the local level, moreover, Ziuganov replied that in regional elections its candidates had won some 46 percent of the vote. But that was far from the whole story, he informed the assembled activists. For in late September 1991, the banned RCP leaders had called upon all qualified party loyalists to enter into government service, "above all in the localities. . . . *Many of them did not disclose themselves to you, and still do not reveal that they are members of the Communist Party of the Russian Federation*."[4] Not surprisingly, the information about this September 1991 directive was also deleted from the more public accounts.

When asked which members of the Central Executive Committee were responsible for "ideological work," the CPRF chairman said that they included above all himself, Yurii P. Belov, and Ivan I. Melnikov.[5] We shall return to the implications of this reply a bit later in this section.

The final query to which Ziuganov turned his attention had to do with the problem posed by the Yeltsin regime's control over television. He conceded that the government officials "use this hellish machine in a downright satanic manner."[6] But he reassured his listeners that the CPRF's methods of person-to-person contacts and one-on-one persuasion were much more effective.

He also used this issue as a launching pad for a discussion of the party's press and ideological positions in general. On the one hand, Ziuganov announced that the CPRF would soon begin putting out a weekly edition of its newspaper, *Pravda Rossii* (which had hitherto been simply an occasional insert in *Pravda*) as well as a local news circular, *Pravda Moskvy*.[7] On the other hand, he recommended a number of already published materials with which all party members should familiarize themselves, including Belov's highly controversial article, "Gosudarstvennyi genii [State genius]: Stalin i Rossiia"; Anatolii I. Lukianov's political analyses; Viktor I. Iliukhin's *Otechestvo v opasnosti* (The Fatherland is in Danger); and his own recent book, *Za Gorizontom*. With regard to the latter, Ziuganov remarked that its focus was "contemporary geopolitics and the struggle of civilizations at the end of the second millennium."[8] As discussed at the beginning of Chapter 5, the crux of the CPRF chairman's geopolitical views was that conflict and competition between Russia and the West, led by the U.S.A., was a permanent and ineluctable feature of the international scene and would continue to be so at least into the early part of the twenty-first century.

Ziuganov closed on the following rather ambivalent but by now familiar note. While he personally preferred "communal property" and "the collective way of life," under present conditions, he declared, it would be impossible for any ruling group "to expropriate everything." Instead, it would be necessary to win the support of the patriotic intelligentsia and indigenous Russian entrepreneurs in order to find specialists capable of governing the country. A "union of state patriotic forces" was thus the order of the day.[9]

The Third CPRF Congress concluded with the election of a Central Committee (formerly Central Executive Committee) of some 140 full members and 25 candidate members, with an additional three dozen or so individuals assigned to the less prestigious Central Control-Auditing Commission (CCAC). On January 22, 1995, the new Central Committee formally approved a nineteen-member Presidium, five-man Secretariat, and CCAC chairman.[10] Heading the list of Presidium members were the three previously top-ranking leaders: Ziuganov as party chairman; Valentin A. Kuptsov as first deputy chairman; and Aleksandr A. Shabanov as deputy chairman. As has been mentioned many times, Kuptsov stood out as a Marxist reformer, especially at the Second CPRF Congress, while Shabanov was Ziuganov's aide in the party's Duma headquarters and a like-minded fervent Russian nationalist.

Before analyzing the political profile of the new leadership bodies, a few more words are in order regarding the growing significance of individuals with higher education in the CPRF. Among the 363 delegates to the Third Congress (chosen according to the norm of one delegate for every 1,400 party members), some 86 percent had received a higher education and 71 had earned an advanced academic degree.[11] Among the former and continuing members of the Presidium, four were known for their academic backgrounds: Shabanov, Valentin A. Koptiug, Kazbek A. Tsiku, and Ivan Melnikov. Shabanov, born in 1935, had spent most of his adult life as a researcher and teacher of physical chemistry at Moscow State University, where he was at one time deputy secretary of the university's local CPSU organization and, during the late Gorbachev era, head of the party organization in the faculty of chemistry.[12] Koptiug was a professor of organic chemistry, a vice-chairman of the Russian Academy of Sciences as well as the head of its prestigious Siberian branch, and widely renowned as a deeply committed protagonist of environmental protection.[13] Tsiku, like Shabanov born in 1935, was a political economist from the Republic of Adygeia, in the Krasnodar region (*krai*), who had been a professor since 1964 and later a department chairman at the Adygeia State Pedagogical

Institute. He was elected to the Duma on the CPRF party list in December 1993.[14]

Melnikov was a younger mathematician from Moscow State University who was born in 1950 into a family of government workers in the Tula region. A CPSU member since 1972, Melnikov had been first secretary of the university's party organization from 1988 through 1991, a time when its members numbered some 8,000 (of whom about half were graduate students and half were teaching and staff personnel). At the 28th CPSU Congress in July 1990 he was elected to the party's Central Committee, and at the first post-congress plenum he was selected as one of five Secretariat members who did not carry the specific designation of secretary (although in mid-1991 he did receive the formal title of "secretary"). Melnikov insisted, however, on keeping his teaching position at the university throughout his involvement in the leading bodies of the CPSU, an unusual request for those times but one to which Gorbachev personally consented.[15]

Melnikov's activity as one of the communists' official defenders during the Constitutional Court's 1992 hearings on the "CPSU case" has already been mentioned in Chapter 3. In January 1995, as indicated in Table 7.1, he was reappointed to the CPRF Presidium and also became a member of the party's Secretariat, which was established for the first time at the Third Congress. At the party's Second Plenum in March 1995 Melnikov was also put in charge of "international ties," in what was probably a move on the part of the leadership to project a younger and more educated image to the outside world.

A fifth academic figure, Nikolai G. Bindiukov, joined the CPRF leadership as one of its new secretaries. Born in 1946 in the Belorussian S.S.R. and an ethnic Belarusan, Bindiukov studied philosophy at Leningrad State University and later (1979–1982) completed graduate work at the Institute of Sociological Research of the Soviet Academy of Sciences. From 1982 until his election to the Duma on the CPRF party list in December 1993, he worked at the Novgorod State Pedagogical Institute, first as a professor, then as an academic administrator, and finally as rector. He was elected to the original Russian Communist Party's Central Committee in 1990 and to the CPRF Central Executive Committee in February 1993.[16] At the party's March 1995 plenum Bindiukov was given responsibility for "ideological work."[17]

Here it should be noted that three additional CPRF loyalists were named to the newly created CPRF Secretariat at the Third Congress: Gennadii N. Seleznev, Viktor P. Peshkov, and Sergei A. Potapov. Seleznev was born in 1947 in the Sverdlovsk region and graduated from Leningrad State University in 1974. A CPSU member since 1970, he became involved early on in both Komsomol work and journalism. He was editor-in-chief of *Komsomolskaia pravda* from 1980 through 1988 and of *Uchitelskaia gazeta* (Teacher's Gazette) from December 1988 until February 1991. He then became first deputy editor of *Pravda* and later, from the August 1991 failed putsch until the October 1993 crisis, its editor-in-chief. In the aftermath of the latter crisis, he was removed by presidential decree from *Pravda*'s top post but remained on its editorial board. And in December 1993 he was elected on the CPRF's party list to the Duma, where he served on the Committee on Information Policy.[18] During the last few months of the Duma elected in 1993, he also served as a deputy speaker. In March 1995, after being appointed to the party's Secretariat, Seleznev was given responsibility for the CPRF's "information policy" and appointed editor-in-chief of its new weekly newspaper, *Pravda Rossii*.

Because Seleznev was elected speaker of the State Duma in January 1996, much more information is available on his background than on that of Peshkov and Potapov. Peshkov, about the same age as Ziuganov with a background in the aerospace industry, was a nationalist-oriented aide to the CPRF chairman and the head of his personal protection service. Almost nothing, however, was known about Potapov beyond his age, which was the same as Melnikov's. At the CPRF plenum in March 1995, Peshkov was put in charge of the coming electoral campaigns and Potapov was assigned responsibility for the party's "organizational work."[19]

Before turning to a discussion of the larger policy-making CPRF Presidium, including its ongoing and newly appointed members, a few more words are in order with regard to the political outlook of the CPRF's new five-man Secretariat. Only Bindiukov may be classified as a Marxist-Leninist modernizer. Perhaps because of this he was appointed to the Secretariat and also assigned to "ideological work," presumably in a move to counterbalance the influence of Ziuganov, Belov, and Melnikov in this sphere. But by the same token, he was not elevated to the party's more powerful Presidium. A member of the RCP's original Central Committee in 1990, Bindiukov mentioned in an interview in May 1995 that he was well acquainted with Viktor A. Tiulkin and had attended meetings of the Russian Communist Workers' Party in St. Petersburg, even contributing his own money to its local newspaper, *Narodnaia Pravda*. He also spoke respectfully of Richard I. Kosolapov, the head of the "Leninist position" group within the CPRF. Most significantly, he drew a sharp distinction between the CPRF's positions and West European social democracy of the Swedish or German type. The latter, he argued, did not aim to create socialism nor did they believe that state property should constitute a larger sector of the economy than private property. He also pointed out that he was one of seven siblings from a rural family, all of whom had completed secondary school and specialized higher education. This, he insisted, would never have been possible in a Western society.[20]

As for his work in the Duma, Bindiukov was an active proponent of legislation to preserve the Lenin Mausoleum on Red Square along with all other memorials to the founder of the Soviet state. His most significant act as a lawmaker, however, was his presentation to the Duma of the CPRF's sensational mid-March 1996 resolution renouncing the Belovezhskie agreements.[21]

Seleznev was the only other CPRF secretary who was not also a member of the party's Presidium. In other respects, however, he differed substantially from Bindiukov. For one thing, in a January 1996 interview he spoke openly of his interest in the "Swedish model of socialism," adding that it had adopted much of what was best in the former Soviet Union[22] (presumably, what Seleznev had in mind was Sweden's extensive social welfare system). For another, he spelled out the ways in which the January 1995 CPRF Program embodied what were once considered controversial "Eurocommunist" positions: support for a multi-party system; the relinquishment of atheism as a prerequisite to party membership; the abandonment of the ideas of a "leading party" and the "dictatorship of the proletariat."[23]

It is also significant that Seleznev, as a post-1991 communist journalist, was associated with *Pravda* rather than with *Sovetskaia Rossiia*. For *Pravda* was, as a matter of editorial policy, evenhanded toward all positions on the post-Soviet communist spectrum (even when it came to the views of Boris F. Slavin, whom Seleznev had hired as a member of the editorial board when he was editor-in-chief), whereas *Sovetskaia Rossiia* was closely identified with the CPRF's nationalist wing and with Ziuganov personally. On the other hand, Seleznev was one of the fourteen signatories of the March 1994 manifesto, "Accord in the Name of Russia," which led to the short-lived movement of the same name championed by Ziuganov. To be sure, the March 1994 manifesto espoused rather moderate political views, and Seleznev did not play a public role in the movement's actual founding the following May. But the new Duma speaker was also associated with the "Spiritual Heritage" society created by Ziuganov's close non-communist colleague, Aleksei I. Podberezkin, in 1994. In short, he appeared to bridge the categories of moderate nationalist and Marxist reformer.

Melnikov, in contrast to Bindiukov and Seleznev, enjoyed membership in both the Presidium and the new Secretariat, thereby suggesting that he had more political clout than they did. Candid and expansive in a June 1996 interview, he was an admirer of Kuptsov and vigorously denied a widely held perception in the Russian media that the first deputy party chairman was somehow "orthodox" in his beliefs. Quite the contrary, asserted Melnikov, who had worked closely with Kuptsov for eight months in connection with the Constitutional Court's 1992 deliberations on the "CPSU case." During that period Melnikov had also had many dealings with members of the Socialist Labor Party, with whom he still maintained contacts and shared many views some four years later. Perhaps the most revealing indication that this younger CPRF leader was a Marxist reformer had to do with his reflections upon the late Gorbachev era. For Melnikov those years, "when everyone was free to speak" his or her mind, were the best of all times in recent Russian history.[24]

As mentioned at the outset of this section, Ziuganov had informed the delegates to the Third CPRF Congress that the party's chief ideologists were himself, Belov, and Melnikov. It is hard to imagine either Ziuganov or Belov agreeing with Melnikov's above assessment of the Soviet Union's twilight years.

The two remaining CPRF secretaries, Peshkov and Potapov, were—unlike Melnikov—first promoted to membership in the Presidium after the January 1995 congress. As already indicated, little concrete information was available about their backgrounds. However, Peshkov, as head of Ziuganov's personal guard as well as the party's committee on electoral campaigns, plainly belonged to the CPRF's nationalist wing. Indeed, in a May 1996 interview he asserted, "The idea that the West is to blame for what is happening in Russia is becoming stronger and stronger. It's just objective reality. . . . [T]he West and the Americans are supporting the weakening of the federation."[25]

Potapov, as chairman of the committee on party organization, may have been more closely associated with Kuptsov, but this could not be affirmed with any certainty. It was clear, however, that Melnikov, Peshkov, and Potapov, as the three individuals who held joint positions on the Secretariat and Presidium, were—along with Ziuganov, Kuptsov, and Shabanov—among the most important CPRF leaders. And our analysis suggests that as a group these six men were fairly evenly divided among Marxist reformers and Ziuganov-style nationalists.

As for the Presidium as a whole, an assessment of the political profile of each and every one of the nineteen members named at the Third CPRF Congress is a bit more problematic. One approach is to look first at this top policy-making body as it evolved between the 1993 and 1995 party congresses, as illustrated in Table 7.1. Its composition changed substantially as a result of the dramatic developments in the autumn of 1993. Soon thereafter, three of the initial seven members named at the February 1993 congress left the Presidium. As discussed in Chapter 5, Ivan P. Rybkin and Mikhail I. Lapshin became central figures in the Agrarian Party of Russia and were elected as candidates on its party list to the new State Duma in December 1993. They were formally removed from the CPRF Presidium at the party's Seventh Plenum, on the eve of the Second All-Russian Party Conference in April 1994.[26] In addition, Svetlana P. Goriacheva, actively involved "from the first to the last day" in the oppositionist deputies' defense of the White House in September–October 1993, returned to her native Maritime region to continue her legal career as a deputy procurator in Vladivostok,[27] a government post which apparently required that she also relinquish her CPRF leadership position. This left Ziuganov, Kuptsov, Belov, and Viktor I. Zorkaltsev among the original members, with Belov long since identified as a staunch nationalist and Zorkaltsev just as clearly positioned as a Marxist reformer.

In the meantime, Kuptsov became first deputy CPRF chairman, and eight new members joined the Presidium during the course of 1993.[28] In addition to Shabanov and Melnikov, whom we have discussed above, three of the newcomers were Duma deputies and three were figures of some stature in the army, military-industrial complex, and the academic world. Of the Duma deputies, we have already had occasion to speak of Kazbek Tsiku, the university professor of political economy from Adygeia, in the Krasnodar region. He was reliably reported to be a Marxist reformer.[29] One of the other two deputies was Valentin I. Nikitin, of Ukrainian origin, who was born in 1948 in what is today Bashkortostan, in south-central Russia. A railway engineer by training, from 1973 onward Nikitin worked in the CPSU *apparat* in the city of Ufa, and he is reported to have become chairman of the Communist Party of the Bashkortostan Republic as early as October 1991.[30]

The other CPRF deputy and new Presidium member was Anatolii V. Ionov, who was born in 1946 in Riazan, southeast of Moscow, and became a metal worker after finishing high school. Ionov became politically active only after the 1991 bans on the CPSU/RCP; thereafter he devoted himself to the reconstitution of both the CPRF and the communist trade union movement. In March 1995 he was appointed head of the party's commission on "work in the trade union movement."[31] While information on Ionov's specific political profile was sparse, he was clearly seen as a vote-getter for he was number seven on the CPRF's central list of twelve candidates in the December 1995 Duma elections.[32] Given his work with trade unions, he was probably closer to Kuptsov than to Ziuganov, but he may well have also shared certain views with the Marxist-Leninist modernizers like Kosolapov.

More solid data were available for the three new Presidium members who were not simultaneously Duma deputies. One of them, Professor Valentin Koptiug, was as already mentioned a renowned scientist and environmental reformer. As for the other two individuals, Georgii V. Kostin, born in 1934 in Voronezh, was a "red director" in the military-industrial complex who was driven from his position by the Yeltsin administration in 1992. Closely associated with Ziuganov since that time, he was named by the CPRF chairman as a likely member of a future opposition government in November 1994.[33]

The other new Presidium member was retired lieutenant general Mikhail S. Surkov. Born into a working-class family in Cheliabinsk in 1945, Surkov rose in the ranks of the Soviet Armed Forces as a political officer. He became a secretary of the party committee in the Chief Political Directorate of the Soviet Army and Navy in 1990 and secretary of the All-Army party committee in March 1991. A CPSU member since 1968, he was elected to the Central Committee at the 28th Congress and became a member of the CPSU Politburo in April 1991.[34] Surkov was one of six top CPSU officials who took part in the Russian Communist Party's August 6, 1991, plenum at which Kuptsov replaced Ivan P. Polozkov as RCP chairman.[35] On the other hand, Surkov's voting record as a Soviet Congress people's deputy was that of a right-wing nationalist opponent of *perestroika*,[36] and at the CPRF's March 1995 plenum he was put in charge of the party's commission on "patriotic education." He almost certainly belonged to Ziuganov's nationalist tendency.

Two more changes in the CPRF's top ranks occurred at the Central Executive Committee's Seventh Plenum two days before the All-Russian Party Conference in April 1994. Shabanov, already a Presidium member ensconced in the party's Duma offices as Ziuganov's right-hand man, was elected deputy chairman of the party. More significantly, Anatolii I. Lukianov now joined the Presidium.[37]

Lukianov, born in 1930 in Smolensk, was like Gorbachev educated in the law faculty of Moscow State University, where he also completed both the *aspirantura* and, in 1979, a doctorate in legal science. Associated for many years with the Presidium of the U.S.S.R. Supreme Soviet, Lukianov entered the CPSU's top echelons during the Gorbachev era. In 1987 he became Central Committee Secretary in charge of administrative organs, from September 1988 until July 1990 he was a candidate member of the Politiburo, and in March 1990, after Gorbachev assumed the newly created position of Soviet President, Lukianov became speaker of the by then much revamped Supreme Soviet.[38] Charged with complicity in the August 1991 putsch and imprisoned from August 29, 1991, until December 1992, Lukianov quickly entered the upper ranks of the reconstituted CPRF. As already mentioned in Chapter 3, he played a key role behind the scenes in the February 1993 selection of Ziuganov as CPRF Chairman. The following December he was elected to the Duma as the communist candidate from the Smolensk electoral distict No. 168, winning over one-third of the votes in a seven-man contest.[39] Lukianov was widely believed by non-communist analysts and rank-and-file CPRF members alike to represent the party's more orthodox Marxist-Leninist tendency.

Of the six individuals added to the Presidium at the Third CPRF Congress, we have already had occasion to discuss the two who were appointed to the new Secretariat at that same time: Peshkov and Potapov. Four, therefore, remain to be identified: Alevtina V. Aparina, Viktor M. Vidmanov, Gennadii E. Gamza, and Leonid A. Ivanchenko.

Aparina was not merely the only woman on the Presidium, but her background is also the easiest to describe of the four last-named members because she was elected to the Duma on the CPRF party list in December

1993. According to the directory of Federal Assembly representatives published in 1995, she was born in the Volgograd region in 1941, graduated in philosophy from Rostov State University in 1967, and later attended the Higher Party School in Saratov. A CPSU member since 1962, she entered full-time party work right out of college and became a secretary of the CPSU's Volgograd regional committee in February 1991.[40] During the period of Yeltsin's ban on CPSU/RCP activity, Aparina became chairman of the Volgograd branch of the Socialist Labor Party with the reported intention of helping to transform the latter into the CPSU's successor organization should the Constitutional Court uphold the president's 1991 decrees.[41] She later actively participated in founding the CPRF in Volgograd, where she became first secretary of the regional party organization. In that capacity Aparina was the exception rather than the rule: for she alone among the several dozen top CPRF activists in Volgograd hailed from the former CPSU *apparat*.[42]

In contrast to Aparina, Vidmanov, Gamza, and Ivanchenko were all former Soviet economic managers who had become prominent business executives in the new order. Vidmanov, born in 1934, was president of the "Rosagropromstroi" Corporation, an agricultural machine-building firm in Moscow. Gamza, born in 1944, was director of the construction enterprise "Avrora," in Blagoveshchensk on the Amur River bordering Manchuria. And Ivanchenko, born in 1942, was general director of the stock company "Svetlana," in Rostov-on-Don. He was also elected in 1993 to the Council of the Federation (the upper house of the Russian Federal Assembly), where he served on the Committee on Economic Reform, Ownership, and Property Relations.[43] Plainly the presence of these individuals on the Presidium was designed to enhance the CPRF's economic expertise and managerial competence. They also lent an air of authenticity to the party's programmatic commitment to a mixed economy in the short term. Whether they could be specifically identified as either Marxist reformers or Ziuganov nationalists was, however, by no means so clear.

The CPRF's Duma Takeover:
The Parliamentary Elections of December 1995

The December 1995 elections to the State Duma were the first to be held under the 1993 Constitution for a regularly scheduled four-year term of office. As in December 1993, the German electoral system was followed insofar as half of the deputies were chosen in single-member districts and the other half were designated according to proportional representation. The latter procedure also incorporated a five percent barrier, the intent of which was to encourage the aggregation of voter preferences into a small number of competing parties. But as we saw in Chapter 5, the result was quite the reverse in 1993, with some dozen or so parliamentary groups eventually being formed in the first Duma. And in 1995 the number of political parties or blocs entering the race jumped from under twenty to over forty. The irony of this situation was that only a very few groups could thus hope to win the required five percent of the party preference vote. The CPRF, with its by then well developed network of regional activists, was in a position to exploit this paradox to its own advantage. In the final count, as will be elaborated below, only four political parties actually exceeded the five percent barrier. The communists were therefore able to parlay their 22.3 percent of the party list vote into a total of 99 of the 225 Duma seats allocated in this fashion.

The CPRF's list of candidates for the party preference vote, which was published in September 1995, was put together with two basic goals in mind: on the one hand, to maximize the drawing power of individuals who enjoyed nation-wide name recognition; and, on the other hand, to ensure that most members of the party's Presidium, Secretariat, and key regional leadership won parliamentary seats. The political profile of the CPRF's central party list (that is, the first twelve names on the federal party list before its subdivision into twenty geographically delineated sub-lists) was suggestive of the party's overall approach.[44] Ziuganov, of course, headed the list, followed by Goriacheva and Aman M. Tuleev. Each of the latter was nationally known and also an experienced legislator. Goriacheva, as we have already noted, resigned as a deputy speaker of the former Russian Congress of People's Deputies in October 1991 (although she retained her parliamentary seat) in an early gesture of protest against the Yeltsin government. Tuleev, likewise a deputy in the Russian Congress and subsequently a member of the new Federation Council from the Kemerovo mining region, had run for president of the R.S.F.S.R. in June 1991, coming in fourth after Yeltsin, Nikolai I. Ryzhkov, and Vladimir V. Zhirinovskii, with 6.81 percent of the total vote. It is also important to note that both Goriacheva and Tuleev, in addition to their widespread name recognition, were among the Russian Congress deputies who occupied the White House, or parliament building, from September 21 until October 3–4, 1993.[45] The CPRF campaign strategists, haunted by the radical left's accusations of passivity, plainly aimed to highlight the role of their activists during that critical turning point in post-Soviet Russia's political evolution.

The second three among the CPRF's top twelve party list candidates were chosen by virtue of their special expertise or position rather than their proven vote-getting ability. They included Valentin V. Chikin, editor-in-chief of *Sovetskaia Rossiia*; Yurii D. Masliukov, the last chief of the Soviet state planning agency, Gosplan, from 1988 through 1990; and Kuptsov who, despite his importance as first deputy chairman and head of the CPRF's Duma fraction *apparat,* had not been elected a deputy in 1993.

The last six candidates among the top twelve were evenly divided among apparent protégés of Kuptsov (the trade unionist and Presidium member, Anatolii Ionov, and Nikolai N. Savelev, a young economist who worked as a consultant to Kuptsov in the CPRF's Duma fraction offices); "non-party sympathizers" and confidants of Ziuganov from the "Spiritual Heritage" research center (Podberezkin, its chairman and a specialist in military-political affairs, who served as a symbolic if not outright link with Ziuganov's right-wing nationalist associates,[46] and former KGB general Valerii P. Vorotnikov, director of a commercial security agency with reported ties to important Russian banking circles[47]); and notable figures from Moscow's wider cultural and professional community (the artist Valerii M. Tarasov and lawyer Yurii P. Ivanov, who took Ziuganov's place in a last-minute December 15, 1995, TV debate with Yegor Gaidar).

Needless to say, given the CPRF's eventual party preference vote and consequent receipt of forty percent of the mandates thereby distributed, all of the above-named individuals were elected to the new Duma. The same was also true of the top four or so candidates on the party's twenty regional sublists, some of whom will be discussed below.

The selection of the CPRF's candidates for its party lists in these territorial election districts (each of which combined several geographically proximate administrative units of the Russian Federation) had a more specific political focus. This was especially the case with regard to the top three persons on each list—those who had the best chance of winning one of the 225 Duma seats allocated according to the party preference vote and whose names would also appear separately on the actual ballots along with the all-national *troika* of Ziuganov, Goriacheva, and Tuleev. Inasmuch as only Ziuganov, Kuptsov, and Ionov from the party's top twenty-one leaders were on the central list of twelve names, the remaining Presidium and Secretariat members had priority on the regional electoral lists (except for Professor Koptiug, who chose not to run for a Duma seat). Six of them were number one in their respective regional *troika* (Aparina, Lukianov, Nikitin, Seleznev, Surkov, and Zorkaltsev), while seven were number two (Bindiukov, Gamza, Ivanchenko, Melnikov, Peshkov, Potapov, and Shabanov). The industrialist Viktor Vidmanov was listed number three, and Kazbek Tsiku and Georgii Kostin were in the fifth spot. The latter two, however, were on lists from heavily pro-communist regional election districts in which they were fairly certain to (and indeed did) win a seat. Belov was the only major CPRF figure who ran exclusively in a single-member district (Volkhovskii No. 98).

Other top candidates in the CPRF's regional electoral districts included Duma deputies who had already acquired a substantial reputation in that capacity (Viktor P. Iliukhin and Professor Oleg O. Mironov); regional party first secretaries (Vladimir I. Tikhonov from Ivanovo and Aleksandr A. Kuvaev, head of the Moscow city committee, among others in this rather large category); national celebrities (Nikolai N. Gubenko, director of Moscow's Taganki Theater, and Petr V. Romanov, Federation Council member and director of the Krasnoiarsk chemical plant *Yenisei*); and, last but not least, persons of some notoriety who were likely to attract radical left-wing voters (for example, the militant armed protagonists of the defense of the White House and the storming of Ostankino in October 1993, retired colonel general Albert M. Makashov and Yurii M. Voronin,[48] as well as the August 1991 putschist, General of the Army Valentin I. Varennikov). As already noted, altogether ninety-nine CPRF candidates would become Duma deputies through the party preference vote mechanism.

There were, in addition to the central and regional party lists, over 160 CPRF candidates running in single-member districts. In some cases they were prominent party leaders who were running simultaneously on the party preference list. In this way the CPRF could take advantage of their widespread name recognition but assign their party list seat (should they win the local contest) to a lesser known candidate. A stellar example in this category was Presidium member and Volgograd regional first secretary, Aparina. In other cases they were current Duma deputies who enjoyed strong local support but ranked somewhere in the middle of the party's regional electoral lists. In other words, the CPRF leadership was not prepared to guarantee them a Duma seat if they lost the local vote. There were also, of course, many other individual candidates judged to have high voter appeal in their home districts. All told, when the votes were in, the CPRF won a total of fifty-eight seats in these local contests.

In early September 1995 the CPRF published its electoral platform, "For our Soviet Homeland."[49] This document was more striking for what it omitted than for what it said. There was no reference whatsoever to socialism or to Marxism-Leninism. Lenin's name appeared only once, directly after that of Peter the Great, in a paragraph extolling the defenders of historic Russian territory from the Teutonic and Mongol invasions through World War II. The existence of a separate party *program* was mentioned only in passing, while the platform focused on the policies of a "people's-patriotic majority" in parliament before the June 1996 presidential elections and those of a "government of people's trust" thereafter. These two steps taken together, however, were actually just the *first stage* in the CPRF program's anticipated *three-stage* transition to socialism. In other words, the party's electoral platform said one thing, its program quite another.

Unabashed populism and appeals to wounded national pride constituted the platform's central ethos. The following excerpts should suffice to convey its flavor. The international roots of Russia's present misfortunes were highlighted and included "*the subjection of the country to the interests of the West, the illegal forced dissolution of the Soviet Union, the loss of strategic allies.*"[50] The new "people's-patriotic majority" in parliament would thus seek to abrogate both the Belovezhskie agreements and those "international treaties and agreements that infringe upon the interests and dignity of Russia."

The policy implications of the latter point were spelled out in a September 30, 1995, CPRF Presidium declaration. It not only denounced recent NATO activities (including those in Bosnia) across the board and affirmed its "negative attitude toward the ratification of the START-2 Treaty," but it also called for "increased defense capability," improvements in the "technical equipment" of the Russian Armed Forces, and a resumption of the production of "contemporary types of armaments in the enterprises of the military-industrial complex."[51] This emphasis upon rebuilding the military-industrial complex was a subject of pointed discussion in interviews with CPRF deputies, particularly those closely aligned with Ziuganov's nationalist views.[52]

To return to the party's election platform, it dubbed supporters of the Yeltsin government the "party of national betrayal . . . the party of Trotskii and Beriia, Vlasov and Yakovlev, Gorbachev and Yeltsin." The linkage of the names of Gorbachev, Yeltsin, and Aleksandr N. Yakovlev with the CPSU's historic heretic, Leon Trotskii, Stalin's notorious police chief, Lavrentii Beriia, and the World War II Soviet general–turned–Nazi-ally, Andrei A. Vlasov, aptly captured the spirit of Ziuganov's conspiratorial worldview.

As for domestic public policy, the eventual "government of people's trust" headed by the victorious presidential candidate of the "people's-patriotic" bloc would undertake a "new economic course" including "extreme measures of direct government regulation." It would restore the social safety net, crack down on crime and corruption, upgrade science and education, curb privatization, and introduce a government monopoly on foreign trade. "As stated in the CPRF Program," continued the document, "*the task of the communists is not to liquidate property-holders but to transform all citizens into real property-holders, co-owners of the general national wealth.*"[53] Everyone would receive for his work as much as he actually earned, "*without the old leveling of incomes but also without the new capitalist racketeering.*"[54] The platform concluded on a threatening note: one could either save the state and national destiny while there was still time, by ballots rather than the sword, or face the alternatives of a "kingdom of criminals" or a country-wide civil war on the pattern of Chechnia.

The CPRF thus headed into the fall 1995 election campaign armed with a platform full of populist promises and a star-studded slate of candidates. It was, to boot, confident that its support would far exceed the five-percent threshold and that the very multiplicity of parties and blocs which began to form by early spring 1995 would work to its advantage.

Just about every point on the Russian political spectrum eventually fielded candidates. Even the radical leftist *Roskomsoiuz* group, which had so condemned the CPRF for "bourgeois parliamentarism" the year before, now entered into negotiations with it in the hope of forming a united left opposition. But because of the CPRF's insistence on dictating the program and terms of such an alliance,[55] the radicals finally created a separate electoral bloc, Communists–Toiling Russia–for the Soviet Union, with its party list headed by the *troika* of Tiulkin, Anpilov, and Anatolii V. Kriuchkov.[56]

Here it bears mentioning that the presence of forty-three parties and electoral blocs on the December 1995 ballot spoke volumes about the democratization of the Russian polity. On the one hand, it was evidence of widespread acceptance of the electoral process in principle. Indeed, every political activist seemed determined to find an outlet to express his or her personal policy preferences, a situation facilitated by the small number of signatures (200,000) required to register one's candidacy.[57] And despite early prognoses of voter apathy, as election day approached ever more citizens indicated that they would go to the polls. Thus, notwithstanding the scheduling of the vote on just about the shortest day of the infamous Russian winter, almost sixty-five percent of registered voters did their civic duty.

On the other hand, the idea that political parties should aggregate individual preferences in such a way as to at least break the five percent barrier in the proportional representation distribution of Duma seats was not yet well understood. At least this was the case among the political hopefuls who created the multiple mini-blocs running for parliamentary seats. Among ordinary voters, however, there were already signs in autumn 1995 of frustration and anger over the unwillingness of the partisan elites to join forces in the public interest.[58]

In addition to the greater lead time and number of contestants, the 1995 Duma election campaign differed from the one in December 1993 in the extent to which electioneering moved decisively from the streets to the media—partly due to the rise in crime, which put a severe damper on door-to-door campaigning. During the four weeks preceding election day, the two state TV networks as well as Russian radio were each required to allocate one hour of free time to every one of the forty-three groups on the ballot. Much more importantly, numerous popular TV talk shows broadcast interviews with or debates between leading candidates, including those from the CPRF.[59] Moreover, while the CPRF was not in a position to buy the additional TV time enjoyed by some other contestants, Ziuganov himself was reported to have held 272 meetings with voters in seventy-two of the Russian Federation's eighty-nine regions. Meanwhile, during the last week before the vote the mailboxes of city apartment dwellers were flooded with campaign literature from all the more serious candidates. While it is not our charge to analyze the election campaign as a whole, it should also be noted that President Yeltsin's hospitalization for heart trouble from October 26 until the eve of the elections added to the overall tone of fair play, especially when compared to the president's dominance of the air waves in the spring 1996 presidential campaign.

When all was said and done, the CPRF was the big winner on December 17, 1995, garnering some 22.3 percent of the party list vote and 157 of 450 seats in the new Duma. This represented a gain of 112 seats and a near doubling of the CPRF's share of the party preference vote compared to its showing in the 1993 parliamentary contest.[60] But communist gains were not limited to the CPRF. The radical left electoral alliance, Communists–Toiling Russia–for the Soviet Union, while winning only one single-member constituency, received an unexpected 4.53 percent of the proportional representation vote (more than the Agrarian Party of Russia or Yegor Gaidar's Russia's Democratic Choice), thereby establishing itself as a substantial challenger on the left to the CPRF. Its showing was all the more striking given the brash maneuvers of local CPRF campaigners who warned crowds at election rallies to urge their friends and relatives not "*to throw away their vote*" by supporting either the Tiulkin-Kriuchkov-Anpilov bloc or the Agrarian Party of Russia.[61]

Meanwhile, the democratic reformers found their voter support greatly reduced. To be sure, the pro-government electoral association, Our Home Is Russia, founded by Prime Minister Viktor Chernomyrdin at Yeltsin's behest, came in third with 10.13 percent of the party list vote and won a total of sixty-five Duma seats. And the Yabloko bloc of Grigorii A. Yavlinskii garnered 6.89 percent of the party preference vote and altogether forty-six deputy mandates. The Gaidar ticket, however, did not even break the 5 percent barrier, mustering only 3.86 percent of the popular vote.

The Gaidar party's resounding beating was a reflection not only of the negative public impact of "shock therapy" but also of faulty campaigning. For example, the TV spots of Russia's Democratic Choice, with their emphasis on comparative Duma voting records, were too detailed to make much sense to the casual viewer. And the last-minute debate late in the evening of December 15 between Gaidar and CPRF candidate Yurii Ivanov, the Moscow lawyer with a facile tongue who ranked ninth on the party's central electoral list, was devastating. In response to Gaidar's technical analysis of the Russian economy, Ivanov charged him with being a new Russian millionaire (which in fact was true) who knew nothing of the plight of the common man.

The center-right and far-right nationalists did not fare much better. Zhirinovskii's Liberal Democratic Party fell from about 23 percent to 11.18 percent of the preference vote and from sixty-three to fifty-one Duma seats. Contrary to the expectations of many observers, the recently formed Congress of Russian Communities won only 4.31 percent of the party list vote. This was partly because its most popular candidate, retired general Aleksandr I. Lebed, was obliged to play second fiddle to his bloc's top-ranking leader,

Yurii V. Skokov, and also bombed in his individual TV interviews with his military greatcoat and cap, poker face and muffled bass voice. And Rutskoi's *Derzhava* movement fizzled out with a mere 2.59 percent of the preference vote.

On the left, however, there occurred a kaleidoscopic realignment of forces—in addition to the surge of support for the CPRF and the relatively respectable showing of the radical Marxist-Leninists. The generally pro-communist Agrarian Party of Russia (APR) fell from about 8 to 3.78 percent of the party list vote and from fifty-five to twenty seats in the Duma, with many previous supporters shifting their allegiance either to the CPRF or to more centrist groups. The same fate befell the Women of Russia bloc which won only 4.61 percent of the preference vote. In other words, when compared to the 1993 party list returns, the CPRF's 1995 gains were to some extent won at the expense of the APR and the Women of Russia, not to mention Zhirinovskii.

At the same time, several entirely new left-oriented formations emerged on the electoral scene. The first was the Party of Workers' Self-Government headed by the famous eye surgeon, Sviatoslav N. Fedorov, and joined by the now ex-communist Boris Slavin, who ranked number eight on its central party list.[62] Basically a social-democratic party, it won a startling 3.98 percent of the preference vote. A second new leftist group was the Power to the People bloc led by former Soviet prime minister, Nikolai Ryzhkov. While it gained nine Duma seats in single-member districts, it won less than two percent of the party list vote, thus reducing its significance in terms of the forthcoming 1996 presidential election campaign.

As the newly elected Duma began its first session in January 1996, the CPRF was, with over one-third (157) of the deputies, well positioned to garner the fruits of victory. Secretariat member Seleznev replaced Ivan Rybkin as speaker of the parliament after a brief bout of inter-party skirmishing during which Yavlinskii's Yabloko fraction supported a candidate of its own rather than joining in a pro-Rybkin coalition that included the Zhirinovskii fraction deputies.[63] At the same time, the articulate and dynamic Goriacheva was elected one of four deputy speakers. Allegations would later appear in the pro-Yeltsin media that there was also infighting among the communists themselves over whom to nominate for the speakership, with Ziuganov backing Seleznev against Kuptsov in a burgeoning power struggle between the CPRF's chairman and first deputy chairman.[64] We shall return to this subject a bit later. For now suffice it to say that such speculation was to be taken with a few grains of salt.

Meanwhile, the 1994 Duma procedures whereby committee posts were distributed according to the party fractions' numerical strength in the parliament were reaffirmed. The CPRF thus gained nine of twenty-eight chairmanships, including those of the prestigious committees on legislation

(Lukianov), economic policy (Masliukov), security (Iliukhin), social organizations (Zorkaltsev), and education and science (Melnikov). Communists also chaired the less important committees on veterans' affairs (General Varennikov) and women and families (Aparina) as well as those dealing with Federation matters and tourism and sports.[65]

Only the four parties that won over five percent of the party list vote were entitled to form Duma fractions (that is, the Chernomyrdin, Zhirinovskii, and Yavlinskii parties in addition to the communists). The CPRF fraction, however, facilitated the creation of Agrarian and People's Power "deputy groups" by delegating some of its own members to them in order to raise their numbers to the thirty-five person minimum required for a share of committee assignments as well as representation in the Duma Council. As a result, the communists acquired not only allies on the Duma Council, where each registered parliamentary fraction or group had a single vote, but also critical leverage over those allies.[66] A third "deputy group" called Russia's Regions, which was made up of independents, was also created, bringing the total to seven.[67] Key Duma committees chaired by non-communists included those dealing with privatization, defense, and nationality affairs (pro-Yeltsin deputies), the budget and international relations (Yabloko), and agriculture (an APR deputy).

On any account, we can conclude that in the 1995 parliamentary elections the CPRF had achieved its two paramount goals. On the one hand, its party headquarters, located as they were in its Duma fraction offices, had been enormously strengthened for the coming 1996 presidential campaign. On the other hand, the CPRF had increased its following to the point where it could be assured of constituting the controlling nucleus of a broader national front electoral coalition in the presidential race.

Ziuganov's Failed National Front Strategy: The Presidential Election of 1996

The two-round Russian presidential contest of June 16 and July 3, 1996 (in which the winner would have to receive a majority in the second-round run-off between the top two vote-getters from the first round), was much more significant in terms of what was at stake than were the Duma elections the previous autumn. This was because the constitutional powers of the presidency combined with the CPRF's stronghold in the parliament would have resulted, in the event of a Ziuganov victory, in domestic instability and renewed East-West tensions. These consequences would have been triggered in part by the communists' reassessment of privatization and market reforms but also by their reemphasis upon the military-industrial complex.

All told, in December 1995 the party list vote for the left-wing forces—including the CPRF, the radical neocommunist alliance, Ryzhkov's Power to the People bloc, and the Agrarian Party of Russia—came to only 32.2 percent of the total. Still, Yeltsin's single-digit ratings in public opinion polls during the early weeks of 1996 and the initial bandwagoning momentum in favor of Ziuganov at that time suggested the possibility of a communist victory. The CPRF, naturally, tried its level best to bring this to pass by adopting Ziuganov's long-preferred strategy of a broad national front coalition of "people's-patriotic forces."

Although Ziuganov declared at the party's post-election Fifth Plenum on January 12, 1996, that the CPRF must "promote its own candidate in the presidential elections,"[68] in fact on January 9, 1996, a so-called "initiative group" organized by Podberezkin had nominated the CPRF leader as its candidate for president. Held in the building of the Union of Russian Writers, no more than 30 of the 200 persons comprising this nominating group were CPRF members.[69] Both the setting and the participants projected the public image that Ziuganov was not a narrow party nominee but a coalition candidate. The members of the CPRF Central Committee were thus presented with a *fait accompli*. The resolution of the Fifth Plenum three days later backed Ziuganov as the CPRF's presidential candidate, but it also specified that the party's most important task was "the creation of a broad bloc of people's-patriotic forces, a coalition of communist parties and organizations of Russia."[70]

The forces backing Ziuganov confronted three basic tasks in the presidential campaign. The first was to neutralize the opposition to a communist victory of at least some of the elite groups in Russian society. The second was to consolidate around its candidate the *entire* left-wing electorate. And the third was to mobilize electoral support beyond the boundaries of that overall left-wing constituency. Here it should be reiterated that the latter, including the CPRF, the Tiulkin-Kriuchkov-Anpilov group, the Power to the People bloc, and the APR, had won only about 32 percent of the party list vote in December 1995.

With regard to its relationship with the Russian political-economic elites, the CPRF followed a policy of conscious restraint in the State Duma, on the one hand, and pursued an outreach policy toward would-be communist sympathizers in the government and business community, on the other. Until the middle of March the communist deputies avoided any kind of skirmish with the executive branch. In particular, they opposed a Duma vote of no-confidence in the government and blocked the Yabloko fraction's attempts to undertake such a step. The CPRF fraction preferred simply to ascribe to its newly demonstrated strength the Yeltsin regime's early 1996 ouster of the pro-Western foreign minister, Andrei V. Kozyrev, and privatization overseer Anatolii B. Chubais.

Meanwhile, trusted CPRF emissaries sought entry, so to speak, into the corridors of power. Vidmanov and Masliukov developed connections with the industrial management sector. Podberezkin was the intermediary with the representatives of the power ministries.[71] And the "red millionaire" Vladimir V. Semago reached out to the "new Russian" business elite.[72]

With regard to the CPRF's second strategic objective, that of consolidating its hold over the generically left-wing electorate, soon after the Duma elections there were indications by Anpilov and Baburin, among others, that they were prepared to cooperate with the Ziuganov presidential campaign.[73] At first, however, these groups stipulated a number of conditions for entering into a coalition with the CPRF. Only as it gradually became clear that there was no alternative to Ziuganov on the left and that he was also Yeltsin's most serious opponent did they withdraw those demands.

Meanwhile, on February 15, 1996, the Fourth All-Russian Conference of the CPRF officially confirmed the party's support for Ziuganov as president. While the decision was taken to back only one candidate, the conference tactfully expressed the party's readiness to back the collection of registration signatures on behalf of Tuleev, who at that time still had presidential ambitions of his own.[74] Soon thereafter, on March 4, a gathering of "people's-patriotic forces" was held to sign an agreement on joint action in support of Ziuganov for president. Although Lapshin of the APR, Ryzhkov of the Duma's People's Power "deputy group," and Oleg S. Shenin of the Union of Communist Parties–CPSU were among the signatories, Anpilov and Baburin declined to participate.[75] Nevertheless, it signaled the formation of a national front coalition the nucleus of which was—in conformity with traditional Soviet-era policy—the communist party. Also evocative of past CPSU/Comintern practice with regard to national front coalitions was the presence of organizational leaders or groups which overlapped in their memberships with the CPRF. These included, for example, the editors of *Pravda* and *Sovetskaia Rossiia*; the Russian Scholars of a Socialist Orientation (RUSO); the Central Committee of the Russian Komsomol; the Agrarian Union of the August 1991 putschist, Vasilii A. Starodubtsev; and so on.

Shortly thereafter one of the more bizarre episodes of the 1996 presidential campaign took place. On March 15, a CPRF Duma resolution to declare null and void the 1991 Belovezhskie agreements, which was put forward by Secretariat member Bindiukov, passed by a vote of 250 to 98. Of symbolic significance only, the parliament's action nonetheless prompted hardliners in Yeltsin's entourage to bloc off and search the Duma building (Sunday evening, March 17) and reportedly to contemplate banning the CPRF, postponing the elections, and/or dissolving the parliament itself.[76] The Duma resolution also resonated widely in the international community, eliciting protests by the U.S. Secretary of State as well as by the heads of most of the former Soviet republics.[77]

The most plausible explanation for why the CPRF's Duma fraction took such an uncharacteristically risky step was that it aimed thereby to broaden support for the party's electoral coalition, especially from the side of the more irreconcilable opponents of the Soviet Union's dissolution. And in this respect it succeeded. At the very next gathering of the "people's-patriotic forces of Russia," on March 17, 1996, Anpilov, Rutskoi, and Union of Officers chairman Stanislav N. Terekhov added their signatures to the agreement on joint action in support of Ziuganov's presidential candidacy.[78] Soon thereafter Baburin also joined the coalition, and Petr Romanov withdrew from the presidential race in favor of Ziuganov.[79]

Nonetheless, the national front coalition remained in many ways an artificial construct. As reported in *Moscow News*, of the 191 signatories to the "people's-patriotic forces" pact as of early May 1996, forty-nine were simply ordinary individuals, while fourteen of the organizations listed consisted of one member only (all communists) and fifteen did not exist at all. Not only that, but a number of signatures were appended by members who were not authorized to do so by their respective associations.[80]

This type of falsification served to underscore the problem faced by the CPRF when it came to its third major campaign task, that of broadening the base of its electoral support. In December 1995, in comparison with the 1993 elections, the CPRF succeeded in more than doubling its electorate, from about 7 to 15.5 million, while the vote for communists of all stripes approached 20 million.[81] The enlargement of the CPRF's electoral support was due partly to voters who had not participated in the 1993 elections (they constituted up to twenty percent of those who voted for the CPRF in 1995) but also in part to the transfer of votes within the opposition. Former Zhirinovskii supporters added about ten percent to the CPRF's 1995 total, while defectors from the APR and the Women of Russia added from three to five percent each.[82] Ziuganov himself had said at the party's January 1996 Fifth Plenum that even a larger turn-out in the first round of the presidential election would add only three to four percent more votes to the CPRF's hardcore constituency.[83]

The upshot of such electoral calculations was that the Ziuganov coalition needed to attract votes from among the undecided and above all from the electorate of the more centrist but anti-Yeltsin parties and candidates. Intense CPRF consultations with presidential candidates Fedorov and Lebed came to naught. Not only were both the latter caught up in negotiations with candidate Yavlinskii over the possibility of forming a so-called "third force" between Yeltsin and Ziuganov; but also, when push came to shove between the two rounds of the presidential contest, each would throw his personal support behind the president. The Ziuganov strategists likewise turned to two other devices to win the support of at least some centrists: a sweeping populist election platform and a moderate if internally inconsistent economic program.

On March 17 Ziuganov presented to the public an electoral platform that contained not a single allusion to Marxism-Leninism and which was not only a far cry from the CPRF Program approved at the January 1995 Third Congress but also differed substantially from the party's fall 1995 parliamentary election platform. If the latter referred to the official CPRF Program only in passing, Ziuganov's presidential platform did not even mention the CPRF. Only four newspaper columns long, it promised to protect "the rights of man" and freedom of thought, religion, and "political parties" as well as the material well-being of all strata of the Russian population.

The basic contours of Ziuganov's thinking were nonetheless unmistakable. He professed belief in the "communist idea that was more than two thousand years old." He urged "timely government support for the high-tech production of the military-industrial complex." He supported "essential changes in the legislation on privatization, the budget, currency regulation, the tax system," and so forth. He backed a "mixed economy" but on condition that the government retain control over those industrial sectors that were most important for the "balanced development and security of the country." He was against the Belovezhskie agreements and the expansion of NATO, and he assured the Armed Forces that they would receive all they needed "for the reliable defense of Russia's borders and interests in the world." He urged constitutional amendments to guarantee the Duma's control over the president as well as each and every one of the government's ministers. And he averred, somewhat ambiguously to be sure, that "the people will forgive the many previous sins of all who . . . work honestly for the rebirth of Great Russia."[84]

On May 28, only three weeks before the first round of the presidential contest, Ziuganov's long-awaited economic program was published in *Sovetskaia Rossiia* and distributed free of charge on the streets of Moscow in the CPRF's *Pravda Moskvy*.[85] Two full newspaper pages in length and probably read by precious few prospective voters, it was subjected to biting criticism in the major pro-government newspapers. In a word, they dismissed it as a wish-list of proposals that called, *inter alia*, for welfare guarantees, price controls, government subsidies to agriculture and industry, reliance on domestically generated investment rather than foreign loans, protectionism, higher expenditures on defense, and lower taxes, but was devoid of any indication of where the funding for these programs was to come from. Still, the program did *not* call for a return to the centrally planned and government-owned economy of the Soviet era.

There were other signs of relative moderation as well. Ziuganov used his ninety minutes of free time on the state-run media to reassure the audiences that a victory by his coalition of "people's-patriotic forces" would mean a return to stability and social harmony rather than radical turmoil. And during the final days before the June 16 first-round vote, the CPRF press reprinted

Western news reports suggesting that a Ziuganov victory would not spell disaster, including an article by the renowned Soviet-era dissident, Andrei Siniavskii, saying that "there is no choice: Yeltsin is more dangerous than the communists."[86]

But there were also contervailing signals, suggesting that Ziuganov and his followers were their own worst enemies. The pro-Yeltsin media had a field day with General Valentin Varennikov's mid-March talk of an unpublished CPRF "maximum program" to be implemented after victory, in what was an unmistakable allusion to the January 1995 official party program. Meanwhile, in his election rally speeches Ziuganov himself constantly reverted to Cold War conspiratorial rhetoric and appeals to the prejudices of the deepest Russian *glubinka* (rural backwoods). He had used this approach in the fall 1995 Duma election campaign,[87] and he employed it to the hilt in the presidential race. In a speech in Smolensk, for example, the CPRF leader expounded upon some of his favorite themes: television was run by "scum who desecrate every holy thing in our history"; industries must be renationalized; the Yeltsin regime was "consciously ruining the country with drink"; and as for the former U.S.S.R., "We will unite!"[88]

The high point of this mixed appeal to social protest and traditionalist obscurantism came at the Congress of People's-Patriotic Forces of Russia, which took place at Moscow's Luzhinki Stadium complex on June 8, 1996. There, flanked by Tuleev, Anpilov, Rutskoi, Varennikov, Starodubtsev, and others, with the ringing of church bells and banners bearing the likenesses of the Savior, Mother of God, and George the Dragon Slayer, Ziuganov identified Gorbachev and Yeltsin as "the two beasts from the abyss sent by the Devil, the first with a mark on his head, the second . . . with a brand on his hand."[89]

The results of the first round of the presidential contest, on June 16, 1996, said it all with regard to the effectiveness of such antics. Ziuganov won 32.04 percent of the total ballots cast and Yeltsin 35.28 percent, with turnout reaching almost 70 percent of all eligible voters. In absolute numbers Ziuganov received more votes than those which the left coalition members had received as a group in the parliamentary elections the previous December. In percentage terms, however, the CPRF chairman had not been able to expand his electoral appeal much beyond Russia's generic left-wing constituency. Meanwhile, the bulk of the remaining votes were divided among Lebed (14.52%), Yavlinskii (7.34%), and Zhirinovskii (5.70%), with almost 3 percent casting ballots for "none of the above."[90]

The dramatic period between the first and second rounds of the presidential race was taken up above all with the Yeltsin team's maneuvers to ensure the president's victory in the run-off with Ziuganov by drawing to his side as many as possible of the preference votes which had gone to the three other major contenders on June 16. Lebed was appointed secretary of Russia's Security Council. The reformist supporters of Yavlinskii were placated by the firing of some of the most discredited members of the president's administration, including those most directly involved in the prosecution of the Chechen War. The second round was even moved from a Sunday to a Wednesday in order to encourage higher voter turnout, especially among the many week-end tillers of vegetable plots on the outskirts of the larger urban centers. Finally, on July 3, 1996, President Yeltsin was reelected to a second term with 53.82 percent (about 40 million) of the votes cast compared to Ziuganov's 40.31 percent (about 30 million), with 4.83 percent (3.6 million) saying a pox on both candidates.[91]

Even before Yeltsin's decisive victory, the opposition bitterly complained about unfair campaign practices, especially with regard to the government's near monopoly on the electronic media and its propaganda barrage alleging that the Ziuganov forces intended to restore the worst excesses of the old Soviet order. The impact of the Yeltsin team's scare tactics was to raise the president's standing from his single-digit public opinion ratings of early 1996 to levels exceeding those of Ziuganov by mid-May[92] and, ultimately, to win him the reluctant second-round support of many of the fundamentally anti-Yeltsin or undecided voters whom the "people's-patriotic" bloc had hoped but largely failed to attract.

However, as we have already seen, the CPRF's official party program made it vulnerable to the Yeltsin campaigners' charges. And even though the mainstream media, including the newspapers, were guilty of exaggerating the potential dangers posed by a Ziuganov victory, the final election results left no room for doubt on one basic point: only forty percent of the Russian voters (including an estimated half of Zhirinovskii's and a third of Lebed's first-round voters)[93] were willing to risk even the partial return to the past which a Ziuganov victory would most likely have entailed. About sixty percent rejected this risk out of hand. And the fifty-four percent who voted for Yeltsin were in fact casting their ballots for the ongoing Europeanization of Russian political culture. On this subject we will have more to say in the next chapter.

Notes

1. Emphasis added.

2. See "Zakliuchitelnoe slovo G. A. Ziuganova na III Sezde KPRF (utrennee zasedanie 23 ianvaria)," in *Informatsionnyi biulleten*, No. 2 (14), February 1, 1995, pp. 23–30. An abridged version of this speech appeared in *III Sezd Kommunisticheskoi partii Rossiiskoi Federatsii (Materialy i dokumenty)* (Moscow: Informpechat, 1995), pp. 63–75. Although this latter version was purportedly taken from "the stenogram" of the congress, there was no reference to the speech's actual delivery *the morning of January 23, 1995,* that is, the day after the congress had reportedly ended. Other more striking omissions will be noted below.

3. "Zakliuchitelnoe slovo G. A. Ziuganova," p. 26. This remark was omitted from *III Sezd KPRF*, p. 67.

4. "Zakliuchitelnoe slovo G. A. Ziuganova," p. 26; emphasis added. This information was not included in *III Sezd KPRF*, p. 67.

5. Ibid., p. 27.

6. Ibid., p. 28.

7. Ibid.

8. Ibid. pp. 29–30.

9. Ibid., p. 30.

10. *III Sezd KPRF*, pp. 118–120; for the members of these bodies, see "Materialy III sezda KPRF," . . . *UZM* (Nizhnii Tagil, Sverdlovsk oblast), No. 1, 1995, p. 48. This special issue was published jointly with a CPRF Central Committee group headed by the new secretary for ideology, Nikolai G. Bindiukov.

11. S. A. Potapov, "Doklad mandatnoi komissii," *III Sezd KPRF*, p. 62.

12. J. B. Urban's interview with Ivan I. Melnikov in the offices of the Duma's Committee on Education and Science (of which Melnikov was chairman), June 11, 1996.

13. J. B. Urban's interview with Boris F. Slavin at the editorial offices of *Pravda*, June 12, 1996.

14. A. S. Barsenkov et al., *Federalnoe Sobranie Rossii* (Moscow: Fond "Foros," 1995), pp. 513–514.

15. J. B. Urban's interview with Ivan I. Melnikov, June 11, 1996. Cf. *Izvestiia TsK KPSS*, No. 8, August 1990, pp. 7 and 59. The "institution of members of the Secretariat of the CPSU CC" was created at the July 14, 1990, plenum; see ibid., p. 7.

16. Barsenkov, *Federalnoe Sobranie Rossii*, p. 245.

17. For this and other personnel appointments at the CPRF's March 1995 plenum, see "Informatsionnoe soobshchenie," *Pravda Rossii*, No. 2 (16), March 30, 1995, p. 1.

18. Barsenkov, *Federalnoe Sobranie Rossii*, p. 473; see also Grigorii Nekhoroshev, "Novomu spikeru blizka svedskaia model," *Nezavisimaia gazeta*, January 19, 1996, p. 1.

19. "Informatsionnoe soobshchenie," *Pravda Rossii*, March 30, 1995, p. 1.

20. J. B. Urban's interview with Nikolai G. Bindiukov in the CPRF Duma fraction's offices, May 26, 1995.

21. *Raznogolositsa*, No. 11 (128), March 11–17, 1996, pp. 31 and 34.

22. Nekhoroshev, "Novomu spikeru blizka svedskaia model," *Nezavisimaia gazeta*, January 19, 1996, p. 2.

23. Ibid.

24. J. B. Urban's interview with Ivan I. Melnikov, June 11, 1996. The authors wish to thank Melnikov for his contribution of a complete set of the CPRF's internal circular, or *Informatsionnyi biulleten*, for their use in this volume.

25. Lee Hockstader, "New Russian Communists Put On a Moderate Face," *The Washington Post*, May 20, 1996, p. A16.

26. *Materialy Vserossiiskoi konferentsii Kommunisticheskoi partii Rossiiskoi Federatsii* (Moscow: 1994), p. 1.

27. "Imia iz spiska," *Pravda Rossii*, No. 17 (31), September 14, 1995, p. 1.

28. Information supplied to the authors by personnel in the CPRF's Duma offices. Cf. the data in *Kto est chto: Politicheskaia Moskva, 1994*, Vol. 1 (Moscow: Pushchinskii nauchnii tsentr RAN, 1994), p. 108.

29. J. B. Urban's interview with Boris F. Slavin, June 12, 1996.

30. Barsenkov, *Federalnoe Sobranie Rossii*, p. 433.

31. Ibid., p. 350; cf. "Imia iz spiska," *Pravda Rossii*, No. 28 (42), November 30, 1995, p. 1. See also "Informatsionnoe soobshchenie," *Pravda Rossii*, March 30, 1995, p. 1.

32. "Federalnyi spisok," *Pravda Rossii*, No. 16 (30), September 7, 1995, p. 1; cf. *Rossiiskaia gazeta*, September 14, 1995, p. 4.

33. See the interview with Ziuganov in *Nezavisimaia gazeta*, November 4, 1994, p. 5. Cf. the interview with Ziuganov in *Sovetskaia Rossiia*, November 11, 1992; the authors are grateful to Robert Otto for the latter reference.

34. *Izvestiia TsK KPSS*, No. 6, June 1991, p. 119.

35. "Results of Plenum Detailed," Moscow TASS International Service in Russian, August 6, 1991; trans. *Federal Broadcast Infomation Service-Soviet Union*, No. 152, August 7, 1991, p. 62.

36. See Giulietto Chiesa, with Douglas Taylor Northorp, *Transition to Democracy: Political Change in the Soviet Union, 1987–1991* (Hanover, NH: University Press of New England, 1993), pp. 62–63 and 286.

37. *Materialy Vserossiiskoi konferentsii Kommunisticheskoi partii Rossiiskoi Federatsii* (Moscow: 1994), p. 1.

38. Barsenkov, *Federalnoe Sobranie Rossii*, pp. 392–393.

39. Ibid.

40. Ibid., pp. 224–225.

41. Information provided by the authors' colleague, Dr. Heinz Timmermann (of the Bundesinstitut in Cologne) based in his June 16, 1996, interview with Feliks Rodinskii, a member of the CPRF's Volgograd regional committee and also a CPRF member on the Volgograd Electoral Commission. Dr. Timmermann was in Volgograd as a European Union observer of the first round of the Russian presidential election.

42. Valerii Vyzhutovich, "Korni travy," *Izvestiia*, March 20, 1996, p. 5. In this respect, the Volgograd party organization was similar to the CPRF's regional organization in Ivanovo; there, too, the post-1991 communist leadership was drawn almost exclusively from rank-and-file party loyalists rather than former CPSU functionaries. This information comes from the authors' in-depth conversations at the CPRF's regional headquarters in Ivanovo, June 13, 1996.

43. See the CPRF's party list candidates for the December 17, 1995, parliamentary elections in *Pravda Rossii*, No. 16 (30), September 7, 1995, p. 3; cf. *Rossiiskaia gazeta*, September 14, 1995, pp. 4–6.

44. For the names of the CPRF's party list and single-member constituency candidates, see ibid.

45. For information on Tuleev, see Barsenkov, *Federalnoe Sobranie Rossii*, pp. 172–173, and "Imia iz spiska," *Pravda Rossii*, No. 18 (32), September 21, 1995, p. 1.

46. See the characterization of Podberezkin in David Remnick, "Letter from Russia: The War for the Kremlin," *The New Yorker*, July 22, 1996, pp. 40–57 at pp.

44–45. Podberezkin, who received a doctorate in "military-political affairs," was also the founder (in 1990) and president of the nationalist-oriented RAU Corporation and editorial house; see "Imia iz spiska," *Pravda Rossii*, No. 20, October 5, 1995, p. 1.

47. Lev Sigal, "Vozhd i dukhovnye nasledniki," *Obshchaia gazeta*, No. 11, April 21–27, 1996, p. 8.

48. "Za kogo golosovat," *Argumenty i fakty*, No. 49, 1995, p. 9.

49. "Za nashu sovetskuiu rodinu!" *Pravda Rossii*, No. 16 (30), September 7, 1996, p. 2.

50. Ibid.; emphasis in the original.

51. "Zaiavlenie Prezidiuma Tsentralnogo Komiteta Kommunisticheskoi partii Rossiiskoi Federatsii, *Pravda Rossii*, No. 20 (34), October 5, 1995, p. 1.

52. See J. B. Urban's interviews with CPRF deputies in their Duma offices, May 1995.

53. "Za nashu sovetskuiu rodinu!" *Pravda Rossii*, September 7, 1996, p. 2; emphasis in the original.

54. Ibid.; emphasis in the original.

55. For the radical left CPs' abortive efforts to reach an agreement with the CPRF on an electoral alliance, see *Raznogolositsa*, Nos. 29, 30, and 34 (1995), pp. 6, 7, and 28 respectively.

56. The bloc's candidates were listed in *Rossiiskaia gazeta*, October 14, 1995, pp. 4–6.

57. Laura Belin, "An Array of Mini-Parties Wage Futile Parliamentary Campaigns," *Transition*, Vol. 2, No. 4 (February 23, 1996), pp. 15–19.

58. The authors knew numerous individuals who waited until the last moment to decide for whom to vote, hoping thereby to discern how to enhance the all-important preference vote of the overall tendency (rather than the specific party) they favored, be that democratic reformist, center-right nationalist, or whatever. The frequent last-minute choice between the parties of Gaidar and Yavlinskii was a case in point.

59. Many argue that the free campaign ads were rather ineffectual, but few analysts have noted the importance of the focused talk show debates. See, for example, Laura Belin, "Television Plays a Limited Role in Duma Elections," *Transition*, Vol. 2, No. 4 (February 23, 1996), pp. 20–23.

60. For the final tally by Russia's Central Electoral Commission released on December 29, 1995, see the "Russia Election Results Supplement," The International Foundation for Election Systems (IFES), Washington, D.C.; cf. *The New York Times*, December 30, 1995, p. 5, as well as the coverage of the elections in *Transition*, Vol. 2, No. 4 (February 23, 1995), passim.

61. Authors' observations at local CPRF election rallies in Moscow; emphasis added.

62. The new party's candidates were listed in *Rossiiskaia gazeta*, September 21, 1995, p. 6.

63. Mikhail Sokolov, "Realnaia istoriia vyborov spikera," *Segodnia*, January 26, 1996, p. 2.

64. See in particular Sergei Chugaev, "Im nuzhen novyi Chernenko," *Izvestiia*, March 21, 1996, p. 5.

65. Petr Zhuravlev, "Fraktsii i gruppy Gosdumy podelili komitety," *Segodnia*, January 20, 1996, p. 1.

66. Thomas F. Remington, "The Balance of Forces in the Newly Elected Russian Parliament," *Post-Soviet Prospects*, Vol. IV, No. 7 (May 1996), p. 2.

67. See "Kolichestvo deputatov v deputatskikh obedineniiakh v Gosudarstvennoi Dume (po sostoianiiu na 17/01/96)," distributed by the Duma *apparat*, January 17, 1996.

68. Gennadii A. Ziuganov, "Ispytanie doveriem: Doklad na plenume TsK KPRF," *Sovetskaia Rossiia*, January 16, 1996, p. 2.

69. Igor Korotchenko, "Gennadii Ziuganov vydvinut kandidatom v presidenty Rossii," *Nezavisimaia gazeta*, January 10, 1996, p. 2.

70. "Postanovlenie V Plenuma TsK KPRF, 'O politicheskikh itogakh vyborov deputatov Gosudarstvennoi Dumy i ocherednykh zadachakh partii,'" *Pravda Rossii*, No. 2, January 18, 1996, p. 1.

71. According to Igor Korotchenko, writing in *Nezavisimaia gazeta*, June 5, 1996, p. 2, Podberezkin had wide-ranging ties "in the Ministry of Defense, the FSB [Federal Bureau of Security], and in the law-enforcement organs. . . ."

72. Lee Hockstader, "Communist Funds the Good Life and the Party," *The Washington Post*, May 20, 1996, p. A17.

73. See, for example, Viktor Khamraev, "Viktor Anpilov gotov agitirovat za presidenta-ziuganovtsa, esli tot otmenit presidentskii post," *Segodnia*, December 22, 1995, p. 2; and Sergei Baburin, "Bez KPRF ne cozdat shirokii narodnyi front [Interviu]," *Pravda*, January 24, 1996, pp. 1–2.

74. "O zadachakh partiinykh organizatsii v sviazi c podgotovkoi i provedeniem vyborov prezidenta Rossiiskoi Federatsii: Postanovlenie IV Vserossiiskoi konferentsii KPRF," *Sovetskaia Rossiia*, February 17, 1996, p. 1.

75. "Soglashenie o sovmestnykh deistviiakh v podderzhku edinogo kandidata na dolzhnost Prezidenta Rossiiskoi Federatsii G. A. Ziuganova ot narodno-patrioticheskikh sil Rossii," *Pravda Rossii*, No. 9, March 7, 1996, p. 1.

76. See Marina Shakina in *Nezavisimaia gazeta*, March 19, 1996, p. 1; Zhanna Kasianenko, "Vzlet 'iastrebov': Na voprosy 'Sovetskoi Rossii' otvechaet predsedatel Komiteta po bezopasnosti Gosdumy Viktor Iliukhin," *Sovetskaia Rossiia*, March 26, 1996, p. 3; and Lee Hockstader, "The Yeltsin Vote," *The Washington Post*, May 26, 1996, pp. C1–C2.

77. James Rupert, "Christopher Censures Russian Vote Rejecting Breakup of U.S.S.R.," *The Washington Post*, March 20, 1996, p. A25.

78. Text in *Pravda Rossii*, No. 11, March 21, 1996, p. 1; cf. Gleb Cherkasov, "Lider KPRF pytaetsia rasshirit krug svoikh storonnikov," *Segodnia*, March 19, 1996, p. 2.

79. "Baburin prishel k Ziuganovu," *Nezavisimaia gazeta*, April 5, 1996, p. 1; "Petr Romanov otkazalsia ot predvybornoi borby v polzu Gennadiia Ziuganova," *Segodnia*, April 4, 1996, p. 1.

80. Yelena Rykovtseva, *Moscow News*, No. 17–18, May 2–22, 1996, p. 2.

81. Ziuganov, "Ispytanie doveriem," *Sovetskaia Rossiia*, January 16, 1996, p. 2.

82. "S kem shagaiut marginaly i za kem idet 'srednii klass'," *Pravda-5*, No. 7, February 16–23, 1996, p. 8.

83. Ziuganov, "Ispytanie doveriem," *Sovetskaia Rossiia*, January 16, 1996, p. 2.

84. "Rossiia, Rodina, Narod!," *Pravda Rossii*, No. 11, March 21, 1996, p. 2.

85. "Ot razrusheniia—k sozidaniiu. Put Rossii v XXI vek," *Sovetskaia Rossiia*, May 28, 1996, pp. 3–4; cf. *Pravda Moskvy*, June 1996, pp. 1–4.

86. "O 'rogatom sillogizme'," *Sovetskaia Rossiia*, June 13, 1996, p. 1; see also "Obviniaet kogo ugodno, tolko ne sebia: Svidetelstvuet amerikanskii zhurnal 'Taim'," *Pravda Rossiia*, No. 21 (67), June 13, 1996, p. 3.

87. See, for example, Jean MacKenzie, "Ziuganov in Nizhny: No More Mr. Nice Guy," *The Moscow Times*, December 5, 1995, p. 1.

88. Lee Hockstader, "Russian Communist Is Talking Tough," *The Washington Post*, April 10, 1996, pp. A1 and A22.

89. See the coverage of this event in *Sovetskaia Rossiia*, June 11, 1996, pp. 1 and 3; the quote from Ziuganov's speech is on page 3.

90. The official results announced by the Central Election Commission (CEC) of the Russian Federation were reported in *The Washington Post*, June 21, 1996, p. A29. The gap between Yeltsin and Ziuganov later narrowed somewhat, as reported by the CEC to the International Foundation for Election Systems in Washington, D.C., with Yeltsin receiving 35.05% and Ziuganov 32.35%.

91. The CEC's official results were reported in *The Washington Post*, July 10, 1996, p. A14. For an informed and balanced account of the presidential campaign as a whole, see Jack F. Matlock, Jr., "The Struggle for the Kremlin," *The New York Review of Books*, August 8, 1996, pp. 28–34.

92. For an excellent analysis, see Richard B. Dobson, "Public Opinion and the Russian Presidential Election: A Communist Resurgence?" (Salt Lake City, Utah: Paper prepared for the 1996 meeting of the World Association for Public Opinion Research, May 16, 1996).

93. See the results of an exit poll of over 9,500 second-round Russian voters, *The New York Times*, July 4, 1996, p. A8.

8

Whither Communism in Post-Soviet Russia?

Boris Yeltsin's decisive victory over Gennadii Ziuganov on July 3, 1996, when he received almost 54 percent of the total votes cast compared to slightly over 40 percent for the communist leader (about 5 percent voted against both candidates), was a source of gratification for the West and a relief for the majority of politically active Russians. All the same, it did not signify either political harmony among those who voted for Yeltsin or the end of communism as a political force with which to reckon. The 32 percent vote for Ziuganov in the first round of the presidential election on June 16, 1996, underscored the extent to which Marxism had experienced a political-ideological revival after 1991 as a result of the Russian Federation's first-hand exposure to unfettered capitalism and the West's post-industrial mass culture. And the additional eight percent of voters who chose Ziuganov over Yeltsin in the second round of the presidential race, their initial preference for a non-communist candidate notwithstanding, suggested the depth of popular disenchantment with both the president and life in post-Soviet Russia.

The Yeltsin camp put what appeared to be a concerted plan of action in effect immediately after the first round of voting, in which the president received only some 35 percent of the votes cast rather than the absolute majority he had confidently (if rashly) predicted a week earlier on the widely viewed television program "Itogi." On June 18 the president appointed Aleksandr Lebed, second runner-up in the first round with over 14 percent of the vote, his national security adviser and secretary of the Russian Federation's Security Council. That same day he dismissed Minister of Defense Pavel S. Grachev, a step reportedly demanded by Lebed as a condition of his joining the president's administration. Just two days later internal squabbling among the Yeltsin forces along with electoral exigencies led to the abrupt removal of Yeltsin's long-time loyalist aides, head of the Kremlin guard Aleksandr V. Korzhakov and chief of the Federal Security Bureau

Mikhail I. Barsukov.[1] The subsequent designation of the controversial former privatization overseer Anatolii B. Chubais (and key figure on Yeltsin's
campaign staff from mid-March onward) as the president's chief of staff set
the scene for future political jousting between Lebed, on the one hand, and
Chubais and the soon to be reappointed prime minister, Viktor Chernomyrdin, on the other. Matters were further complicated when Yeltsin's re-
curring heart trouble forced his withdrawal from day-to-day governance
pending medical treatment.

The situation on the communist side was little better. Although evidence
of outright fracturing occurred only at the edges of the former people's-
patriotic electoral bloc, the three basic tendencies comprising the CPRF's activist core showed signs not only of renewed vitality but also of mutual demarcation from one another. On the one hand, Ziuganov and his nationalist
associates within and beyond the CPRF undertook to transform the spring
1996 people's-patriotic coalition into an enduring political organization,
distinct from the CPRF and renamed the People's–Patriotic Union of Russia
(*Narodno–Patrioticheskii Soiuz Rossii*). The proponents of this new entity
seemed to have in mind the creation of a centrist or center-right, welfare-
oriented nationalist movement rather than a communist-centered national
front organization.

On the other hand, a number of communist activists grouped around
Valentin Kuptsov, who were generally a decade or so younger than the
CPRF's first deputy chairman, sought to strengthen the party organizationally while reforming it politically and programmatically. Not notably more na-
tionalistic than ordinary Russian citizens, they presumably looked to the experience of the East-Central European communists–turned–social democrats
as a possible pattern to emulate (in 1996 Poland, Hungary, and Lithuania
were governed by center-left coalitions headed by former communists).

All the while, the doctrinaire Marxist-Leninists—now divided among the
ultra-leftist communist parties of the *Roskomsoiuz*, Viktor Anpilov's Toiling
Russia movement (which had joined Ziuganov's people's-patriotic bloc during the presidential campaign), and the Marxist-Leninist modernizers within
the CPRF—stuck to their ideological guns. Just as the Yeltsin campaign tactics had, in their eyes, vindicated the Leninist maxim that the dictatorship of
the bourgeoisie would use all methods, legal and illegal, to maintain its
power, so too they clung to the belief that the proletariat would in due time
rise up to throw off its chains.[2]

On the questionable character of the presidential campaign's methods,
there was full agreement among the oppositionists. Kuptsov, in his major
post-election report to the Eighth CPRF Plenum on August 6, 1996,[3] set
forth a list of campaign abuses many of which were apparent even to impar-
tial Western observers. He pointed, first of all, to unprecedented Western in-
terference on behalf of the sitting president, including not only the granting

of multi-billion dollar loans to shore up the Russian economy but also the dispatch of American political consultants, or "image-makers," to advise Yeltsin's campaign staff.[4] The Americans, claimed Kuptsov, could hardly have participated "without agreement at the highest level and the influence of special agencies." Secondly, he stressed the presidential campaign's unauthorized use of government personnel and funds as well as direct pressure upon local administrators (i.e., "Tammany tactics," in the words of one American analyst) to influence the election outcome.[5] Thirdly, Kuptsov blamed the government's "totalitarian" control over the mass media, which, he argued, "fully substantiated the Leninist thesis on the dependence of the SMI [means of mass information] on the money-bag."[6] Last but not least, the CPRF first deputy chairman accused the Yeltsin regime of manipulating the Central Election Commission and falsifying outright the election results, which was the one charge denied by most Western observers.[7]

Otherwise, the divergencies among the various Russian communist tendencies were substantial indeed, as evidenced by their respective proposals for improving their political prospects. We shall therefore turn to a brief examination of those proposals as well as to an analysis of the sources of CPRF support among Russian voters during the 1995 and 1996 elections.

Chto delat? Alternative Political Strategies

However much the communist opposition agreed on the underhandedness of the Yeltsin campaign, its various currents differed perceptibly on what to do next. This question, a matter of considerable discussion even before the final election results were in, took center stage in connection with the projected formation of the People's–Patriotic Union of Russia. Kuptsov, in his report to the Eighth CPRF Plenum, bluntly noted the "sharp discussion" of this initiative at a meeting of the party's Presidium on August 5, 1996.[8] Other speakers at the Eighth Plenum of the Central Committee the next day expressed a wide range of dissenting views.[9]

On the specific issue of the party's relationship to the People's–Patriotic Union of Russia, Kuptsov took the customary communist "frontist" approach. In a nutshell, he declared that the CPRF should be the "nucleus of the movement, its vanguard." On other organizational questions Kuptsov expressed similar traditionalist ideas. He called for an "exchange of party documents," that is, a review of party members' credentials, prior to the Fourth CPRF Congress scheduled for the spring of 1997. He emphasized the importance of discipline in the CPRF's Duma fraction, insisting that the fraction's work should be "under the clear-cut control of the Central Committee and Presidium." And he spoke of moving party cadres into work in government agencies and other social and political organizations.[10] Most worrisome from the viewpoint of those who might favor the development of a broadly based left-of-center government of the East-Central European type, Kuptsov accused potential center-left coalition partners such as Grigorii Yavlinskii and Sviatoslav Fedorov, not to mention Lebed, of collusion with the Yeltsin regime. By supporting the president in the second round of the election, he declared, they had dispelled "the illusions of some of our comrades regarding the possibility of a union with the so-called soft liberals and self-proclaimed 'social democrats.'. . ."[11] Assertions like these contributed to the widespread view among non-communist Russians that Kuptsov represented the CPRF's orthodox wing.

In fact, however, Kuptsov's prescriptions for improving the CPRF's political fortunes were quite innovative, starting with his admission of the party's inadequacies during the election campaign. With regard to the pro-Yeltsin media's standard caricature of the communists as orthodox revivalists, he said: "Frankly speaking, we did not succeed in disavowing these false premises."[12] He therefore called for a thoroughgoing renewal of the party's "programmatic documents" so as to deprive the "anti-communists" of the possibility of denouncing the CPRF as "lacking in perspective." Kuptsov proudly summed up the party's programmatic evolution already achieved since 1991: its reconsideration of the optimal type of "property relations" (read mixed economy); its rethinking of "internationalism" to include both national and "general-civilizational" (*obshchetsivilizatsionnye*) aspects; and its rejection of ahistorical leaps in national development (read premature revolutions?). He then went on to declare:

> We have rejected the unjustified closedness of our ideology, when in the name of the "purity of Marxist-Leninist ideology" many constructive and productive ideas were swept from the threshold. We have begun to understand that human civilization was pluralistic from the beginning: this is the natural state of things, and only through interaction with other ideological tendencies can one confidently move forward.

"Communist ideology," Kuptsov continued, "is not dead but living, open to innovations and systemic development."

Kuptsov's suggestion for bringing about the CPRF's renewal was just as open-minded. He called for an "all-party," indeed an "all-national," discussion of just what the CPRF should stand for, of what should constitute "the program of a *contemporary party of socialist orientation*,"[13] of who should be considered its allies, and of how the party, once elected by a majority of voters, might guarantee "the democratic rights and freedoms of citizens."

Conspicuously absent from Kuptsov's reflections on the CPRF's programmatic innovations, let alone his recommendations for further progress along these lines, were the ideas and methods espoused by Ziuganov. While Kuptsov insisted on the protection of the Russian Federation's national interests, he did not extol "Great Russia" and he did not speak of the inevitable clash of civilizations. Nor did he mention such notions as *sobornost* or the other unique characteristics Ziuganov attributed to ethnic Russians over the centuries. Above all, he did not arrogate to the party leadership the task of formulating the CPRF's new programmatic documents. As stated above, he left that to the rank-and-file members themselves. As he pointed out in his Eighth Plenum report, the changes that had already transpired had taken place "without the pressure of the *nomenklatura* and the influence of the *apparat.*" In other words, he gave evidence once again of the pervasive rejection of *diktat* from above among many post-Soviet Russian communists, their insistence on implementing as it were the democratic facet of "democratic centralism" in internal party affairs. A telling illustration of this phenomenon had to do with the CPRF's refusal to enter into any kind of coalition government under Yeltsin: on that score, Kuptsov announced, "the opinion of the base organizations is for now unanimous."

In sharp contrast, an unsigned article in the same mid-August issue of *Pravda Rossii* which published Kuptsov's report conveyed a very different message from the first deputy chairman's. It announced that the CPRF Presidium had approved a "note" from the party's ideological department dealing with the "political study and education" of communists and their supporters. (The ideological department, it may be recalled, was directed by the relatively orthodox Secretariat member Nikolai G. Bindiukov.) The article described the "note" as containing the following points.[14] The elections of 1995 and 1996 showed that not all party members possessed sufficient theoretical training. Recent documents of the CPRF and the "bloc of people's-patriotic forces" should therefore be carefully studied, on the basis of the "Marxist-Leninist methodology of understanding reality." To that end party organizations, under the direction of their first secretaries, should examine a series of problems (none of which warrant enumeration here inasmuch as, unlike Kuptsov's proposed topics for all-party discussion, they in no way suggested a fundamental revision of the 1995 CPRF Program). The punch line was that "the CPRF CC leadership requested the Central Council of the RUSO Society [the Society of Russian Scholars of a Socialist Orientation] to help party organizations get a handle on political study and the broad political education of the population." As mentioned at the end of Chapter 6, the RUSO Society was at least partially responsible for the doctrinaire Marxist-Leninist slant of the program officially approved at the Third CPRF Congress in January 1995. In other words, if Kuptsov had opened the door to a wide-ranging rethinking of communist principles and goals, the party's more orthodox Marxist-Leninist wing was ready to slam it shut.

The foregoing discussion indicates the extent to which two of the three main tendencies evident within the CPRF's top echelons since 1993 remained coherent and influential in the post-presidential election period. But what about Ziuganov, the CPRF's chairman and the standard-bearer of the "people's-patriotic bloc"? His speech to the Eighth Plenum was curiously bland, although the ideas he expressed were vintage Ziuganov, both with regard to what had gone wrong in the elections and what should be done thenceforth.[15] He spoke of both the marginalization and "alienation" of ever wider strata of the population as well as the "fascisization" of the regime. Like Kuptsov, he called for "renewing" the CPRF's "programmatic documents" and eliminating their "still existing elements of orthodoxy," but he also specified the importance of incorporating within them the "values of Russian civilization." While referring in passing to reliance on what was best in the "communist, socialist, social-democratic, and people's liberation movements," he declared that "one should not fear appealing to national traditions and even starting out from positions of *'creative conservatism.'*"[16] He announced that the time had come to form a "shadow cabinet" to lead a future "government of national interests." Above all, he reiterated the importance of winning over the intelligentsia, uniting it around "the Russian idea as the integrating value."

Unlike Kuptsov's report, moreover, Ziuganov's address was devoid of self-criticism.[17] Nor did he mention the need to search for new ideas regarding appropriate changes in the CPRF's programmatic outlook, let alone call for participation by the rank-and-file party membership in such a search. In this context it should be noted that a few days earlier Ziuganov had disclosed that during a recently reported week-long vacation he had in fact completed a book called *State Ideologies*, on which he had been working almost ten years.[18] To the outside observer this suggested once again Ziuganov's unbounded self-confidence in his own theoretical prowess.

The blandness of Ziuganov's Eighth Plenum address was doubtless related to the fact that the founding congress of the People's–Patriotic Union of Russia was set to take place the following day. His primary concern on both occasions was thus to articulate a set of positions which might unify non-communist nationalist-oriented oppositionists whose views and organizational sources of support were widely divergent.

The People's–Patriotic Union of Russia (PPUR), founded on August 7, 1996, can best be described as a blend of conservative populist nationalism in its programmatic declaration and a better organized version of the short-lived spring 1994 "Accord in the Name of Russia" movement. The basic intent behind this undertaking was to prepare for the forthcoming autumn 1996 elections for over fifty regional governors and about half that number of representative assemblies. Its formal declaration of purpose thus had a two-fold thrust. On the one hand, it appealed for the restoration of the full range of Soviet-style welfare entitlements. On the other hand, it called for the satisfaction of both the moderate nationalist goal of protectionism for domestic producers and the hardline nationalist demands for reinvestment across the board in the military-industrial complex as well as "countermea-

sures against the subversive activity of foreign states' special services."[19]
These policies were wholly consistent with Ziuganov's pre-election platform,
and Ziuganov himself was, as agreed beforehand, unanimously elected chairman of the new movement's coordinating council. Five co-chairmen were
also chosen: film director Stanislav Govorukhin, Agrarian Party leader
Mikhail Lapshin, and Aleksandr Rutskoi—all three of whom had been key
figures in "Accord in the Name of Russia"—as well as the "Spiritual Heritage" leader Aleksei Podberezkin and the Kemerovo mining region's charismatic politician, Aman Tuleev.[20]

What lent some credence to the potential viability of this new organization was the leadership role of Nikolai I. Ryzhkov in its planning and implementation. Ryzhkov had been Gorbachev's long-time prime minister; he
was the first runner-up behind Yeltsin in the 1991 R.S.F.S.R. presidential
election, winning almost seventeen percent of the total vote; and he was
currently the leader of the People's Power group of Duma deputies. He
thus projected a public image of experience and statesmanship. Furthermore, from the time the PPUR's organizing committee was established
under Ryzhkov, he had emphasized the need for Ziuganov to distance himself from the CPRF as well as the parity and equal rights of all groups entering into the PPUR.[21] On the latter point he was seconded by Andrei V. Fedorov, political adviser to Aleksandr Rutskoi's *Derzhava* movement, who
on July 11, 1996, publicly called for strengthening the projected union's
"non-communist make-up, above all in the persons of Rutskoi, Baburin,
and Govorukhin."[22]

Such, however, was not certain to be the case, despite Ryzhkov's designation as head of the executive political committee of the PPUR's coordinating council and his delivery of the opening report to the founding congress.
For one thing, the Russian All-People's Union led by Sergei N. Baburin announced on the very eve of the congress its refusal to take part in the gathering, fearing communist domination of the proceedings.[23] (Baburin was no
doubt informed of Kuptsov's insistence, at the CPRF's Eighth Plenum, on
the communists' "vanguard role" in the new entity.) Furthermore, of the
327 delegates who actually attended the inaugural session, over one-half
were members of the CPRF or its frequent allies.[24] At the same time, just as
the diverse groups joining together in the People's–Patriotic Union of Russia had been rent by political rivalries in the past, they were likely to be so divided again.

At this point it should be emphasized that the multiple currents comprising the CPRF, in contrast to the PPUR's components, had in the past been
distinguished more by differences of principle than by power rivalries. Their
activism in the post-Soviet communist movement, as we have so often mentioned, was the result of political conviction rather than the personal careerism that characterized so many upwardly mobile members of the old

CPSU elite. The collapse of the Soviet order, moreover, elicited ideological self-doubt rather than the fanaticism associated with the early Bolsheviks. Commitment to a common cause had thus been, at least so far, a source of unity in diversity, something which many non-communist Russian publicists tended to overlook.[25]

This is not to say, however, that the potential for schism within the CPRF did not exist, especially in the wake of the political self-questioning and brain-storming brought to a head by the 1996 presidential election defeat. There had always been a fault line running between the inward-looking chauvinism of Ziuganov's closest circle and the latent internationalism of large sectors of the rest of the party. The latter notion, it should be empha-sized, had precious little in common with "proletarian internationalism," the ubiquitous slogan that the Soviet superpower patriots had used to browbeat the Moscow-centered world communist movement into backing the Krem-lin's foreign policy under Stalin, Khrushchev, and Brezhnev. Here we are speaking instead of the internationalist solidarity that had bound together the early Marxists and continued to resonate among important sectors of the European communist movement throughout the Soviet era. Simply put, it was the idea that working people were united across state borders and ethnic boundaries by the common cause of their joint betterment. This sentiment remained alive and well among some groups of post-Soviet Russian commu-nists, both within and outside the CPRF. When combined with the Marxist reformist tendency within the party's upper echelons, it reinforced the po-tential for the evolution of a communist-turned-social-democratic formation in contemporary Russian politics.

Communist Electoral Support: Past Sources, Future Prospects

Data on voting results and opinion polls relating to the Russian parliamen-tary elections of December 1995 and the presidential contest of mid-1996 are in substantial agreement on the following major points.[26] First of all, the CPRF won substantial support south of the 55th parallel overall and, in par-ticular, in some regions along the Volga, in the rural farming areas of the *Tsentralnoe Chernozeme* (the fertile agricultural zone of European Russia to the west and south of Moscow), and in the Northern Caucasus. These were provinces where the communists won a plurality in the Duma elections and Ziuganov generally won a majority in the second round of the presidential race. Secondly, the CPRF did poorly in the large urban centers and not much better in medium-sized cities and even in the administrative centers of the farming regions. Thirdly, the older the voters, the more likely they were to vote for the CPRF. In the second round of the presidential election, for example, an exit poll of 9,510 voters indicated that the vote for and against Ziuganov was about evenly divided among people aged 45 and older, while as voters declined in age from 44 to 18 they were more likely to favor Yeltsin.[27]

What is important for our discussion are not detailed statistics but an analysis of the basic cleavages within the Russian electorate, namely, the rural-urban gap and the generational divide. With regard to the former, Ziuganov's stress on the power and glory of Great Russia, his diatribes against contemporary Western mass culture, his gawkish overtures to Orthodox believers, his insistence on the unique spiritual and collectivist qualities of Russian national character through the ages—combined of course with his populist campaign promises—clearly elicited a positive response among rural inhabitants.

Historic Russia had been, after all, populated largely by Orthodox peasants ignorant of the outside world and suspicious of their own Europeanized elite. With Stalin's forcible collectivization of the Russian countryside, the most enterprising and capable individuals fled to the industrializing cities, that is, if they managed to escape being branded as kulaks and exiled to the borderlands of Siberia or Central Asia, where survival was the exception rather than the rule. Those who remained on the farm were, euphemistically speaking (and perhaps even genetically), the dregs of Russian peasant society. Their offspring became accustomed to life in the sheltered confines of the state-run agricultural complex where personal initiative was rarely rewarded and often penalized, and tending one's own kitchen garden was the surest path to relative well-being. Just as the Stalinist regime embraced the peasantry's innate suspicion of the outside world, moreover, it limited the rural inhabitants' exposure to the modernizing ethos of the newly industrialized urban centers. In short, the peasant villagers remained the most victimized social stratum in the evolving Soviet economic order (except, of course, for the Gulag inmates). That they would in due time freely vote for a presidential candidate who exalted the memory of the *vozhd* who had so tyrannized their grandparents can only be called, as suggested in Chapter 5, "Stalin's revenge."

Some contemporary analysts of Russian society viewed Ziuganov's "quasi-intellectual"[28] booklets as a continuation of the Westernizer-Slavophile controversy which was so central to the intellectual history of nineteenth-century Russia. But it seems equally appropriate to interpret the syncretic and chauvinistic writings of the CPRF chairman as the product of someone who grew to maturity in the backwaters of a rapidly modernizing but economically imbalanced society, split between a traditional (albeit state-run) rural sector and an industrially developed, highly educated, and ever more outwardly oriented urban sector. Ziuganov's public praise of the "*Tsentralnoe Chernozeme*" as "the real Russia—the most civilized, the most educated, the most prosperous, the most diligent,"[29] his depiction of Gorbachev and Yeltsin as "the two beasts from the abyss sent by the Devil—the first with a mark on his head, the second . . . with a brand on his hand,"[30] his conspiratorial insinuation that German Chancellor Helmut Kohl after meeting with Yeltsin in September 1996 "had spirited out of Russia the means of controlling [its] nuclear forces"[31]—all of these declamations marked Ziuganov as the product of traditional peasant society, a man of the rural past, not of the post-industrial future.

Turning to the many pro-Ziuganov voters forty-five and above, the post-1991 decline in their economic fortunes and certitude, their frequent loss of social status, and the surge in street crime and other threats to health plainly outweighed their expectations of future betterment, especially in view of Russia's markedly lower longevity rates compared to the West. Too old or too set in their ways to acquire new skills, they yearned for the relatively greater security and predictability of life under the old regime. The opposite, however, was the case among the younger urban dwellers. For them the freedom for Russia to join the rest of the modern industrialized world appeared much more important than the temporary material setbacks and uncertainties of the "transition" from dictatorial communism to a democratic free-market polity. This was true of most youth in their late teens and twenties, with few family responsibilities and a compelling urge to see the world from which their parents and grandparents had been cut off. It was likewise the case for many in their thirties, for whom occupational retraining and holding down two jobs at once gave promise of a more satisfying life in the future than that known by their parents in the present or past.

The CPRF's post-election analysts plainly understood the implications of the above voting trends for the future of their party, even if they did not publicly expound upon them. The rural population (excessively large by Western standards) was bound to shrink as privatization and technological innovation spread to Russian agriculture and redundant workers left for urban areas and new occupations. By the next scheduled national elections in the year 2000, moreover, older voters opposed to the new order would inevitably decline in numbers, to be partially replaced by a newly middle-aged cohort more accepting of the post-Soviet changes.

Meanwhile, in their summer 1996 assessments of what to do next, communist spokesmen articulated yet another sobering conclusion from the 1995–1996 election results: namely, the painful fact that the industrial working class had for the most part *not* voted for the CPRF candidate. As Kuptsov put it to the Eighth Plenum, "So far the basic mass of trade unionists and, consequently, their leaders have not viewed our party as a reliable partner." Blaming this primarily on inadequacies in the party's work, he recommended that the CPRF Presidium create "the position of secretary for the workers' movement."[32] Ziuganov also briefly mentioned in his Eighth

Plenum speech the importance of strengthening the party's work "in the industrial centers and big cities, in the labor collectives."[33] And Ryzhkov, in his opening address to the PPUR's founding congress, frankly conceded that "we cannot answer the question of why the starving [sic] Ivanovo region and other regions of the Russian North voted for Yeltsin."[34]

Considerations such as the above obviously underlay the generally recognized need to revise, or "renew," the CPRF's program and to create a broader based opposition coalition. Yet, besides excoriating Yeltsin's campaign tactics, none of the CPRF spokesmen really addressed the other side of the coin to which Ryzhkov alluded in the above-cited passage: that is, why did so many Russians vote for Yeltsin?

Russia's Communists at the Crossroads

In late summer 1996 the answer to this question as well as any assessment of alternative future scenarios pertaining to Russia's communists called for reflection on the changed character of Russian socio-political orientations over the preceding decade. What had transpired had amounted to nothing less than the Europeanization of Russian political culture. Epitomized by Gorbachev's somewhat inchoate ruminations on "our common European home" in the later 1980s, the compass of the Second Russian Revolution had pointed due West.

To be sure, the sixty percent of the Russian voters who cast their ballots against Ziuganov in the second round of the 1996 presidential election were painfully divided among themselves. This was already evident from the fractiousness of the reform-oriented groups competing in the December 1995 parliamentary elections. There were those who shared the *laissez-faire* economic policies of the traditional European liberal parties and others who favored policies closer to those of the center-left formations that had alternated in power with center-right conservatives in one after another major European state after World War II, beginning with the Labour Party's victory in Great Britain in 1945 and continuing with the German Social-Democratic Party's assumption of the chancellorship in Bonn in 1969, François Mitterrand's election as president of France in 1981, and so on. There were also the non-communist nationalists who were more concerned with Russia's international clout and the plight of ethnic Russian minorities in the former Soviet republics than with socio-economic policy. Above all they wanted Russia to take her historic place among the great nations of Europe, and they often viewed with ambivalence, distaste, or outright mistrust the American superpower across the seas.

All these differences notwithstanding, the second round of the 1996 presidential election presented the Russian voters with the raw choice of continuing on the path of joining Europe, broadly defined, or returning to a militarized and possibly closed society. For whatever the positions of the various CPRF tendencies on a mixed economy and democratic procedures, and however much the Yeltsin campaigners distorted those positions, one thing was clear: the domestic rhetoric of the CPRF and the "people's-patriotic bloc," as articulated publicly by Ziuganov in his election plat-forms and during his multiple cross-country campaign jaunts and privately by his closest supporters, was fundamentally anti-Western and unabashedly in favor of restoring the power and prestige of the former military-indus-trial complex. By the same token, whatever the divergencies among the Russian voters who on July 3, 1996, cast their ballots for Yeltsin, they shared one point in common: they opted for the ongoing Europeanization of the Russian Federation, including, it seems safe to surmise, the contin-ued redirection of economic resources away from the bloated military ex-penditures of the Soviet era.

Russia's communists were thus plainly at a crossroads after the 1996 elec-tion. The basic question they faced was how to come to terms with the path of development chosen by the politically active majority of the Russian citi-zens. Viewed from a broader European perspective, Ziuganov and his closest associates, in pushing for the formation of the People's–Patriotic Union of Russia, appeared to be opting for what one could call a "Gaullist" solution to the partisan fractiousness and wounded national pride so widespread in the Russian body politic. The rule of General Charles de Gaulle (and his suc-cessor Georges Pompidou) from 1958 until 1974 had constituted a conserv-ative but welfare-oriented nationalist solution to the problems posed by France's humiliating 1940 defeat by Hitler's armies, her postwar loss of em-pire, and the weakness resulting from the Fourth French Republic's fractious multi-party parliamentary system. De Gaulle's vision of French *grandeur*, which included bucking U.S. hegemony in Europe, distancing his nation militarily from NATO, and asserting a special role for Paris in the interna-tional politics of that Cold War period, resonated well with the French peo-ple's ingrained self-image of cultural superiority within Europe. To our knowledge, Ziuganov never referred to the Gaullist model. But he was doubtless correct in surmising that for many Russians a comparable path of evolution might well appear very attractive: hence his constant emphasis on "state patriotism." The problem with this hypothetical analogy, however, was that Ziuganov was no Charles de Gaulle—not in experience, not in charisma, not in intellect. The role of a Russian Gaullist might someday be played by Lebed or an as yet unknown political figure, even one from among the CPRF's ranks, but certainly not by Ziuganov.

By way of contrast, the announced intent of the CPRF's Marxist reform-ers to rethink the goals and functioning of a "contemporary party of socialist orientation" through a membership-wide debate brought to mind the process of incremental transformation undergone by the former communist parties of, say, Italy and Hungary. The fact that the political parties which evolved from both these nations' former CPs were by mid-1996 major partners in their respective coalition governments could hardly have escaped the notice, let alone the interest, of the more innovative and internationalist figures in the CPRF. The public insistence by Kuptsov and others on their party's "vanguard role" in the PPUR may therefore have been intended as a way to thwart the development of what was in their view an unacceptable and potentially rival strategic alternative.

All the same, Kuptsov's out-of-hand dismissal of future cooperation with the spring 1996 "third force" presidential candidates, Lebed, Yavlinskii, and Fedorov, because of their support for Yeltsin in the second round of the presidential race, was potentially self-defeating. Alone, the CPRF could not hope to form a government by democratic means. If the Marxist reformers rejected, as they had by implication, the path of the conservative nationalist oppositionists, they had little choice but to reach a working arrangement with some of the center-left formations on the Russian political scene—at the national level, in the regions, or in both arenas. At the same time, it was incumbent upon them to eschew ties with the ultra-leftist Marxist-Leninist groups and to tame, as it were, the Marxist-Leninist modernizers within their party's ranks.

The failure to devise a workable center-left reformist or, for that matter, centrist or center-right nationalist alliance strategy that included important sectors of the CPRF could spell the opposition's political isolation into the foreseeable future. More than that, such a denouement might consign post-Soviet Russia to the fate of post-fascist Italy. In the late 1940s, it is well to recall, Italy's citizens voted into power a U.S.-backed regime, many of whose members were at the very least associated with the former fascists. The postwar Italian Christian Democratic Party and its various centrist allies governed for more than forty years, with frequent insider switches in ministerial posts lending a veneer of democratic legitimacy to a political class rife with corruption, clientelism, and in some cases covert ties with the Italian *mafiosi*. The First Italian Republic became, in a word, a prototypical "blocked society" in which a normal democratic alternation in power of opposing political coalitions was precluded by virtue of the opposition's "communist" identity. One could only hope that the analysts among the CPRF's diverse tendencies would bear in mind Italy's "blocked" past as they pondered their own strategic choices for the future.

Two potential alternative strategies seemed to have emerged in embryonic form within the CPRF in the post-election season of 1996: what we have called the "Gaullist" solution and the East-Central European option. The People's–Patriotic Union of Russia was groping toward the first: a centrist, even conservative socially oriented nationalism that would assert Russia's role as a great European power on the basis of historical precedent and ethno-cultural preeminence. But the PPUR could scarcely hope to attract widespread electoral support without dispelling the specter of retrogression to a militarized autarchic society which Ziuganov's own writings as well as his domestic rhetoric in the 1996 presidential election campaign suggested.

The CPRF's Marxist reformers seemed instead to be looking tentatively in the direction of the East-Central European communist–turned–social-democratic parties. This, in turn, raised the possibility of a center-left scenario which would entail Russia's closer integration with Europe on the basis of transnational ties, for example with members of the Socialist International, and shared post-industrial values.

Each of these prospective paths of development bore promise of attracting a number of other Russian political groups to its side and of thereby posing a potentially successful future challenge to the victorious "Yeltsin camp" of 1996. But the eventualization of one or the other path would require recognition on the part of their respective protagonists that they could no longer coexist in the same organizational home. Ironically, the CPRF seemed to have given rise to two mutually incompatible tendencies in much the same way that its progenitor, the CPSU, had done within Soviet society as a whole. In the latter case, the alternatives in their starkest form were to stick to the inward-looking, militaristic, and economically stultifying status quo or to join the rest of the industrially developed world. The bulk of the population of Russia and of most of the Soviet republics in Europe chose the latter, as did the majority of Russian voters five years after the demise of the U.S.S.R. But few would venture to argue that the majority of those who voted for Yeltsin in 1996 were happy with the corruption, criminality, and economic uncertitude which characterized the post-communist Russian Federation. In the final analysis, responsibility for the eventual development of a democratic system in which opposing coalitions might alternate in power without undue threat to social stability rested in no small measure with the CPRF and the strategic choices it was poised to make as 1996 drew to a close.

Notes

1. "Shake-up in Russia," *The New York Times*, June 21, 1996, pp. A1 and A8; see also the extensive coverage of these developments in the major Russian newspapers, *Segodnia*, *Nezavisimaia gazeta*, and *Izvestiia*, June 19–22, 1996.

2. In July 1996 the Russian Communist Workers' Party removed Anpilov from the leadership of its Moscow branch for indiscipline; see "Informatsionnoe soobshchenie," *Trudovaia Rossiia*, No. 10, 1996, p. 1. For RCWP leader Viktor Tiulkin's assessment of the elections and Ziuganov's collaboration with Russian capitalism, as well as his favorable comment on the CPRF Marxist-Leninist modernizer and RUSO leader, Ivan P. Osadchii, see his article, "B kita li korm?," *Trudovaia Rossiia*, No. 12, 1996, pp. 1–2.

3. "Itogi vyborov, ikh uroki i zadachi partii," *Pravda Rossii*, No. 24, August 15, 1996, pp. 1 and 3.

4. For an excellent piece of investigative reporting on this topic, see Lee Hockstader and David Hoffman, "Yeltsin Campaign Rose from Tears to Triumph: Money, Advertising Turned Fortunes Around," *The Washington Post*, July 7, 1996, pp. A1 and A22.

5. For a compelling argument on this account, see Daniel Treisman, "Why Yeltsin Won," *Foreign Affairs*, Vol. 75, No. 5 (September–October 1996), pp. 64–77.

6. For Western reports on this phenomenon, see Lee Hockstader, "Russia Media Stack the Deck for Yeltsin: Fearing Return to State Control, Press Ignores Communist Candidate," *The Washington Post*, April 3, 1996, pp. A1 and A15; and by the same reporter, "Yeltsin Paying Top Ruble for Positive News Coverage," *The Washington Post*, June 30, 1996, pp. A1 and A21.

7. See, for example, *Report of Observations: Election of the President of the Russian Federation, 16 June 1996* (Washington, DC: IFES [International Foundation for Election Systems], 1996). See also *Report of Observations: Repeat Voting Election of President of the Russian Federation 3 July 1996* (Washington, DC: IFES, 1996).

8. "Itogi vyborov," *Pravda Rossii*, August 15, 1996, p. 3.

9. See the excerpts from those speeches in ibid, pp. 3–4.

10. Ibid., p. 3.

11. Ibid., p. 1.

12. For this and Kuptsov's subsequent comments, see ibid., p. 3.

13. Emphasis added.

14. See "V TsK KPRF," *Pravda Rossii*, August 15, 1996, p. 4.

15. Gennadii Ziuganov, "Oni ne pobedili, a my ne proigrali," *Pravda Rossii*, August 15, 1996, p. 2. The text also appears in *Sovetskaia Rossiia*, August 8, 1996, p. 3.

16. Emphasis added.

17. Ziuganov did expound on certain tactical errors committed by CPRF campaigners in a lengthy interview in *Nezavisimaia gazeta*, August 2, 1996, pp. 1 and 5; the interviewer was Ivan Rodin.

18. Ibid., p. 5.

19. "Deklaratsiia dvizheniia NPSR," *Sovetskaia Rossiia*, August 10, 1996, p. 2.

20. Ibid.

21. Interview with Ryzhkov in *Nezavisimaia gazeta*, July 30, 1996, p. 2; the interviewer was Sergei Mulin.

22. Andrei Fedorov, "Gennadii Ziuganov: Pobeda na fone porazheniia," *Nazavisimaia gazeta*, July 11, 1996, pp. 1 and 5 at p. 5.

23. Gleb Cherkasov, "Sergei Baburin opacaetsia kommunisticheskogo diktata v NPSR," *Segodnia*, August 9, 1996.

24. As reported by Vladimir Isakov in *Sovetskaia Rossiia*, August 13, 1996, p. 2, the CPRF had 82 delegates, Lapshin's Agrarian Party 54, Shenin's Union of Communists–CPSU 22, Terekhov's Officers' Union 7, and Anpilov's Toiling Russia 4.

25. For examples of Russian news commentaries on political infighting among the CPRF leaders, see the articles by Sergei Chugaev in *Izvestiia*, March 21, 1996, p. 5; April 13, 1996, p. 2; May 21, 1996, p. 2; and June 8, 1996, p. 2.

26. For some excellent analyses of the election results, see Robert W. Orttung and Scott Parrish, "Duma Votes Reflect North-South Divide," *Transition*, Vol. 2, No. 4

(February 23, 1996), pp. 12–14; Dmitrii Oreshkin and Vladimir Kozlov (of the "Mercator Group"), "Odin prezident-dve strany," *Segodnia*, July 10, 1996, p. 5; Mikhail Gorshkov, "Poslevybornaia Rossiia: obshchestvo trekh tretei," *Nezavisimaia gazeta*, August 8, 1996, p. 5; and Sergei Gostev, "Itogi reshaiushchego goloso-vaniia," *Nezavisimaia gazeta-stsenarii*, No. 7, July 1996, pp. 1–2.

27. The exit poll was conducted at 118 voting stations throughout Russia by Mitofsky International in cooperation with CESSI Ltd. (Institute for Comparative Social Research) and published in *The New York Times*, July 4, 1996, p. A8.

28. We are indebted to Robert Vincent Daniels for suggesting the use of the term "quasi-intellectual" in this context.

29. See the interview with Ziuganov in *Nezavisimaia gazeta*, August 2, 1996, p. 5.

30. See chapter 7, p. 172.

31. Michael R. Gordon, "Yeltsin Team for Surgery Seeks Advice from Abroad," *The New York Times*, September 13, 1996, p. A5.

32. See Kuptsov's report in *Pravda Rossii*, August 15, 1996, p. 3.

33. Ibid., p. 2.

34. See Ryzhkov's address in *Sovetskaia Rossiia*, August 10, 1996, p. 2.

Bibliographical Note

Our research for this book was complicated by several circumstances. Most important was the fact that the various components of the communist movement in post-Soviet Russia initially operated under conditions of semi-clandestinity. Even though the 1991 ban on communist activity was lifted in late 1992, the Communist Party of the Russian Federation remained fearful of renewed suppression during the first months after its reconstitution in February 1993. That situation was aggravated by the temporary state of emergency decreed by President Boris Yeltsin following the bloody confrontation between the parliament and president in October 1993. As a result, it was for some time difficult to discover even the full composition of the leadership bodies of the CPRF. If it was somewhat easier to obtain information about the more radical neocommunist parties, that was perhaps because of their working premise that the regime would be as ready to employ force against them as they were to respond in kind.

Furthermore, in the case of all of the post-Soviet Russian communist parties, the publication of party newspapers, even weekly or monthly "flimseys," was hampered by perennial financial problems. Again, this did not seem to affect the smaller Marxist-Leninist formations quite as much as it did the CPRF because of the latter's far larger membership. While a monthly with a circulation of five to ten thousand copies was sufficient for the former, the CPRF sought to publish a party organ with a print-run of some four hundred thousand. It did not actually succeed in doing this until the spring of 1995.

Whatever their publication outlets, moreover, most of the Russian communist parties took care to conceal the nature of their internal party discussions and controversies. Stenographic accounts of the debates of party meetings and leadership bodies were simply not available, at least for the time frame covered by this book. This made the need for personal interviews with leading activists of the various communist groups much more essential than it might otherwise have been.

Primary Sources

From the start of the post-Soviet Russian order, both *Pravda* and *Sovetskaia Rossiia* retained their left-wing orientation. *Sovetskaia Rossiia*, however, expressed the nationalist thinking associated with CPRF chairman Gennadii Ziuganov and his likeminded associates, while *Pravda* was open to all points on the spectrum of left-wing thinking, from orthodox Marxism-Leninism to the social-democratic reformism of Sviatoslav Fedorov's Party of Workers' Self-Government. After the reconstitution of the CPRF, both of these major dailies, each with a circulation of several hundred thousand copies, included the CPRF's periodic two-page insert, *Pravda Rossii*. (Over the course of two years, however, there were only fourteen such inserts.) When the CPRF was finally able to begin publishing *Pravda Rossii* as a regular four-page weekly newspaper in March 1995, it was initially folded into both the above mainstream dailies each Thursday for distribution. By autumn 1995, however, it was included only in *Pravda*, reportedly as a means of boosting the sales of the latter.

Meanwhile, during 1993 the most important outlet for information about the CPRF was the weekly or bi-weekly *Glasnost*, a multi-page news journal which was published by former CPSU *apparatchiki* grouped around Oleg S. Shenin, the founder in March 1993 of the Union of Communist Parties–CPSU. *Glasnost*, for example, published the fullest account of the debates which took place at the February 1993 CPRF Congress. Soon, however, it became largely a mouthpiece for Shenin's own organization, and when it resumed publication after the October 1993 crisis, its circulation dropped from some one hundred fifty thousand to about thirty thousand.

In addition to *Pravda Rossii*, the CPRF published, from 1994 onward, booklets devoted to individual party congresses, conferences, and important plenary sessions of the Central Committee. Ordinarily they included all the important speeches and resolutions related to the meeting in question. In mid-1994 the party also started publishing a bi-weekly *Informatsionnyi biulleten* containing miscellaneous items of interest to the CPRF's Duma deputies and staff as well as its regional activists.

Ziuganov was by far the most prolific writer among the post-Soviet Russian communist leaders. We refer repeatedly in this book to the following four items: *Drama vlasti* (Moscow: Paleia, 1993), *Derzhava* (Moscow: Informpechat, 1994), *Za Gorizontom*, and *Rossiia i sovremennyi mir* (the last two were both published by Informpechat in 1995). He subsequently came out with several additional volumes of collected speeches and articles, most of which had already appeared in the press.

With regard to the smaller neocommunist parties, each one had its own central organ as well as, in some cases, regional ones. As already mentioned, *Glasnost* became for all practical purposes the journal of Shenin's UCP-CPSU. Aleksei Prigarin's Union of Communists (and its separate Moscow city organization) published the monthly newspaper *Golos kommunista* (a "flimsey" of four to six pages), which we found the most useful for purposes of research. Besides laying out its own political views, it also disseminated a number of documents relating to the Russian communist movement in general. The Russian Communist Workers' Party published a monthly organ in St. Petersburg, *Trudovaia Rossiia*, edited by Viktor Tiulkin, and another one in Moscow called *Molniia*, edited by Viktor Anpilov. In terms of documentary information, the first was more reliable than the second. Viktor Kriuchkov's Russian Party of Communists likewise came out with a monthly, called *Mysl*.

Secondary Sources in Russian

For developments from 1989 through 1993, when the CPSU dissolved into competing factions that later evolved into separate neocommunist formations, we consulted a number of documentary collections and handbooks. Among them were *Kto est chto: Politicheskaia Moskva 1994* (Moscow: Pushchinskii nauchnyi tsentr RAN, 1994); *Politicheskie partii sovremennoi Rossii: Informatsionnye i analiticheskie materialy ob obshcherossiiskikh partiiakh i obshchestvennykh dvizheniiakh (1990–1993)*, first ed. (Moscow: Izdatelstvo "Rossiiskaia politicheskaia entsiklopediia" [ROSSPEN],

1993); Vladimir Pribylovskii, *Slovar novykh politicheskikh partii i organizatsii Rossii* (Moscow: Informatsionno-ekspertnaia gruppa "Panorama," 1992); *Rossiia: partii, assotsiatsii, soiuzy, kluby: Sbornik materialov*, 10 vols. (Moscow: "RAU-Press," 1992–1993). For a useful article dealing with this same time frame, see Sergei F. Cherniakhovskii, "Kommunisticheskoe dvizhenie v eltsinskoi Rossii: Ot raspada k konsolidatsii," *Rossiia XXI*, No. 1–2 (1994). For an invaluable biographical handbook on the leaders of Russian political groups during 1991–1993, see *100 partiinykh liderov Rossii: Prilozhenie k informatsionno-analiticheskomu sborniku "Obozrevatel"* (Moscow: RAU-Corporation, 1993).

Several handbooks or edited volumes dealing with political parties and leaders from late 1993 onward should also be noted. Information on the Duma deputies elected in December 1993 is available in A. S. Barsenkov et al., *Federalnoe Sobranie Rossii: Biograficheskii spravochnik* (Moscow: Fond "Foros," 1995). In addition, we frequently consulted Nikolai Gulbinskii and Marina Shakina, *Afganistan . . . Kreml . . . "Lefortovo": Episody politicheskoi biografii Aleksandra Rutskogo* (Moscow: Lada, 1994), and *93. Oktiabr. Moskva: Khronika tekushchikh sobytii* (Moscow: Vek XX i Mir, 1994). For our purposes the most useful Russian daily newspapers were *Segodnia* and *Nezavisimaia gazeta*. We also regularly scanned *Raznogolositsa: Inform Press Ekspress*, the weekly press review of the Institute of Scientific Information on the Social Sciences of the Russian Academy of Sciences. This invaluable source, which began publication in 1993, includes information on all the Russian political parties, blocs, and movements.

Secondary Sources in English

Almost nothing has been published in English on the communist movement in the post-Soviet Russian Federation. For background information on the overall Russian political context, we consulted articles, monographs, and collective volumes far too numerous (as well as often only indirectly related to our subject) to mention separately in this bibliographical note. Several, however, warrant specific mention: John B. Dunlop, *The Rise of Russia and the Fall of the Soviet Empire* (Princeton: Princeton University Press, 1993); Graeme Gill, *The Collapse of a Single-Party System* (Cambridge: Cambridge University Press, 1994); Jeffrey W. Hahn, ed., *Democratization in Russia: The Development of Legislative Institutions* (Armonk: M. E. Sharpe, 1996); Peter Lentini, ed., *Elections and Political Order in Russia* (Budapest: Central European University Press, 1995); and Thomas F. Remington, *Parliaments in Transition* (Boulder: Westview Press, 1994).

About the Book and Authors

Less than five years after President Boris Yeltsin's ban on communist activity in Russia, the Communist Party of the Russian Federation (CPRF) rose from the debris of the former Communist Party of the Soviet Union to win over one-third of the seats in the lower house of parliament in December 1995 and to challenge Yeltsin for the presidency itself in mid-1996. This groundbreaking study analyzes the CPRF's evolution as it sought to reshape its program and practice to fit the realities of post-Soviet Russia while also battling the more orthodox Marxist-Leninist groups on its left. The authors examine the CPRF's origins, internal factions, and electoral strategy during the parliamentary and presidential contests of 1995 and 1996. They address in particular the nationalist thinking of CPRF chairman Gennadii A. Ziuganov as well as the political profile of leadership and official program that were endorsed at the Third CPRF Congress in January 1995. The CPRF's alternative strategic choices and prospects in the aftermath of the critical 1995–1996 electoral season are also assessed.

Joan Barth Urban is professor of politics at the Catholic University of America. **Valerii D. Solovei** is senior researcher at the Gorbachev Foundation in Moscow.

Index